VICKY EROTIC TALES

Volume I

Pensacola, Florida, EEUU, October 2024

Library of Congress Catalog
Names: Rodulfo, Juan
ISBN: 979-8-3305-2230-9 (paperback)
ISBN: 979-8-3305-2170-8 (e-book)
ISBN: 979-8-3305-2231-6 (hardcover)
First edition
Layout by Juan Rodulfo
Cover art by Guaripete Solutions
Production: Aussie Trading, LLC
books@aussietrading.ltd
Printed in the USA

*"Why should I be ashamed
to describe what nature
was not ashamed to create?"*
Pietro Aretino

vickytoys.com

CONTENT

PREFACE

Welcome to a world of sensual exploration, where desire knows no bounds. This collection of 28 erotic tales, adapted from the first two seasons of the popular podcast, invites you to delve into the depths of female sexuality.

Each story, penned by the talented Vicky, is a journey through the labyrinth of passion, intimacy, and pleasure. From tender encounters to wild abandon, these narratives celebrate the diversity of female desire and the power of connection.

Prepare to be captivated by the evocative language, vivid imagery, and raw emotion that permeate these pages. As you turn each page, you'll discover a world of erotic possibilities, where fantasy meets reality.

In the age of technological marvels, where the lines between the artificial and the human blur, we present to you Vicky Erotic Tales, Volume I. This collection of 28 lesbian stories, originally brought to life by a British female AI voice, is a testament to the boundless potential of human creativity and machine intelligence. The Podcast is available at: vickytoys.com

Each tale within these pages is a digital dream, woven from the threads of desire, passion, and intimacy. The AI voice, a vessel for countless untold stories, has breathed life into these narratives, transforming them from mere text to immersive auditory experiences.

As you journey through these pages, you will encounter a diverse range of characters and scenarios, each one a reflection of the multifaceted nature of human sexuality. From tender romances to intense encounters, these stories celebrate the beauty and complexity of female desire.

We invite you to immerse yourself in this world of erotic fantasy, where the boundaries of reality and imagination intertwine. May these tales ignite your senses and awaken your passions.

This book and podcast are defined by three concepts:

Eroticism, in the context of this book, refers to the exploration and expression of sexual desire through words and imagery. It involves the arousal of sexual feelings through suggestion, symbolism, and allusion. Eroticism is not solely about explicit depictions of sexual acts, but rather the art of evoking sensuality and pleasure through language and narrative.

Lesbianism is a sexual orientation where individuals are primarily attracted to people of the same sex, specifically women. It encompasses a wide range of identities and experiences, including but not limited to lesbian, gay, bisexual, and queer. Lesbianism celebrates the diversity of female sexuality and the unique bonds that can form between women.

Onanism, often referred to as masturbation, is the act of self-stimulation for sexual pleasure. It is a natural and healthy part of human sexuality, regardless of gender or sexual orientation. Onanism can be a solitary practice or incorporated into partnered sexual activity, and it can be a source of physical and emotional satisfaction.

*"What is erotic,
like taste in art, is subjective."*
Kelly Borsheim

vickytoys.com

THE SECRET BEACH

Two hours of Googling, three hours of driving, and then one hour of hiking in the 40 degrees Celsius weather.

All of it to find this secret beach.

And there she was, sitting in the very middle of the beach, her long tanned legs spread in front of her as she leaned on her hands behind her back, not a single care in the world.

I guess I'm not going skinny dipping today after all.

This really makes me sad because it was the only reason I bothered finding the secret beach where nobody was going to be.

I sigh but still make my way down the rocky path leading to the beach. If I came all this trouble to be here, at least I'm going to enjoy it.

As my feet reach the sand, the girl turns her head, half of her face covered with dark sunglasses. Slowly, her lips curl into a smile as if I was a friend she was waiting for all along.

I was still not used to the friendliness of locals.

She says something in Italian, too fast for me to decipher. When I don't answer, she grins wider and repeats herself in English, "Not many people know this beach. Especially those who are not locals."

The way her lips move, and words come off her tongue, rich and teasing, makes the hairs on my body rise with pleasure. Now that I'm closer to her, I can better see her body in a bikini, the tan lines over her hips looking very attractive.

I'm grateful I wear sunglasses so she can't see my eyes roaming her body freely. The way her nipples are peeking through her white bikini top, triangles barely holding her breasts in, the way the muscles in her legs shift as she wiggles her toes makes me feel a certain type of way.

Right then, I realize she's still looking at me, smiling and waiting for the answer. I clear my throat.

- "I did Google for hours to find the location," I say, a smile curling the corners of my lips as well. "I hope you don't mind if I join you."

She laughs then, tilting her head backward, and I watch as her long chestnut hair spills over her shoulder and back, beachy waves glittering in the sunlight.

- "Not at all," she says. "It's always nice to have company."

She pats the sand by her side with her hand, indicating for me to settle. And I oblige. I feel her eyes on me, watching every move.

- "Are you going to sit in your jeans on the beach?" she asks, her voice full of amusement as she eyes my jeans and white shirt over the top of her sunglasses.

I rub my palms over my thighs, biting on my lip. I mean, she's the only one here I might as well undress. It's silly sitting on the beach in full clothing in this weather.

But as I once again steal a sideways glance at her body next to mine, the long legs and tight sun-kissed skin, something inside my stomach twists.

She's so damn attractive.

I don't think I can sit next to her with my pale legs and jiggly thighs. This trip was not planned, hence the lack of my beach body.

- "Come on, you don't have to be uncomfortable around me," she offers, more gently as if she could read my thoughts. "It's only you and me, and I think you're hot."

The sudden honesty in her words throws me off, so I laugh.

- "I'll close my eyes if that makes it easier," she suggests and removes her sunglasses. We lock gazes, her hazel eyes hooded and intense.

Sparks fly through my body, and I feel my nipples hardening.

- "Alright," I agree, interested in playing this game.

- "But then you'll need to guide me into the water," she suddenly adds. I blink, lips parted. But then I nod.

- Sure, why not?

She does as she promised and closes her eyes. Her thick eyelashes are so long, they rest on her cheeks as she keeps her eyes closed, still facing me.

Slowly, I rise to my feet and unbutton my white shirt, letting it fall on the sand next to my feet. My jeans are next, and I unzip them, letting them slide off my hips and thighs before I step out of them.

The gentle breeze caresses my thighs, my naked belly, and chest, and my nipples harden even more. It's a good thing she's not looking.

- "Ready?" I ask.

She nods, rising on her feet with her eyes still closed, and reaches her hand. I immediately take it in my palm, feeling her hot flesh, and she laces our fingers together.

I smile to myself as we walk through the sand towards the turquoise water. When the cool water touches my toes, I chuckle.

Oh, how I've missed the feeling of the sea wrapped around my skin.

We charge deeper into the sea, tiny waves crashing into our thighs as we walk, and I glance at her to find her eyes still closed, a calm expression settled in the beautiful features of her face.

Once the water reaches our waists, I stop, turning to her.

- "Thank you," I say. Heat surges up my chest, neck, and face as the feeling of shame and embarrassment rises to the surface.

- "You know, when you take one of the senses away, the others become more intense," she says, grinning once more.

- Yeah, that's what I've heard.

Does she feel the cool water wrap around her middle way more intensely now that she can't see? How would it feel if I grazed my fingers up her arm?

Without another thought, I reached her with my hand, trailing the very tips of my fingers through her collarbone, to her shoulder, and down her arm. Breath hitches in her throat, her nipples peeking through more, and suddenly my throat is dry.

Oh, God, she's gorgeous.

I let my hand drop, unsure whether she shares the same feelings.

Before I could think about it too much, her hand finds my face, and her fingers trace my jaw before making their way down my throat to my chest. When she trails the path down the track between my breasts, I shiver.

I wish her tongue was in place of her fingers.

- "Close your eyes," she says, her words barely a whisper, and I obey.

Her hand moves lower, and my heart drums in my chest like crazy as she trails the circle around my navel. I don't breathe. I can't breathe.

Water swirls, and then I feel the heat of her body close to mine. Her breath is on my lips, and before I know it, she kisses me. Soft and sweet.

Fire surges through my body, and I take her face into my hands, letting her tongue part my lips and deepen the kiss. She tastes like the sea, and I can't get enough of her soft tongue in my mouth.

I want it everywhere.

Her hands wrap around my waist, pulling me in closer to her, and I don't think about anything for a moment. I don't think about the rolls she can clearly feel. I don't think about the cellulite as one of her hands dips lower and squeezes my ass.

I gasp, and she chuckles before another hand does the same.

I don't stop her when her fingers slip under the line of my bikini bottom, teasing me and sending spikes of pleasure between my legs. She finds the knots and unties them, letting the bikini bottom fall in the water. Suddenly, I'm very aware of my nakedness as the cool water caresses my bare pussy.

I move my hand down from her face to her neck and untie the knot there, letting her top slide down. She moans into my mouth as my palm cups her breast, kneading it slowly.

I bit her bottom lip, dragging it between my teeth, and she moans some more, bucking her hips into me. Without letting her lips escape me, I find the sides of her bikini bottoms and free her off them.

With one hand, I grab the back of her thigh and guide her closer to me, intertwining our legs together. And then, I roll my hips, letting my sensitive clit rub on her. I moan as warmth rolls off my body, and she picks up the movements, her hips moving in slow, long teasing rolls.

The water cools our heated bodies as we move together, gasps and moans escaping through the rushed kisses. My lips hurt from kissing, but I don't stop.

I can't get enough of her.

She's the one to break the kiss, though. I don't want to let her lips go, so I inch forward, eyes still closed as I search for her, but then I feel her lips on my neck, gently nibbling on the skin there.

I let my head fall back, inviting her to taste me everywhere, and she trails her tongue down my throat, and the heat between my thighs gets even harder to bear.

- "Oh, damn," I whisper as she nips at my neck with her teeth, first carefully testing to see my limits. When I don't push back, she chuckles and sinks her teeth deeper, sucking.

I moan, weaving my hand into her hair, pushing her head into me as our hips roll, and I'm overwhelmed with sensations. When she picks up the speed and the rhythm of her hips changes, becoming more erratic and needy, I know she's close.

With one hand, I palm her soft breast, squeezing it, and then my fingers find her pebbled nipple. She seems to like a touch of pain, so I squeeze it between two fingers, rolling it, and she whimpers.

- "Don't stop," she begs me, breathless once her mouth finds mine again, and I do the same with her other nipple, squeezing it and twisting it slightly.

The warmth inside my belly builds faster, and I can feel myself on the very edge of an orgasm. Suddenly, she gasps, every muscle in her body going taut, and I push her closer to me, holding her to me as she comes.

Once I feel her body relax, my hands cup her ass, and I let myself ride her thigh harder, faster. I let my head fall back as I moan, feeling my orgasm as warm waves roll through my thighs.

We're both breathless, holding each other in the water, eyes still closed.

When I finally peeled my eyes open, I find her close to my face, eyes hooded. Slowly, a smile blooms on her beautiful face as she says, "There are more secret beaches to explore."

There is a promise in her words. And I can't help but smile, ready to explore every single one of them with her.

"Sex is a spiritual experience."
Deepak Chopra

THE VIDEO CHAT

My boss, Julianne Billing, sits in her pristine gray and yellow home office completely unaware of what I have going on under the table. It's thrilling to tell the truth. I've never done anything like this before – hadn't much considered it an option really – but when the video chat tone started going off right as I was getting close, I made the rash decision to throw on a shirt and answer. It wouldn't be odd for me to look a little disheveled for our video meetings since starting to work from home but usually I'm not naked from the hips down with a vibrator inside me. And, usually, it's a lot easier to ignore the pretty curve of her lips with her signature bright pink lipstick during work meetings. And the way her eyes crinkle in the corners when she tells bad jokes she thinks are funny.

Now, I'm having trouble staying on topic as she tells me about the new project, she's putting me on. In my defense it's near impossible to concentrate on anything but the steady rumble inside me and the fresh wetness pooling between my legs. I rock forward to shift the vibrator to a different spot. When it presses so perfectly against me, I have to cough to hide the moan that tries to escape.

- "Goodness, that didn't sound good," she says worriedly after my coughing fit, "Are you feeling alright?" Always the concerned mom-friend.

- I nod, "Fine, fine, sorry about that, just a tickle." She watches me closely for a moment longer and I can't help but imagine her with that same intense expression as she hovers over me in my bed. She would probably enjoy being on top, she looks like the type, acts like it despite her soft, peppy aesthetic; I would definitely enjoy her atop me, maybe grinding on a vibrator between us.

I push the scene aside, and the pulse of hot desire that flows through me, when she clears her throat and gets back to arranging whatever papers she has on her desk. Julianne glances at the screen, at me, and clears her throat again, "Well, that's just about everything I needed to tell you. Do you have any questions?"
I move my hand between my legs where she can't see, ready to give in to the building sensation inside me but not wanting to see her go just yet. "Just one," I answer, sliding my finger between my warm, swollen folds.
- "How have you been staying sane this week?"
She pauses, blinks at me; I have to admit I love catching her off-guard. There's a pinch in her brows as she tilts her head curiously, but she answers anyway, "You know, the usual stuff, keeping my apartment in order and taking care of my dogs and stuff. You?"
- "I work out a little, get my heart pumping often," I say; it's not a lie, masturbating is essentially a workout. And my heart is sure beating fast as I circle my clit and think about pink lipstick stains on my skin, a trail down my neck and a smear of it on each of my breasts.
- "That's good," she smiles, "I have to admit I'd get next to no exercise if I didn't have to walk my dogs." The laugh she gives me is soft and a little guilty, but I love it just the same.
I don't say anything back, focusing on keeping a pleasantly neutral expression while I work myself closer.
- "Anyway," she tucks a bit of dyed-blonde bob behind her ear, "I should let you go; you've got some work to do now."
- "I do," I grin at her, "Have a good day, Julianne, don't work too hard." She smiles back at me, laughing again but it's bigger this time, "You too, Mell."
I let her sign off first and as soon as the screen changes back I prop both my feet onto the edge of the table and

get my other hand in on the action too. I run the tips of two fingers between my legs, coating them in my ample wetness before sliding them both into me. The bottom of the toy isn't far inside so I push it further until the upward stretch is almost too much and then curl the tips of my fingers into the sweet spot it had been pressing against.

My body rolls into the sensation. I work my clit faster, letting my body rock as much as I can as I rub my fingers against my g-spot over and over.

The scene from earlier comes back but now Julianne is moving her lips down farther and farther until her warm mouth is around my clit, her lips soft and her tongue insistent. I moan, flicking my clit like I imagine her tongue would.

I sink into the motion, let myself drown in the thought of her pleasuring me, and soon the growing intensity of my orgasm is reaching its height. I clench tight around the toy and my fingers until the vibration and pressure is too much.

I come with a choked cry as searing white waves course through me; my orgasm goes on and on and it's all I can do to keep my fingers moving to work me through it. When I finally stop to let myself relax it's almost too much to pull the toy, still vibrating, out of me as it sends another wave of painful pleasure through my body.

I'm panting after, slouched over the chair, wondering when I'll be able to safely see Julianne in person again. All this isolation – and my not-so-new desire for her – has me itching to get well within six feet of her.

A while later I get a text from her saying that was fun Mell, but I want to see you NOW! I text back all in due time babe.

"The erotic is applied only to the viewer –
the artist is solely responsible for the passion."
Kris Courtney

VACATIONS IN MALLORCA

I promised myself this would be a vacation I'd never forget.

Finally, after a very long time of parental persuasion, my friends and I were allowed to spend the summer holidays alone. Our summers were usually spent in boarding schools with strict teachers and little enjoyment. One more thing that was sure to make this holiday unforgettable – my 20th birthday.

Us five girls planned an amazing trip to Mallorca, Spain. Our flight came in early Saturday afternoon, and our host was a gorgeous girl, with long, dark hair, a pierced nose and tongue, and an evenly tanned body in a red bathing suit. I was immediately awe-struck by her.

She took us to her house that was already jam-packed with people who were laughing, dancing, smoking, and of course, drinking. A quiet wave of panic crept underneath my skin – all those people were so confident and sexy, and to be honest they kind of scared me.

We left our stuff in our room and joined the party. Everyone was mingling, people were kissing on the couch, men casually passed joints as women chatted and laughed in their clingy summer dresses. I stood in the corner watching over everything like a movie scene when suddenly our host came to me and began dragging me to dance.

I completely froze and told her I was still tired from the trip. She sweetly laughed – "What you need is some stress relief... like a good orgasm." I couldn't believe what I had just heard and couldn't help but blush and turn my head away from her. She threw her head back in laughter, but not in a way to communicate that she was at all joking.

My eyes trailed her neck down to her breasts that were rising and falling as she teased me. I felt a sudden surge of warmth between my legs, a weakness in my knees, and my breath rapidly shortening. She looked at me with a fiery spark in her eyes and whispered, "Don't tell me you've never had an orgasm?" Her lips brushed my ear and neck, and the air of her confidence took me in completely. I shook my head, "I'm not sure I know how to." I couldn't believe I was being this honest and raw with a stranger, but it felt right.

Slowly, she took my hand and led me to her room. Closing the door behind her, she said with a wink, "We need to relax you a bit, or you'll never get laid and that would make for a very boring holiday." Her hands started gently running up and down my body, from my hair to the back of my neck, down my shoulders, and gently tickling my back and waist.

I started to really feel the heat; my cheeks burning and wetness coming through my panties as she unbuttoned my summer dress. I closed my eyes as the dress slid off my shoulders, her lips on my neck.

She started licking and kissing my breasts, gently running her hands all over what felt like every inch of my body. My nipples perked up, but my whole body was completely stiff. She laid me down on her bed, still kissing me and making small bites down and down my stomach.

She grabbed my panties with her teeth and pulled her hands behind my back lifting my ass to easily remove my panties. Her hands trailed my legs and inner thighs and climbed up to my sex, stopping just an inch before. She climbed back on top and looked me in the eyes as her fingers massaged my lips and opened them slightly. I moaned as she slid her two fingers into my mouth, wetting them. Those two wet fingers found their way down to my other lips, and lightly caressed my hotspot without touching it.

Her tongue found mine, and I got dizzy as her fingers and tongue sparked so many sensations in my body that I never knew I could feel. Suddenly, she got on her feet, smirked at me and said:

- "First, you need to know what you like. Do you like me?"

- "Yes," I breathed.

- "Would you like to see me naked?" She said with a coy smile.

- "Yes" I almost moaned.

- "I have one condition... touch yourself while I take my clothes off," she said.

I got completely red and hot, both in my face and my body... I grabbed my breast with one hand and wet the fingers of the other and started stroking my pussy. She twirled and slid her bottoms down, dancing to the music from the living room. Her skimpy red bathing suit didn't leave much to the imagination, but I was absolutely amazed by her.

I was completely and utterly turned on and I slid my fingers inside me. A moan escaped my mouth, and I could feel her watching me as I lost myself.

I looked at her as she opened a drawer, pulling out a small pink gadget.

- "Do you know what this is?" she whispered.

I nodded my head and continued falling deeper into myself.

- "You're about to get blown away," she says while removing my hand from my sex, turning on the toy and bringing it close to my clit. I felt waves of intense pleasure passing through me the closer she brought the toy. She surprised me by pressing the toy around my clit, and I let out a loud scream of pleasure that I had never felt before.

- "Stop, please, stop!" I beg, but she just smiled and continued to play with the toy... and me.

This crazy wave kept building from my clit and went through my whole body. The more I moaned and sighed, the more she pressed the toy to me, and suddenly, I burst into a loud, overwhelming peak of pleasure, my body trembled, my back arched, and I quickly grabbed a pillow to muffle out the loudness of my sounds.

She pulled herself up to me, kissed me strongly, and put the toy into my hand... "Join the party when you're ready," she said as she walked away.

*"To love and be loved is
to feel the sun from both sides."*
David Viscott

SLEEPOVER WITH ABBEY

- "Hey, mum, I'm home!" shouted Abbey as we got to her house, "Lizzy is here."
Abbey lived in a nice house, big considering there were only the two of them. I knew that her mum had a job working with a bank doing something managerial.
- "Hi girls," called Abbey's mum from the kitchen, "You have a good day at school?" As many of you will know, this is part of the standard line of questioning for parents when their kids get in, mine asked all the time.
- "Fine, Ms. Kingston," I said, "Thanks again for having me over." She was always happy to have me round, I knew that, but it's always polite to say thank you.
- "Oh, you're always welcome round here, Lizzy, you know that" she replied whilst putting some pots away. Abbey's mum always finished work early on a Friday, one of the perks of being the boss she had told me once.
- "We'll be up in my room, mum," called Abbey as we shot our way up the stairs.
- "Ok, I'll give you a shout when dinner is ready!"
We dumped our bags at the bottom of her bed and freshened up; we took turns in her shower and changed into some fresh clothes. Our dress code for sleepovers was whatever was most comfortable; it had started off the first time as a pair of jeans but as their house was always so warm and toasty, this eventually consisted of just some cotton boy-short pants and a thin T-shirt.
Abbey's mum always bought the nicest shampoos and conditioners, for me a sleepover at their house was like staying in a posh hotel; I tried the fruity one this time and it was fantastic. After drying my hair, I felt like one of those models from the adverts, swishing my hair around, because I'm worth it.
Her bedroom was a lot bigger than mine, she had a king-size bed, a walk-in closet, in-suite bathroom and

a proper dressing table, I was always jealous. It had also recently been redecorated by her mum with an old-English style with bedside lamps and French wallpaper, very classy.

We spent the rest of the afternoon painting each other's toenails, surfing the internet for celebrity gossip and then went downstairs for dinner.

Ms. Kingston was a cool mum; Abbey and she were very close and seemed so much alike it was funny. They laughed and smiled the same way, and were joking all the time, they were both so happy it was infectious. Something else that never occurred to me at the time was the fact that we spent most of our time around her house not wearing many clothes. It sounds odd but modesty was never an issue, so I guess it just didn't seem unusual after a while, the two of us going downstairs for dinner in just some pants and a t-shirt; even her mum lounged around the house at times in just her underwear. Advantages of having such a relaxed, female-only environment I think, it was a nice atmosphere.

After helping with the washing up, I thanked her Ms. Kingston again and we carted armfuls of snacks and drinks from the kitchen upstairs to her room for the evening matinee.

- "Right, what's the main attraction tonight then?" said Abbey, as I ruffled through my bag for the DVD. I threw her the case and waited for it, she took one look at the cover and pulled a face. "Not another horror movie! Oh God," she moaned, "You know they make me jump!"

- "Yeah, I know," I grinned, "That's the fun of them though. Come on, it's got to be better than some of those cheesy, Rom-Coms we keep watching," I replied. I could tell she was mulling it over. "Ohhh, go on then," said Abbey reluctantly, she might have been the bossy one out of the two of us, but she was willing to compromise from time to time, I think that's why we got on so well.

The film had been on for about an hour and was not one of the better ones we had seen together, neither of us were really watching it and we ended up both lying on her bed flicking through magazines. As at some point it inevitably did, the talk eventually turned to boys and sex; we were both having a laugh talking about some of the guys at school.

- Have you ever played that game Marry, Kill, Screw? If you haven't, it's basically where one of you picks three people that you both know, and the other has to choose which one they would marry, which they would kill and which they would... you get the idea. I was purposely picking names of some of the more unattractive guys we knew from school for her to decide on, this was earning me a barrage of playful shoves from Abbey.

- "Why have you got to be so mean, Liz? At least I always leave you with a good looking one to fit in there somewhere!" she complained.

- "Yeah, I know," I said smiling back. I was mean but it was only playful teasing.

The game ran its course and when we got bored of it, we eventually returned to chatting about guys and sex again. Abbey and I were both virgins, we had never been all the way with a boy, although recently we had both experienced some 'intimate touching', well, more like clumsy fondling really, by a couple of guys at the same party.

- "You ever kissed another girl?" asked Abbey, completely out of the blue.

This threw me for a second whilst my brain worked out what she had just asked me.

- "What?" I replied, slightly shocked at the sudden change of direction. I looked at her, but she had her gaze directed at her magazine, her bottom lip poking out.

She waited until I'd turned back and started flicking through my magazine again. "Kissed another girl, you know," she asked again. I wasn't sure how to reply.

- "Well, I kissed you at Rachel's brother's party last month?" I replied. This had only been a playful type of kiss, you know the sort, not a proper one but I think I knew what she was hinting at. She closed her magazine and rolled onto her side, facing me. I could tell she was looking directly at me, but I just pretended to carry on reading some article on dating tips.

- "Come on. You know what I mean, not like that," she said playfully, giving my shoulder a nudge.

- "Err, no I haven't," I admitted, but starting to wonder if Abbey had. "Have you?" I knew she hadn't, I'm sure she would have mentioned it to me by now, we did spend every waking hour of the day together practically.

- "No," she replied in a quiet voice, 'Ha, I knew it!' "Wondered what it would be like though, you know? Different to kissing a guy."

Wow. We had never actually discussed this sort of thing before.

- "Hmmm," I mumbled, not sure how to respond, "Probably, yeah."

Had my best friend just admitted to me wanting to kiss another girl? Properly kissing a girl? I think she had. She was still looking at me, I could practically feel her gaze on the side of my face.

- "Lizzy, you don't think that's, weird, do you?" she said, tucking her hair behind her ear.

- "No, of course I don't," I replied, trying to act all cool and nonchalant about it.

I really didn't think it was weird at all, I had just never put any proper thought into it before. This is the first time our conversation had headed in this direction, and it struck me that there might be more to Abbey than she had let on to. She fancied girls? Knowing that her mum was now with another woman and having met Julie and seen how nice they both were, I was in no way homophobic in any sense.

- "Well, for one thing girls smell better," she carried on, that one made me giggle, I couldn't help it. "And they have softer lips."

I suppose she had a point. I felt I honestly did want to join in the conversation, even if just to be a bit nosey and find out how much she had been thinking about this, but I wasn't sure how to.

All I could manage as a reply was:

- "Yep." I don't know why but at this point I could already feel my mind betraying me, now I was thinking about it. Girls do have softer lips. Would that make them better kissers? I wondered what Abbey's lips feel like, what they taste like. The quick peck we had shared was nothing really. I knew she liked to wear strawberry lip gloss, so they tasted like strawberries. Yeah, that would make sense.

Then it occurred to me, I had sort of phased out for a while there thinking about kissing my best friend, and the conversation had petered out to a silence. Had she just asked me something else?

Then, I felt it.

Abbey and I were always playfully pushing and shoving each other, hugging each other as girls do and had even given one another back massages at past sleepovers which were fun. The recent subject matter, however, had thrown me a bit and had left me unprepared for when her fingertips caressed slowly down my back, the softest sensation of touch through my t-shirt. It sent a shiver down my spine that slowly travelled all the way to my toes, it was unexpected, but electric.

She was lying facing me, she was barely twelve inches away; I could smell the vanilla shampoo she had used in her hair; it was lovely. I had goosebumps on my arms and could feel a strange sensation begin to wash over me, a kind of mixture between tension and anticipation. We had just been talking about kissing girls and now she was caressing my back, was she just being friendly or was she coming on to me?

- "Lizzy," she whispered.

- "Hmm?" I mumbled, pretending to still be flicking though the magazine which now held none of my attention.

- "Can I ask you something?" She was resting her head on her left hand, her head propped up.

- "Sure," I replied. What the hell she was going to ask me now? Abbey lifted her right hand to the side of my face and gently brushed my long hair back behind my left ear. I almost jumped out of my skin when the back of her fingers touched my cheek. I'm sure I flinched that hard that the bed shook, she scared the hell out of me. I think I might have even squeaked.

- "Are you okay?" she asked, giggling, "You look really, I don't know, nervous." She was obviously enjoying something, smiling at my discomfort.

- "I'm fine," I wasn't, "It's just this movie. Things jumping out of the dark, you know?" I replied, trying to put a reassuring smile on, we weren't even watching it. I reached over to the remote and turned it off. She'd only brushed my hair back and I'd nearly wet myself.

- "Oh right, okay," said Abbey, "You're sure? You almost had a heart attack."

- "Yeah, I'm okay. Thanks," I replied, as she softly replaced her right hand on the top of my back just below my neck. With the TV now off, it all went quiet. I considered staying mute, wondering if she would just

change the subject. "So, what did you want to ask me?" I enquired quietly after a little while. 'Liz, get a grip!'
I think I was secretly hoping it was going to be something sexual; God only knows what was going on now, but I felt excited. I was also beginning to get quite hot; I could feel my skin warming up, my cheeks flushing, they were bright red. It was warm anyway but now it was as if the temperature of the room had suddenly jumped. What was wrong with me? She'd only brushed my cheek.
- "Oh, mmm, I was just wondering if... you know," whispered Abbey softly, rubbing her fingertips slowly between my shoulder blades. It should have been a soothing, relaxing sensation, but all it was doing was getting me worked up.
- "If what?" I said distractedly after a moment, still pretending to find the content of the magazine utterly fascinating. I couldn't have told you what was written on that page if my life had depended on it.
- "Mmm, oh it doesn't matter," she replied after a few seconds, shrugging it off. Abbey had never had a problem asking me anything before, she was usually upfront and forward about it. This really had me intrigued now.
She had asked me a couple of weeks before if I shave 'down there', and after a bit of prodding and encouragement I had admitted that I did. I told her that I thought it felt cleaner and fresh and she'd just said "Oh, okay." Last week in the middle of a toenail painting session she had asked me if I masturbated, we'd had to change her duvet cover after I sprayed lemonade all over it. She'd had to wait until I was taking a drink didn't, she?
- "No no, go on. It's ok," I said, genuinely intrigued. "You can ask me, we're friends." I wasn't sure where

this was leading, but if she asked to borrow my favorite top it was going to be a real letdown.

- "Well, I was wondering if you had ever thought another girl was... sexy." She drummed her fingertips on my back.

- "Well, I err, there are loads of girls at our school that are pretty good looking I suppose" I mumbled, "You know what it's like when the sun comes out. All the short skirts, skimpy tops and sunglasses." It went quiet again. That hadn't been what she meant, but I was a little nervous and had automatically deflected the question by turning it into something more innocent.

- "No, I mean, not that way. You know, attractive," whispered Abbey. I could feel as she shuffled a little closer to me, her breath on the side of my face, as if she wanted to make this discussion even more private even though there were only the two of us there.

- "I'm, not sure really, maybe," I stuttered after a second or two. It had been a serious question, and I felt obliged to flash a quick look in Abbey's direction so that she didn't think I wasn't ignoring her.

She had her head tilted behind looking towards her headboard, lips slightly parted. She was very beautiful, her soft golden hair flowing over her shoulders. Was she looking at my ass? 'Oh my god!' I turned back quickly, maybe she hadn't seen me, seeing her, checking me out. She was checking out my ass! 'Breathe Lizzy, in, out, in, out.'

My eyes shot open as I felt Abbey's hand start to glide down the middle of my back again, ever so slowly working its way down my spine. She stopped just where my t-shirt ended. Just where a friendly back massage would end, where they had always ended.

- "Yeah?" she said, leaning even closer. There wasn't much room left now, we were almost touching. Had her mum left the heating on too high? I couldn't take my eyes off the magazine, I just kept looking at it, I was terrified of what would happen if I turned to look at her. Would she lean in for a kiss?

My body was reacting on its own, my heart was beating so hard I wondered whether Abbey could hear it, and not just that. The realization of the situation hit me, it seemed other things had made their own minds up and were letting me know whatever was happening was a good thing. I could feel the beginnings of a tingling sensation between my thighs, I felt hot and swollen. It was scary and excruciating at the same time. Things were snowballing. Abbey's lips brushed my left ear so slightly I thought I had imagined it until she whispered into my ear, two words.

- "I have."

A sudden intake of breath gave me away, it was hardly anything at all, but I couldn't help it. I knew it, she knew it, and I knew she knew it too. It was the green light she had been waiting for, confirmation that her subtle advances towards me had been welcome after all.

She leaned even closer, her breasts just brushing against my arm. "There's this one girl I have liked for a while," whispered Abbey, every barely uttered syllable now shooting straight through my brain to my pussy.

'Oh god, what the hell is happening to me? I'm getting turned on by my best friend!'

"I've wanted so badly to tell her how I feel but was afraid that she might not feel the same way," she continued softly. Her hand started to head south, slowly caressing over my right ass cheek; at this point I had to bite my bottom lip to keep from moaning. "She goes to our school," whispered Abbey, very gently gripping and squeezing me through my panties. I could feel her bare leg rubbing against mine.

Who was she talking about? It was me, wasn't it? Please God let it be me! I had lost all hope of calming this situation down now, my body wanted this so badly and wherever it was going, I was along for the ride.

- "In fact, you won't believe this, but she is lying on my bed... right... now." The last word was whispered so quietly into my ear.

- 'Yes!' My brain screamed, I felt lightheaded like I was going to pass out.

I had never been so aroused in my entire life, just her hand gripping my ass was wonderful. She was so confident and in control. I was a nervous wreck.

I felt a soft, warm sensation as Abbey's lips slowly closed over my ear lobe, she began to suck and nibble it gently. It felt wonderful, utterly divine. A tingling sensation had started to cover my whole body as she began to squeeze my ass more firmly.

'Have some courage girl, you can do it. Tell her what you're feeling.'

- "I...I...think she likes you too," I managed to whisper out between gulps of air. I was breathing, I could feel my lungs actually taking the air in, I just couldn't catch my breath. The magazine had long since ceased its usefulness and was now merely a prop. I gave up the act. I had gone from heterosexual to God knows what, in the time it took to say those words.

Abbey stopped when she heard that, her soft lips releasing my ear. I couldn't see her, but I could tell she was smiling, I just knew it instinctively. I still hadn't the courage yet to move, I just lay there propped up on my elbows as Abbey slowly caressed me, it was so surreal.

She started to kiss, very gently, the top of my arm and shoulder as she slowly, very tenderly, slipped her right hand under the waist of my panties. I had my eyes closed now, the feel of her warm hand on my bare ass was incredible, indescribable, unbelievably sensual. She caressed me tenderly before running her hand between my cheeks, her middle finger dipping into the crevice. I exhaled deeply as my head dropped forward, my hair hanging down, "Oh God."

Her finger slid gently over my hole, tickling, she could tell what effect she was having on me, the conflict between my wavering reluctance and my body's reaction to her attention. It felt so wrong and yet so right. My back arched involuntarily, my ass lifting slightly from the bed as her fingers reached lower and lower. Slowly, so slowly, her fingertips worked their way to that spot, that ultra-sensitive patch of skin just below my pussy. I felt like I was going to explode.

Abbey was purring now; it was so seductive. She continued on and the second her finger reached my opening; it was like a switch being flicked. My head shot up and I rolled over onto my back quickly, her hand slipping out of my underwear. I could feel the heat radiating from my face like a hotplate, I must have been glowing bright red, my T-shirt riding up at the bottom. I felt faint. The only sound in the room now was my heavy breathing, my chest was heaving as I tried to catch my breath.

Abbey started giggling as I looked over to her through the hair now covering my eyes, "Are you alright Lizzy? You look like you're going to pass out." She smirked, her perfect mouth flashing perfect teeth.

I looked back to the ceiling and released the huge breath of air I had been holding, blowing the hair out of my face. I had my arms extended over my head, hanging just over the edge of the bed.

- "I'm... I'm ok, just really, really hot." I smiled, looking at her from the corner of my eye. Had I bottled it? The adrenaline was pumping through my body like nothing I had ever felt, my hands were shaking. My attempt to

appear calm about this situation was failing miserably. Abbey was never one to turn down a challenge, she never had been. She slinked herself over to me slowly and lay on her side again, looking at me. I had to admit that she really was the most beautiful girl I had ever seen, her gorgeous blonde hair flowing over her shoulders, framing her face as she looked down at me.
- "Well, that was getting interesting," she said, smiling.
- "Mmm, hmm," was all I could manage, nodding my head, my lips superglued together. I had no idea what to say, or even if I could speak properly if I tried.
- "Mmm, hmm," she mimicked, still smiling, "Would you like a minute to cool down, baby?" Baby? I could tell she was loving this.
Abbey reached up and walked her index and middle finger up my bare arm, "I'll tell you what, why don't we take it really, really slow and see where it leads, hmm?" she whispered as she raised herself up and leaned forward, slowly bringing her face towards mine.
I felt as our lips touched, she was so soft, so warm, so inviting. Her tongue gently teased my top lip, enticing me to join in the fun, this was the most erotic thing I had ever experienced. My brain had shut out everything but the two of us, the only things that existed in the whole world, were her lips, and mine. I tentatively reciprocated the affection, and our tongues met, it felt so new yet so forbidden as our passion took over.
As our lips parted I realized I'd had my eyes closed the whole time, and now opened them to see Abbey's face just inches from mine, her deep blue eyes staring into me. I was falling for her. I wanted more and plucked up the courage to lean up into the next kiss, feeling more comfortable, more secure, happy. She was so gentle and loving. Our tongues danced in each other's

mouths, our lips pressed firmly against each other, a cocktail of velvet soft flesh and strawberry lip gloss.

I was right, strawberries.

She ran her fingers through my hair which sent tingles down my spine. Slowly she slid her hand behind my head, lifting me further into herself as our kissing got even more heated. I couldn't get enough; I wanted it all. She softly lowered my head back to the bed and after what seemed like an eternity lost in her embrace, I felt her shift and her hand reach down and begin to slide up under my t-shirt. The goosebumps were back as her fingertips burned a path in my smooth skin, up over my stomach and chest to my heaving breasts. It was hard to breathe. Her lips soothed my tension as her fingers brushed slowly over my left nipple, it was so firm, so sensitive, I almost climaxed right then from the sensations.

- "Mmm, you like that don't you, Lizzy? You are a naughty girl," she whispered into my mouth; I could barely mumble my reply at that point, my mind had removed my ability to read earlier, now it had decided to prevent me from stringing more than two words together as well. Those two words though, 'naughty girl', I felt overwhelmed.

Abbey was in complete control; I had no control whatsoever. She began to tease me, to circle my nipples with her fingertips, slowly rolling them between two fingers before tugging gently. She bit my bottom lip, playfully pulling it between her teeth as I looked into her eyes, this was so intense, so sensual.

We didn't have to say anything, our bodies were doing all the talking. Her eyes, oh god her eyes. It felt like she was looking into my soul, I could have dropped and fallen into those two blue pools, losing myself in them forever. She flashed me a devilish grin and in one swift movement, I felt her throw her right leg over my body to straddle me. She sat up and looked down at me from up high. She was so beautiful, her golden hair framing the face of an angel. My angel.

I looked down and could see her hard nipples poking out under her shirt. The most sensuous and erotic feelings washed over me as I noticed the warmth radiating from between her thighs on my stomach, her ass pressing down onto my mound. She reached down and took hold of the bottom of my t-shirt. A little panic started to set in when it hit me that she was actually undressing me, I had never been properly naked in front of her before, but I wouldn't have stopped her for anything.

She very slowly pealed the shirt up exposing my breasts, then up over my head where she stopped and released it. I could hear her removed her own top and threw it on the floor. I was lying with my arms over my head and my t-shirt half off, covering my face like a shroud. I couldn't see anything but could feel her as she leaned forward and began to gently kiss me through the material. The feel of her warm mouth through the shirt was intriguing and unbelievably sexy; I couldn't move my arms with the shirt where it was, and I couldn't move my body with her sat on me.

I was restrained.

As Abbey leaned lower, her breasts pressed and rested on mine, the heat was intense, the feel of her bare skin, her body pressed against me. She was lying on top of me, trailing kisses down my covered face to my bare neck, one of my most sensitive areas. As she planted small kisses on my collar bone and shoulder, and very slowly slipped a hand down over my stomach and under the waistband of my panties.

- "Oh fuck!" I whispered intensely, wriggling.

She only ran her fingers over my pussy for the briefest of moments, but I could feel straight away how wet I was down there, and so could she. Abbey withdrew her hand slowly, I didn't believe it, but I could hear her licking her fingers, my hearing now felt intensely sensitive to all the sounds around me. Abbey had just tasted me.

I jumped slightly as she began to run her hands up my sides, slowly up over my smooth armpits, under the arms of the T-shirt and up further over my head all the way to my wrists. She had freed me, in more ways than one.

Resting her head next to mine, she whispered sensuously in my ear, "Is all that girl-good for me?" I could have died happy at that moment.

My top fell discarded to the floor as she slid her hands back down my arms to my chest and encircled my breasts. I could not describe the feelings that ran through me, lifting my head and looking down to see my best friend slowly lower her head and gently run her tongue around one of my nipples before sucking it into her mouth. Her own were so hard.

My back arched involuntarily at the sensation of her warm lips enclosing over me, the feeling of her tongue circling my stiff nipple took me to new heights. I had played with my breasts and nipples before when masturbating but this was something else; the feeling was focused, warm and intense. My pussy was now throbbing, I felt so wet I was sure I could feel it trickling out of me, soaking my panties. Every time I squirmed; I could feel my moist lips slipping against each other.

I could have laid there forever, floating on a carpet of sexual ecstasy. After Abbey had licked, sucked and nibbled me senseless, she started to slowly run her tongue down my body. She slipped downward to my stomach, gently kissing, licking and scraping her teeth on my skin. I looked down and she looked up, our eyes meeting.

- "Oh Abbey!" I moaned passionately as she slid her body down further, my legs were forced apart by her knees. I tried to prop myself up on my elbows and look at her; my head swam, and I felt dizzy. I knew what was coming, was she really going to go down on me? As she reached the top of my panties, she looked up again into my eyes and smiled the most beautiful smile I had ever seen, the look radiated love and lust at the same time. I felt so happy, so loved.

She glanced back down to the wildfire burning between my legs and looked back up to me, her smile transforming into a mischievous grin. I looked down and blushed beetroot red as I realized why she was smiling; my panties were absolutely soaked. A huge wet patch was clearly visible. Instinctively I tried to cross my legs to cover myself, but Abbey reached up and held my legs firmly open at the knees.

- "A, A, Abbey..." I stuttered.

- "Shhh," she whispered, 'It's okay, Lizzy, just relax."

I could hear her breathing deeply through her nose as she bent lower, taking in my scent; I didn't know whether to feel embarrassed or aroused. She started to softly kiss my inner thighs, working closer and closer. The anticipation was killing me, I wanted to feel her so badly.

An eternity passed before she eventually leaned forward and ever so slowly licked all the way up the length of my pussy through my panties, tasting me. The sensation was tantalizing, it tickled and only served to make me even hotter. "Oh my God," I moaned.

Using her hand, she started to rub my clit which was throbbing hard now. I could hear Abbey moaning quietly, it sounded like she was purring again, it was so fucking hot. I could tell she was enjoying this as much as I was. If I had been wearing a pair of knickers or a thong instead of my boy-shorts, I have no doubt that she wouldn't have had the patience to remove them and would just have pulled them to one side. Or maybe just ripped them off. Her fingers slipped over the waist of my panties, and she started to slip them off, this was the last barrier between us. As I lifted my hips to assist her, my red, swollen, hairless pussy coming into view, I suddenly realized the situation I was in. Naked, lying on my best friend's bed with her about to... This was unbelievable.

Abbey carefully pulled my legs up towards my chest and then parted them spreading my pussy lips wide open, I was completely exposed to her now, I felt so vulnerable. It hit me almost immediately, I could smell the sex in the air, that unmistakable aroma of female lust. She held my legs there for a moment and just stared at my pussy, her face radiated a carnal lust and desire. I have small, light pink pussy lips which get puffy and swollen when aroused. They were swollen now and screaming for some attention. As she lowered her head between my soft thighs, she slowly suckled my lips into her mouth.

- "Oh fuck, Abbey!" I cried as powerful sensations took over. Completely new sensations. "I can feel you, it's so good."

- "Mmm," Abbey mumbled, her mouth full of my most private area, "You taste delicious, baby."

She sucked my labia into her mouth and pulled them gently between her lips before releasing them. I could feel everything, I could hear everything, a powerfully sexual, wet sucking sound emanating from our coupling. Little shockwaves spread out from my clit as she started to blow on it.

- "Oh fuck!" I cried, "Oh my god, Abbey!" My clit was throbbing so hard I was sure it was about to explode like a miniature stick of dynamite; I looked down one more time to see her looking up at me with those beautiful blue eyes as she again lowered her mouth to my womanhood.

After what seemed forever, she sat up with the most lustful look on her face and started to slip her own panties off. I never knew but Abbey was completely shaved as well, her smooth, bald pussy was such a turn on. I could see her arousal glistening. My head dropped back to the bed. Her mouth felt hot like a river of molten lava running over me, yet so soft like the caress of liquid silk, her beautiful mouth making love to me. I was lost.

Gradually, she worked her way back to my clit, her tongue now a jackhammer flicking across my hood. As her mouth went to work, my mind closed up shop; I couldn't focus on anything but this.

- "Fuck fuck fuck, oh my god!" I moaned loudly. I had never dreamed anything could feel this good. I could hear Abbey moaning as well, slick, wet sounds telling me that she was rubbing her sopping pussy with a passion. I threw my head back and forth moaning in pure ecstasy, my best friend's head buried between my thighs and my hands now holding her there. This already felt better than any orgasm I had ever using my own fingers, and I hadn't even come yet; I was in heaven.

The only way to describe the next few minutes is bliss; Abbey devoured my sex utterly and completely as she fingered herself, her own hole filled with wetness. She licked, nibbled and sucked my every crease, crevice and fold like her life depended on it, like mine did. Her fingers began to probe my pussy, first one then two started to slip in and out as she continued to devour me.

- "Abbey, I'm going to come! Oh my god, Abbey!" I moaned loudly.

Abbey reached her hands up over my thighs and put her fingers either side of my clitoral hood and gently pulled back exposing my nub; I could feel her fingers slipping slightly on my skin from the mixture of her saliva and both of our sexual juices. The second she took my exposed clit into her mouth, she sucked hard and swirled her tongue around it; my reaction was instant and intense, an explosion between my legs. I couldn't hold on any longer.

- "Oh, fuck fuck fuck, I'm coming!" I shouted, as she shushed me to keep quiet.

Time stopped.

All my muscles cramped up, my hands gripping the duvet so hard my knuckles turned white. My toes curled and my feet turned in; it felt like my whole body was held together and connected by a series of elastic bands that had all just been pulled and tightened at the same time. My eyes clamped shut as my back arched and I started to shake uncontrollably. The intense, almost painful focus of pleasure between my thighs started to spread throughout my body as I lay there, vibrating.

I have no idea how long it lasted but the greatest sense of release and relaxation spread over my body as my muscles began to unfold and a fuzzy warmth spread to every inch of my body from head to toe. I realized at that moment; this had been my first real orgasm.

When I opened my eyes, the room was spinning. I felt dizzy and disorientated. I was covered in a sheen of sweat and could feel rivulets running between my breasts. I was throbbing. I barely had enough strength left in me to lift my head to see the delicious creature that had just made me a woman, she was propped up on her hands and knees between my legs, the biggest smile on her face.

- "Oh my God, Lizzy," she said, and started giggling at the realization of what had just happened. The look on my face must have been a picture because we both burst out in hysterical laughter.
Suddenly there was a loud knock at her bedroom door, after the quiet atmosphere in the room it sounded like a bomb going off; I almost jumped out of my skin.
- "Are you girls ok in there?" called Abbey's mum from the other side of the door. We looked at each other, my face a perfect expression of total panic. She didn't have a lock on her bedroom door.
- "We're fine, mum, thanks," shouted Abbey, no trace of hesitation in her voice. I was frozen.
- "Erm, okay, are you sure? Can I get you some more drinks or something?" she called back.
- "No were good thanks, mum," replied Abbey looking directly at me, "We're just having a nibble." My eyes shot open as I looked at her, she just flashed that devilish grin at me as she licked her lips.
- "Okay, well I'm off to bed now, see you both in the morning. Don't stay up too late."
- "Night, mum," called Abbey. She nodded at me.
- "Goodnight, Ms. Kingston," I managed to squeak out. As I heard her mum's bedroom door open and close in the hallway I collapsed back and started breathing again, I'd almost had a heart attack, I felt faint. If she had opened the door then, what would she have seen? Oh God! What she would have seen was her daughter's best friend, lying completely naked, spread eagle on the bed, with her daughter between my legs covered in my juices.
We just looked at each other again, Abbey's smile disarming my worries, and we started laughing. She crawled up the bed and cuddled up to me, it was the best hug I had ever had. I began to laugh so hard that I

was crying. She just held me, our warm bodies melted together, so peaceful.

When things had settled down and my breathing had calmed, she cradled my head in her hands and kissed me softly. It was so beautiful. I could smell our lust everywhere, her hands, her lips, it was intoxicating.

- "I can't believe we just did that," I whispered to her.

- "I can't believe you just screamed out you were coming at the top of your voice," she chided, smiling before nudging me.

I looked at her as what she just said dawned on me, my contented smile fading. "Oh my God. Oh my God! I did! Did your mum hear us?" Panic was setting in.

- "No, I don't think so," Abbey replied. I wasn't sure, but she was reassuring.

Abbey was running her fingertips leisurely over my chest and after what had just happened, I had no inhibitions about my body with her.

- "That was really intense. I've always wanted to do that," Abbey said dreamily, "So, tell me, what did it feel like to have your best friend eat your pussy?" The way she whispered into my ear was all it took to perk my interest again. I could already feel a tingling sensation begin to spread.

The only thing I could think of saying as I looked at her was:

- "It was amazing."

- "Hmm, that's good to know," she said as she pulled me up, "Now it's my turn!"

- "What?!"

*"The good thing about masturbation
is that you don't have to get dressed up for it."*
Truman Capote

PARTY AT THE BEACH

Megan was our host, Kimberly's cook. A sexy twenty-year-old nymph that had seen me naked for the last four days as I lay out by the pool, walked the short beach, or through the house. She was an island beauty with mocha skin, black eyes, and cornrowed hair in braids. Her body was always covered in a loose tunic, bare underneath though I had not seen her other assets yet.

Megan cornered me a few times during our visit, and we kissed. Yesterday she caught me in the kitchen and pushed me against the wall, slipping her fingers between my legs and teasing my clit. I moaned into her mouth, pushed her away, and ran from the room, thrilled but shocked at her boldness.

Tonight, she was attending the party, finding me, pulling me to her into a dance. We were dressed similarly in thin tunic dresses and bare underneath. As we danced, our attraction grew strong. Megan was rubbing against me, with only our thin dresses separating us. I could feel her hard nipples and the heat of her pussy pressing against my thigh. We locked eyes, kissed more deeply, and began to grind harder on each other.

Megan pulled away, looking at me. I shivered as I looked into her lust-filled eyes. "Come with me," taking my hand, pulling me outside by the pool. Megan held me tight and kissed me hard, then quickly pulled my short tunic over my head, dropping it on the lounger beside us. I stood naked, shaking, then reached down and pulled the tunic off her succulent young body.

We looked at each other, lust overtook us, and we pressed our breasts together, feeling our nipples poking into each other's skin like bullets. Our breathing became rapid as our hands roamed all over. Our kisses grew more passionate. Lust took over, and there was no turning back. What was happening inside the house meant nothing to us; the two of us were all that mattered.

Megan stepped back and gasped:

- "Oh God, girl, I need to fuck you now." She took my hand, and we ran, stumbling our way through the sand and grabbing each other until we came to the water's edge and collapsed in the small waves holding each other tight, kissing passionately as more small waves spilled over us, caressing our bodies.

The woman lover in me took control, and I felt pure lust for this nymph. I pushed her back on the sand, ready to show her how I felt, when another small wave crashed over us, wetting us completely.

My mouth found Megan's, and we kissed with great passion. Megan moaned as her legs spread wide, welcoming me between them. I slipped down until our mounds pressed together, and I began to grind my wet mons against hers, fucking her in a kind of a throbbing motion.

Soon, I was moaning, as was Megan. We kissed again, then I slipped down her body, kissing and tasting the salt water on her skin as another small wave wet us. I took her nipples in my mouth, first left, then right, sucking them, nipping them, biting them as Megan whimpered, putting pressure on my head, urging me to move further down. I resisted; I was not finished playing with her breasts.

After more urging, I slipped down, and my breasts and mound rubbed against her salty skin on the rough sand, sending sweet sensations through my body. I kissed down her chest to her tight young belly, and my tongue teased the tight knot of her outie belly button. I moved down, kissing and nipping her salty skin above her mound.

Megan spread her legs wider as she began moaning and squeezing her firm full breasts. I licked her open slit and looked up at her. Our eyes locked, and above the noise of the surf, I said, "Megan, I am going to fuck you so hard you will explode coming harder than your young body has ever experienced!"

I needed no reply as I pushed her thighs apart, and her hips rolled forward. I lay the tip of my tongue on the tight bud of her asshole and rimmed her. Megan moaned and shivered as I tapped her star a few times, then licked across her taint, finding her hot open hole, pulsing, wet with her sweet cream and salty water. I teased her opening, making Megan moan loudly. I continued my travels, slithering my tongue through her meaty lips and separating them, finding her hard bean peeking out from its hood.

I flicked it, making Megan moan in her sexy island voice:

- "Oh God, mam, yes, please suck my clit, make me cum."

Who was I to refuse her request? I closed my lips on her clit and sucked it as I tapped on it with my tongue, knowing that Megan would soon explode. I pushed two fingers into her pussy and fucked her hard, driving my fingers into her hot center. Soon Megan was mumbling local words I did not understand, but I knew what they meant. I sucked her clit hard, lathing her with my tongue as my two fingers found her G-spot and took her to heaven.

Megan grabbed my head as her hips bucked against my face, and she exploded. I pulled my fingers out, and my mouth quickly covered her whole mound as she squirted stream after stream of her cream, filling my mouth full. I swallowed as fast as I could, but her cream spilled out of my mouth and mixed with the small waves as they covered us with warm salty water.

Young Megan collapsed back on the sand, gasping for air as I laid my head on her rising belly, feeling her rapid breathing slowly calm. My job was done. I had fucked the beauty to an incredible orgasm that she will never forget, and neither will I.

A larger wave crashed over us, and we knew the tide was rising. Megan pushed me away, stood, and pulled me up. "To my room, mam; I need to fuck you now."

We ran along the sand to a small cottage beside the big house. We stopped at the outdoor shower to wash off the salt. We embraced and kissed passionately. The cold water shook me out of my sexual haze. I had a sudden thought of my husband, where was he? Did he know? Was he looking for me?

Megan shook me back when her fingers worked between my legs into my hole. I spread my feet and rolled my hips forward, leaning back against the wall, letting her take me. All thoughts of my husband cleared from my head.

Megan leaned against me, kissing me as her fingers fucked me. My breathing was ragged as I wrapped my arms around Maris, holding her tightly. She turned the water off and pulled me, dragging me inside. She quickly dried me and herself and pushed me to her bed. I fell back, and she crawled over me like a cougar. She looked down into my eyes, "You are so beautiful, mam; I need to love on you now. Please accept me as your lover and let me pleasure you."

My God, what a declaration! I was speechless. My heart was beating wildly. My body was tingling, and my pussy was so wet that my leaking cream ran down my crack over my asshole.

I reached up and pulled Megan down, kissing her and surrendering myself to her.

I must say, beautiful, sexy women have laid me this week, but none of them could compare to the soft, sensual loving I received. I came for more than an hour, finally crashing into sleep with my beautiful lover lying on me, warming my whole body with hers.

Sexual heaven could not be better than this.

*"Eroticism is like a dance:
one always leads the other."*
Milan Cundera

COLLEGE ROOMMATE

When I started college I had a sweet roommate, Sara. We were both in the liberal arts college at our university, and by virtue of this ended up with a lot of free time. Back then I still smoked a lot of weed, and we both spent a fair amount of this free time by sitting around smoking together. Sara had a ridiculous bong shaped like a mushroom... anyway I digress.

One of her friends at the time, Moley, stopped by often to smoke with us.

I'd always suspected that I might be bisexual but never had a chance to test it out until college. Moley was the first girl I ever developed a real crush on. She was striking. Equal parts sexy and intimidating, I felt butterflies when I talked to her. She was taller, with olive skin and sweet maple brown hair. She had lots of piercings, including her nipples as I would find out later. Her pupils floated in the frozen blue sea of her eyes, and I was smitten immediately. I've never met another person to this day with eyes like that.

Moley was mostly Sara's friend, so at first, we only saw each other when Sara was around. I wasn't sure if she was interested in girls-- and besides, I had never really tried flirting with a girl before. It sounds ridiculous but I wasn't exactly sure how to go about it.

Maybe a few months into our first semester of college, it was me, Moley, and Sara all sitting in the dorm smoking. Obviously, you're not allowed to smoke weed in a dorm. We always used that ridiculous towel under the door technique that never works.

Anyway, on this day we were smoking a lot. I was seriously smacked when Sara decided we needed liquor too just to make it a memorable night. Memorable for what exactly? I'm not sure. I guess that's just the nature of early college. Sara declared that she'd walk to the liquor store with her fake and pick up a bottle of Rosé. Again, very college freshmen behavior.

So, Sara left, and for the first time, it was just me and Moley. We got to talking about this or that when suddenly she broke the banter.

- "Gaby, I just have to ask you... are you like interested in girls at all?"

I paused for a moment, unsure of how to reply.

- "Yeah, I guess I am... I'm not a virgin or anything," I laughed, "but I've never been with a girl. If that's what you're asking?" I was staring into those chilling blue eyes of hers, and she was staring back. A good sign.

- "Would you ever want to be with a girl-- like that?" She posed back to me, sliding closer to me on the bed. I felt her electrifying presence wash over me, and before I could say anything we were kissing. Her lips were full, and God damn she was a good kisser. One of the best I've ever experienced. It started off gently and lightly. Just each of us softly embracing the other.

- "How long do you think that booze run is gonna take?" She broke away and asked me.

- "Long enough." I told her and pulled her back to melt into me. Fuck! I was groping her breasts lightly over her shirt and she was doing the same to me. I confirmed then that I was absolutely into women.

Moley started massaging my ass gently as our kissing got more intense. She pushed me down on the bed and was on top of me, starting to slowly grind herself into me. I tried to angle my pussy up to meet her and I was in heaven, even though the clothes. Our tongues were swirling together now, and I was pulling her hair, forcing her closer to me.

She started taking off my shirt, and I felt myself getting wet. We stopped for a moment and just looked at each other. Like we were searching in each other's eyes for some affirmation. Whatever it was, we found it, because she ripped off my shirt and started sucking on my tits. God. Then she was kissing her way down my stomach, and I was bucking my hips up towards her. She pulled down my skirt and panties and was tracing around my pussy with her fingers. I couldn't wait for her to enter me.

- "Please Moley, please..." I moaned to her, and she just smiled, planting a gentle kiss on my entrance.

- "Oh fuck..." I whimpered as she started fucking me with her tongue. Every few seconds she'd alternate to gently licking at my clit and force a finger gently into me. Before long she was a knuckle or two deep.

- "You're tight, Gaby..." She whispered to me. "So tight. Can I fuck you?"

- "Please." I breathed to her.

So, she pushed a finger all the way into me, and I sighed, pushing my hips to her. She began with that single finger and then two, building a nice pace. God this girl knew what she was doing. She'd go back in, working with her tongue, then come back up to kiss me, all the while making nice work on my dripping pussy with her fingers. I was completely incapacitated, a heaping mess of moans and little cries.

She had me entirely under her control and I barely cared. Moley took her fingers out my pussy and forced them into my mouth to muffle my cries of pleasure.

- "Suck on them." she demanded. I complied, sucking on my own juices like a fucking slut as she started fucking me again with her other hand.

- "Oh god I'm close Moley." I'd been trying to work on her pussy too, but she kept moving my hands back to her tits under her shirt. They were easily both handfuls, and I wanted to see them so badly.

- "Please can I look?" I moaned to her.

- "If you cum like a good girl I'll let you." She whispered in my ear. I was bucking my hips on her fingers now, building up closer and closer to an orgasm.

- "Good, good." She kept whispering. "That's it Gaby, goooood girl."

That's all it took to send me over the edge into a goddamn mess. I was coming all over her hand as I held my own tits tight in my palms, grasping them firmly and riding out the orgasm.

- "Jesus…" I said to her, "I want to make you cum too, please!!" I told her, frustrated. I felt genuinely bad I hadn't made her feel so good too.

- "Gaby don't worry!" She laughed. "That was so hot for me. We don't have time, Sara will be back soon, I'm sure. Why don't we just agree to make it a more regular thing?" She mused, starting to pack the bong, as I laid a mess on my dorm bed.

And Sara was back soon so nothing more happened that night. Moley and I did have a lot more fun that semester and even sort of dated.

"Don't knock masturbation.
It's sex with someone I love."
Woody Allen, Annie Hall

THE SALESGIRL

I'd popped into a new store on the way home from work. I didn't really need anything; I just wanted to browse and relieve the stresses of the day.

I wandered the aisles grabbing a couple of skirts and tops to try them on with before heading into the changing area. Instead of individual cubicles with a curtain for privacy, it was open plan, with opaque dividers creating personal spaces.

Stripping down to my undies I hung my trousers and blouse on a peg and slipped into the first skirt. Just above the knee, it would be stylish but warm for the autumn months. I added a clingy roll-neck top and moved to the large wall mirror opposite to assess the finished look.

My usual indecisive self-took over, and I frowned at my reflection.

- "It looks good on you, honestly, just add some boots with a bit of a heel to them."

I turned to look at my advisor, a smiling, curly-haired blonde stood before me. Sheer black thigh highs and heels were all she wore. She had a blouse on a hanger in either hand while her full curvy breasts stood proudly bare.

- "Do you think so," I asked, whilst trying to keep my eyes on the bubbly stranger's face.

- "Yes; what size are you – I'm a six, try mine if you want." She dipped a hanger toward a pair of smart black boots lying behind her.

- "I'm a five, but if you don't mind."

- "No, go ahead, sorry if I'm intruding. I'm Vivian by the way."

- "I'm Patty, and thanks for your help."

I slipped the boots on; the leather was soft and expensive. I could feel the warmth of Vivian's feet as I pulled the zips up and distant memories, long forgotten, started to rise in my subconscious.

I turned back to the mirror, Vivian was right. My legs looked good, and with the heels lifting my hips the skirt hung so well.

- "See, evening or day, that's a good look on you."

I nodded my agreement, "Yes, I'm sold, you should get commission," I giggled.

- "One more suggestion, it would look amazing without the bra."

I could feel my face coloring as the heat moved up from my neck, "Oh," was all I could manage.

- "Sorry, too much? I don't have much of a filter." Vivian only looked mildly contrite.

Suddenly, grabbed by a desire to shake myself up, I pulled the roll neck off and slipped out of my bra.

The girls looked good; 34DD, large stubby brown nipples. pulled the roll neck back on.

- "Good, eh?" A broadly smiling Vivian had moved to stand alongside me at the mirror, "They look awesome."

The clingy soft roll neck was hugging my curves, tenting over my rigid nubs, "Yeah, they do, thanks."

My eyes were drawn to Vivian's breasts, her pale pink nipples now engorged and rigid. I could feel my pussy moisten.

Our eyes met. "Let's get out of here and maybe have a drink?" I smiled at the bubbly stranger who was igniting such long-dormant desires within me.

We dressed and I took the bra off, letting my girls move around under my blouse.

Vivian had a short skirt and a snug chunky knit sweater, and her legs looked amazing in her boots.

We paid for our purchases and headed for a wine bar across the way.

We took a booth in a quieter corner of the bar and started to chat. It turned out that we had a lot more in common than just big boobs. We both enjoyed modern country music and loved espresso martinis.

I worked as an office manager for an insurance company nearby, and she held a similar role for a planning company.

More importantly, we were both in a relationship.

As we got to know more about each other, we worked our way through a charcuterie board and an assortment of olives with freshly baked bread. Plus, several more Martinis.

In almost no time the evening had passed, and we had chatted like longtime friends, giggling and indulging in smutty innuendo, like a couple of naughty teens.

Reluctantly I commented that it was nearing closing time, and we would have to wrap things up.

- "I don't know about you, but I'm really not ready yet. We could grab a cab to mine if you'd like?"

Vivian's eyes were firmly fixed on my tits, as she made the offer. It was all too obvious that she had more than coffee in mind.

I let our eyes meet, holding her gaze, as I slowly raised my hands to cup my breasts through my shirt before pinching and stretching my nipples.

Vivian smiled and made a show of licking her lips, and then raised her sweater giving me, and anyone passing a clear view of her long, swollen nips and firm smooth orbs.

Moments later we were in a cab heading to her place. I'm sure the cabbie could smell the aroma of aroused horny woman as he drove. His eyes spent more time on his rearview mirror than on the road ahead. Hardly his fault as we spent the entire journey with tongues locked and pawing at each other's tits.

Pausing just long enough for Vivian to pop her door lock, we stumbled into her apartment.

I stepped out of my heels, almost toppling as I was pulled toward the living room.

Vivian's apartment offered some stunning views of the town and nearby river.

Did I take any notice? No. Did I care? No. My eyes were fixed on Vivian, as she pulled her sweater off before dropping her skirt.

She stood before me in a visibly wet red thong, those sheer black thigh highs, and of course those sexy black knee boots.

- "I'm rather overdressed," I observed. Even to me, my voice sounded dry and wobbly.

- "Yes, you are, so fix it, girl."

Very slowly I started to unbutton my blouse, starting at the bottom to keep my tits hidden as long as possible.

As the last button popped, I shimmied, letting the girls peek from behind the fabric before moving on to unfasten my trousers.

Kicking them off, I stood there in an equally wet thong and a white blouse that parted to flash my tits with every move I made.

Vivian had pulled her sodden thong aside and was openly rubbing her pussy. She was wet, audibly wet. Sticky sucking sounds accompanied her fingering.

I gazed on. In college, I had fucked lots of girls. My roomie had made a move one drunken evening, and I went with my curiosity and never looked back until college was over.

My memories were coming alive, and my cunt already was. I could feel my juices running down my thigh.

Stepping forward I knelt before Vivian, gripping her hand to stop her fingers from moving.

Nuzzling her wet swollen slit, I flicked my tongue across her fingers, taking my first taste of her tangy nectar.

Vivian moaned aloud as I pressed my face into her pussy, letting her juices dribble down my chin.

Cupping her arse cheeks in my hands, I knee-walked forward until her legs were against her couch.

Slowly I pushed, toppling her until she rested with her arse on the edge of the seat.

Again, we locked our eyes, ensuring that we were on the same track.

I tugged her thong down her legs and saw that the lacey red scrap of cloth was coated in her thick cream.

I left the thigh highs and boots in place; she looked so fucking hot.

Draping her legs over my shoulders, I leaned forward and attacked her cunt.

I peppered her lips with kisses, I licked her lips before sucking them into my mouth. I flicked her clit with my tongue before forcing it between her folds.

My reward was a face coated in tangy girl cum. She had one of the wettest cunts I've ever played with, every tremor seeming to release another trickle of cum.

When I slid two fingers deep inside her, she bucked and groaned, her heels drumming against my bare back. I could feel her heels scuffing my skin, the slight pain driving me on.

Eventually, I drove her over the edge, and with a neighbor waking screaming, those warm nylon-clad thighs clamped around my head.

I couldn't move. I swallowed all that I could, but my face was coated, and thick creamy cum dribbled from my mouth. It was even up my nose, making breathing an effort.

My hand lightly slapped her thigh until she relaxed her grip on my head.

Released, I dabbed at my eyes and nose as I sucked in a deep breath.

- "Holy fuck, Patty, that was amazing, I just knew you were a girly girl at heart."

With breathing re-established, I moved to sit beside Vivian.

I watched as her body relaxed from its high, her skin and eyes glowing from her huge cum. A deep wave of satisfaction passed through me. I still had it if I wanted to use it.

Vivian took my hand. I could see her kitchen clock; it was just five hours since we'd met and yet I felt so close to her. Part of me wondered if this was genuine passion or just a desire to fuck and be fucked.

I looked at my new friend's face, the curly blonde hair, the piercingly bright blue eyes, the smooth, blemish-free skin. She was quite stunning.

A broad smile engulfed her face, and my heartbeat faster.

Standing, she turned her back to me, bending forward to unzip her boots. She bent far more than was necessary, ensuring that I got a close-up of her gooey cunt and neat pink pucker.

Turning back to face me, she placed a foot on the armrest, the action opened her cunt wide, releasing another trickle of cum. Slowly she teased her stocking down. My cunt throbbed in response.

She repeated the action with her other leg, another gape, another trickle, another spasm of anticipation from me.

Vivian knelt before me in the same spot that I had occupied minutes before. This time it was my turn to have my skimpy thong removed.

I could feel the warm damp cloth passing over my bare toes as Vivian tugged it free.

Our eyes met as she raised it to her nose, inhaling deeply before licking my cum from it.

- "Oh, you smell and taste delicious, I can't wait," she sighed as she crawled to straddle my lap.

Her hands slipped my blouse from my shoulders, before she gripped my nipples, tugging and stretching them mirroring my lustful actions in the bar.

- "Ooooooooooooh Fuck yes," I moaned in approval of the abuse. My nips are hotwired to my clit, and any pain there, triggers so much pleasure in my core.

- "I knew you'd like that," Vivian smiled in delight before slipping her hand between my thighs and plunging a finger deep between my folds. Ordinarily, it might have hurt but I was so wet she could have put her entire fist in, and I wouldn't have cared.

I surrendered to her, slipping sideways to lie along the couch, legs spread, one foot on the floor, the other over Vivian's shoulder.

With her fingers stretching and fucking my aching cunt, she went back to sucking and licking my breasts. Teasing my tender tit flesh before her teeth grazed my nipples and then her warm wet mouth sucking for all she was worth.

Adrift in a sea of pleasure I rode one orgasm, and then the next. I couldn't say how many times she made me cum, or everything that she did; my eyes were closed, my mind freewheeling.

I slowly focused on her lips, sweet with wine, they locked with mine as our tongues met.

Breaking away, she gave me a knowing look, "I reckon you can manage one more cum, a real doozy,"

I had my doubts but nodded my agreement.

With that Vivian stood, still holding my ankle to keep my legs apart.

A series of swift stinging slaps hit my throbbing cunt lips. Nobody had done this since college, yet she knew instinctively what I needed.

I bucked and moaned in delight, an enormous cum building from deep inside me.

Just as I thought I could take no more, she pulled her masterstroke. At some point, she had tucked a stocking deep inside my cunt, and now she slowly pulled it out. The rough lacey band dragged across my lips and clit.

She literally blew my mind, short-circuited my body, fried my cunt. I spasmed, screamed, and bucked as I let go.

It took me a while to float back to earth, to find myself cradled in Vivian's arms, a throw pulled over us.

My body ached, my pussy was tender, but in such a good way, I hadn't felt so alive in years.

- "Welcome back gorgeous," Vivian smiled down at me,
- "How about a warm shower, and then bed."

We shared the shower, tenderly soaping and caressing each other, mindful that we were both rather sore and abused.

Vivian took me to her bed, and we snuggled like lifelong lovers, spooning with a familiarity we shouldn't have had.

Now we stay over most nights of the week, either my place or hers. It's just nice to give the neighbors some respite.

Next month we're moving into our own place.

I always take Vivian shopping with me, and like her, I seldom wear a bra these days. She confessed over breakfast that first morning that she had fallen in love with my girls as soon as she saw them in that changing room and decided to try her luck.

I'm so happy that she did.

*"It is sexual energy which governs
the structure of human feeling and thinking."*
Wilhelm Reich

BABY STAY

It's easier said than done, wouldn't we all agree? It's been 3 years since the day I met her, back at our college graduation.

While we waited for our ceremony to start, we talked about everything possible. Ultimately, we exchanged numbers and sat next to each other laughing like old friends during the ceremony. Since that day I've been totally into this girl.

First it was just friends you know, we would hang out sometimes, movies, dinner, clubs, but never anything more than friendship. Her smile made me smile; her voice brought joy because it meant she was near. Seeing a car similar to hers made me wonder what she was doing. She was amazing, perfect in every way possible.

Anything she needed, anything she wanted, anything I could give was hers. What's worse is she never took advantage of it. You know when someone's a jerk to you, you can try and get over them because they're jerks. But with her she was the perfect friend, never a taker and always a giver. A great listener and always had time for me as I had for her.

Why didn't I ever go for it? Simple, in my life great friends are hard to come by. Hell, good friends are hard to come by period. I wasn't just attracted to her because of her looks, we were friends above all.

I had seen her go through shitty break ups with girls who didn't deserve her and all I could do was hold her and tell her it would get better. She loved with all her heart and when it broke it was hard on her. I was the one who held her hair when she threw up from drinking too much after a breakup. My bed was the one she shared when she didn't want to be alone. Now here she was again with another girl who didn't deserve her and treated her like crap.

I could tell you every detail about her and never miss a beat. From the tip of her toes to the top of her head. Long brown wavy hair, always done. When she's having a hard day, she pulls it back into a ponytail. Her eyebrows arch into a sharp peak and her eyes are soft and brown in an almond shape, giving her an exotic appeal. She has a tiny scar on her nose that she hates but I love it. I have a similar one on my chest. Her lips are so fucking luscious, not that I would know right. But I mess with her all the time I tell her she's Jay-Z's cousin, because they're so big. Damn I would give anything to bite down on one of those.

Her breasts are so beautiful and perfect, a handful each, definitely smaller than my own. She's envious of my large breasts that I say are each as big as my head. My only answer is she can have them any time she wants. She always laughs, but I'm so serious. She's perfect the way she is, and I would never change anything about her.

I finally saw her come down the stairs from her place and she smiled when she saw me. That smile makes my heart warm, and I smile automatically. She was gorgeous in black skintight jeans, and her Burberry Brit Shawl-Collar Belted Coat. I was with her when she bought it, and I had wondered what she would look like with only the coat on and nothing underneath. The outfit was completed with a pair of solid black Louboutin Heels. She was wearing almost a whole paycheck worth of work for me, her birthday present to herself.

Lisa, her girlfriend, looks pissed as usual. Taylor, like most women I know, likes to look good when she goes out and takes forever to get ready. When I wait, I play video games to pass the time. Over the last 3 years she

has bought me a Wii and a PS3 to entertain myself when I wait for her. Lisa on the other hand just goes around grumbling about how long she's taking. She's not allowed to touch my toys.
- "Hey Jackeline, hey Doll." Only person who calls me Doll. I don't think I've used her name since we first met actually. She's shorter than I am standing at 5'3" and I'm 5'8", so her way of greeting me is not the usual kiss on the cheek. She wraps her hand around my neck and kisses it.
- "Hey Sugar, Lisa."
- "MJ. Jackeline" No, she doesn't like us.
- "Hello ladies, everyone ready." Taylor jumped in the back seat and Lisa walked away, wasn't she coming, not that I minded if she didn't. "Lisa?"
- "Nah."
We didn't really like her, so Jackeline took off with nothing else said. Turns out Lisa had a job that night, she was an on-call security guard and had to work at a concert tonight. So, we had fun without her, and I later found out that Taylor was done with her and her crap. It had become obvious to Taylor that she would only be on-call to work when Taylor wanted to spend time with her outside of the bedroom. So, she was done with her. Fine by me.
That night she stayed in my bed after we all came home from the movies and dinner. Jackeline was my roommate and stayed in her own room. I had a guest bedroom, but I knew she preferred to sleep with me. This part is torture on me but what can I say I'm a glutton for punishment. Every time it's always the same, she wakes up curled into me, with my arms around her and won't let me out of bed until we absolutely have to.
- "Sugar let me up, I have to go to the gym." She's practically on top of me with half of her body on my

right side, her leg wrapped around my right and her right arm on my stomach, yup she was making it difficult not to feel aroused, horny, WET.

- "No, you look fucking amazing Doll, toned, tanned and trim as perfect as can be." Now she was tracing the muscles on my stomach.

- "If I stayed out of the gym every time you wouldn't let me out of this bed, I wouldn't look this good." She laughed and looked into my eyes, why can't she see how much I want her.

- "I wouldn't love you any less." She kissed my neck.

- "Sugar please." I tried to move but she's so quick to hold me down. "I really can't stay." I tried to roll away.

- "But baby it's cold outside." Please don't call me that I can't take it.

- "I've got to go away, it's time for me to leave you know that." I was pleading, begging for her to understand what she was doing to me. Why was she so comfortable with me?

- "But baby it's cold outside." Snow will never keep me indoors and she knows that better than anyone.

- "It's nice enough for me to work out." Now I was caressing her back, I don't think this is getting me any closer to the door.

- "I had been hoping that you'd stay. I'll hold your hands, they're just like ice." I'm cold blooded, Doctor's say I have poor circulation, however she is like an oven all the time nice and warm, makes my skin instantly feel better.

- "I should really get going." I tried to roll her over, but she just rested more of herself on top of me.

- "Beautiful, what's your hurry, listen to the heater roar. Doll, please...don't hurry." Why couldn't she see how much I wanted more, more than just words and hugs but her lips on my own. Her body in my arms for me to make her feel loved and protected but because I was more than just a friend.

\- "How about some lattes?" She instantly sat up; she knew my weakness. She made the best lattes around and I had bought her an expresso machine, at her request, for her to have at my house.

\- "Put some music on while I make your favorite." She had fallen asleep in my dress shirt from last night after I had taken it off and she had undressed into her undies. It barely covered her upper body and just enough of her lower area for me to see her panties.

\- "Just a quick cup, I really have to go."

\- "Baby, it's bad out there." She leaned on the frame and gave me her best pout. Those lips were the death of me and those big puppy dog eyes, could force me to do anything.

She went out and it took all of me to not want to just touch myself in this bed she had just vacated. I could smell her wonderful scent, lavender, and vanilla, I have no idea how she does it but that's how she smells. My shirt will have her scent when she takes it off. I can still feel the warmth of her touch on my skin, and legs wrapped around mine. I could feel the moisture from her lips on my neck. I had my chance to leave and get ready and I didn't.

I didn't need to go to the gym, but I had to get away from her. If I expected this friendship to stay intact, I needed to make a run for it. She had a key and could lock it up when she left, hopefully before I got back. As I got up to shower and get dressed, she came back mugs in hand. I didn't even manage to get off the bed, so I sat on the edge and turned on a playlist on my iPhone whatever was on my playlist last.

\- "Say, what's in this drink?"

It was her favorite playlist, of course right, not to mention the best music for being romantic.

- "No way you're going anywhere. You know your eyes are like jade stones."
I wish I knew how to break this spell. Why is she saying this and just watching me?
- "You roll out of bed; your red hair looks amazing and perfect."
- "What are you up to Sugar?"
- "Mind if I move a little closer."
At least I'm gonna say that I tried to keep this friendship safe, but she's just irresistible.
- "What's the sense in hurting my pride."
I smiled and patted the bed next to me.
- "I really can't stay."
- "Baby don't hold out." She set both of our cups on the nightstand.
- "I simply must go." I knew that I should leave, but I wasn't moving, on the contrary she was holding my hands in hers.
- "But, Baby, it's cold outside." She placed her right hand on my neck and kept my hands in her left.
- "You're so nice and warm."
- "Look out the window at that storm." I was so occupied with leaving I hadn't noticed I really wasn't going anywhere. It was snowing.... a lot.
- "Jackeline will be suspicious." What am I saying?
- "Man, your lips look so delicious," Tracing them with her thumb. "Strawberries with whipped cream waiting to be licked." I was just staring at her lips as if she was describing the thoughts in my mind about her own.
- "Gosh your lips look delicious."
- "Maybe we should finish our drinks". I placed my hands on her thighs, the hem of her panties to be exact.
- "Never such a blizzard before." She took her free hand to my neck, begging me to look at her but I wanted nothing more than to take off that shirt and kiss her entire body.

- "I've got to go."
- "Oh, baby, you'll freeze out there." But I'm burning up here. "It's up to your knees out there."
- "But don't you see."
- "Your eyes are like emeralds, look at me, let me see." I looked up at her big brown eyes, pleading for her to see what she was doing, begging her to let go of me. Never had she been this insistent. Never had she been this intimate, this close. This couldn't be, she was lost for sure, she didn't know what she was doing to me.
- "How can you do this thing to me?" She took my hands in hers and placed them on her waist, returning hers to wrap around my neck, pulling me to her as I placed my leg up on the bed.
- "My life has been a long sorrow; do you know why?" She was fine, calm, and collected, while I was a bomb ready to blow.
- "I really can't stay."
- "Get over that. It's cold out there." She was begging me for something I couldn't see, but the tear-filled eyes rooted me to this bed. "Can't you stay a while longer baby?"
- "Well... I really shouldn't." I looked away from her and she pulled my head right back.
- "I'll make it worth your while baby." She leaned in and my world was flipped upside down in that one instance. Her lips were everything I had wished for, soft and delicate, hesitant but persistent. I wrapped my arms around her waist. She pushed herself onto me and I used one hand to set us down gently so as to never disturb our lips, once on the bed I rolled on top of her. Holding myself up in one hand and undoing her shirt with the other, she was mine for today if tomorrow she ran away, today she was mine. The first few buttons from the bottom led me to her soft stomach, sensitive as she felt my cold fingers on her warm body. A moan

escaping her mouth into mine. Going straight to the consciousness of my mind, letting me know she wanted more.

I worked the rest of the buttons and felt her silky soft skin, the tops of her bosom, extracting a moan from me at being so close to having the woman I had dreamed of for so many restless nights. Was this really about to happen, but I couldn't just let it happen. I didn't just want one time, if that's what it was, I had to stop.

- "Open your eyes, Sugar." I was worried about the answer I might get, but I needed to know. I stroked her face with my free hand.

- "MJ, what's wrong?"

- "What are we doing beautiful?"

- "I thought it was obvious."

- "We're friends, I don't want to lose you."

- "Then don't screw me over and just screw me. I know it's taken us a while to get here but damn it I've wanted this from that day three years ago when you walked onto that field."

I needed nothing else; we were just too lost to find each other then but we're here now and she won't regret waiting.

I thrusted my hips downward applying direct pressure to her mound as I kissed her with all the love and lust, I had for her.

- "Ahh, do that again..." Damn the way her eyes roll back and stretches her neck leaving one succulent piece of exposed neck. I just had to bite down as I worked my hips one more time and sucked hard.

- "Are you sure that's how you want it?" I whispered into her ear, then nibbling on her lobe.

- "No... damn I want you.... I'm not sure of anything but that I love you." She loved me no matter how many times she said that, and I had hoped to hear it in a different context.

- "Fuck, are you trying to make me fall in love with you, because let me tell you I've already fallen." She finally looked at me with a sincere look of happiness I hadn't seen in a while.
- "You better be good in bed, because I don't plan on ever being with anyone else."
I worked my hips in a circular motion with a downward thrust, making sure to hit the spot that would make her know she would not be let down.
- "I'm not one to brag but you're gonna have to call in tomorrow and the day after. I've been dreaming of this for 3 years Sugar. Believe me I'll be better than good."
I sat up and admired her gorgeous body, sexy with curves in all the perfect places, the exact opposite of me. I pulled my shirt over my head as she sat up and took off hers. I was going for my pants when she kissed the first one then the other nipple. There was a look of awe in her big brown eyes. Holding my breasts in her hands tenderly massaging them both, gently squeezing, but never going back to my nipple. Finally, after I thought she could not possibly have been any more delicate, she was hungry for more.
She looked up and a big smile formed on her face, she was going for her prize. My nipples had been waiting patiently for their turn, well they were standing at attention to be exact. She took one into her mouth and bit while instantly pinching the other, I gave up on sitting up and fell forward, she never stopped lavishing attention to either breast. I was in a state of bliss, and every moan escaping my body was a testament to her skill. She closed her eyes and just had her way with me, I realized I would let her do anything to me as long as she was in my bed.
I finally pulled away, she began to pout, and I stood to pull off my pants. Then I took off her panties. She was.... mine. Everything, her hips, her thighs, her lips,

she would be mine and I would be the one bringing her pleasure and adoring her body.

- "I have never seen a tastier looking pussy in my life." She looked hungry and I was definitely on the menu.

- "I have, it's between your thighs."

As I went to enjoy my breakfast, she stopped me just as I was about to taste it.

- "No, I know how I want it...our first time." The sincerity in her voice was special. "I want to see your face, I want to feel your body on top me, I want to feel as much of you as possible."

She pulled me up to her and I rested my body on top of hers, placing one leg between her thighs and working my right hand to her neck. I leaned down and bit her neck; I was claiming my prize, marking my territory. I let up and worked my hand down her body as my lips found hers.

There was a need now, a hunger it wasn't tentative or new it was the want to have more. I found the small strip of hair leading me to the land of treasures. I moaned instantly feeling how wet she was. Inserting one finger into the slickness that were her juices, so lost in the sensations that when she lifted her knee into my pussy, I moaned her name.

- "Fuck me. Say that again." I worked two fingers into her center feeling every inch of her that was available to me. "Please Doll, say it again for me." I was done, from this day forward I would never find anyone else who could make me do anything they wanted.

- "Taylor, make love to me."

- "I am so in love with you." The way her breath sounded next to my ear was music to my fingers. Starting a rhythm, forcing her body to dance with me. Her fingers found their way inside me, and we became one. Dancing on this bed, making love playing the music from our hearts for our bodies to move too.

Our bodies moving together, harder, faster reaching every inch of pleasure attainable. I could feel her body tensing and her fingers jerking forward inside me. She was going to push the button and make me cum all over her hand. As if she was listening to my thoughts the dam inside her burst.

- "YES, YES, YES!" Sending me into a world of euphoria.

- "Oh God, TAYLOR!" Her fingers managed to keep moving inside me and I felt my body react to her. Grinding down on her hand working my hips downward applying pressure to my own hand inside her and hers inside me.

She had a mischievous smile as I worked my body on top of her.

- "Fuck, what's with the smile sugar?"

*"To be brave is to love someone unconditionally,
without expecting anything in return."*
Madonna

THE PAINT

Elaine is one of my best girlfriends. I first met her when I was twenty, at a house party. Back then, her hair was pink and spiky, and I remember she was wearing these large dangly geometric earrings. The thing is, the 80's had been long over- but I really dug her retro look.

She wasn't the first girl I experimented with, but she was the first girl that I really had anything special going with. That night, I had no idea that she was even into girls. Especially since she was hanging on the arm of this lanky dark-haired guy with an eyebrow piercing.

The two of them were going at it pretty hot and heavy, like some kind of high school make-out session. As it happened, I found out later that she had just graduated, and he had just dropped out of alternative ed. He was joining this local alt/punk band which she thought was totally cool. I could see that they weren't going anywhere- the band or the couple, but I kept my mouth shut. There was really no reason to do otherwise.

We didn't hook up that night, but we talked during the time that alternate boy was hanging with his bandmates. I was in college, studying art and I told her that I would love to paint her sometime. She was kind of shy about that, she didn't feel that she was especially pretty, and she felt sort of awkward. I let her know that I thought she had the perfect face for portraits, and that she wouldn't have to do anything other than sit still and keep me company while I painted her.

- "You mean I don't have to sit perfectly still the whole time?" she asked me.

- "Of course not, just when I'm sketching out a certain feature, and that's the shortest part of the process."

She agreed that it wouldn't be much different than what we were already doing and that she would do it, if

I really needed her to help me out. I told her that I really did. What I meant was that I really wanted to, but she didn't seem ready to believe it.

In the weeks that followed, we came to know each other pretty well as I rendered her likeness onto the best quality canvas I could afford. She was frustrated by the fact that I wouldn't let her see it until it was finished, but she seemed to enjoy our sessions as much as I did. We found out that we had a lot in common; similar values and politics, interest in the arts- Elaine was into photography and fashion design, similar taste in music (band-boy notwithstanding). One thing that we never discussed was my growing attraction for her. She never hinted at any tendencies toward bisexuality, and I didn't want to take a chance of damaging our friendship or scaring her off, so I didn't say anything. But I felt the heat in the room whenever she was around. I knew the excitement whenever I thought about her, or the anticipation of seeing her again. Part of me didn't want to finish the painting; part of me had this irrational fear that when the painting was finished, I'd never see her again.

But I did finish the painting. I remember the day quite clearly. She came in that day with her pink hair spiked up and those same geometric earrings she wore the first time I had seen her. She was wearing head to toe green, and it made me think of a nature spirit, the way her tiny body floated around the room and her musical little laugh echoed around in my head long after the sound had dissipated from the room.

At first, she sat quietly while I added the finishing touches. She knew that I was almost done and there was something almost magical about it that we both understood. It was almost as if we were holding our breaths in anticipation, knowing that the finished product was so close, so fragile that we didn't want to do anything to slow it down or break it at the last minute.

- "OK," I finally said. "You want to come, see?"

Her eyes lit up. "It's ready?" she asked tentatively.

I nodded and she ran to my side. When she looked at the picture, I heard her inhale suddenly and then she was silent for a moment or two.

- "You made me look so- beautiful," she said in awe.

- "You are beautiful," I answered. She looked at me with her eyes shining. Something passed between us, I felt I knew what it was, but I was afraid to name it. A moment that seemed it could have gone anywhere if one of us had had the courage to seize it. But neither of us did, and the moment passed.

- "You're very talented," she told me. I wondered if the moment had happened at all.

- "I think this is my best work," I told her.

- "Can I see some of your other stuff?" she asked, looking eager.

- "Sure, let's do that while this one dries. It always looks a little different after the paint dries."

I took her over to my cupboard and we started looking through my canvases. I didn't have many yet, most of the pictures I had painted in high school were in boxes painted on heavy paper. Most of the canvases, even, were from school assignments. We flipped through my meager collection. Elaine seemed impressed with everyone.

- "Wow!" she told me, "I don't think I could ever be that talented."

- "What are you talking about?" I asked her. "You're a photographer! And you design clothes."

- "Yeah, but that's different. Photography's not really a talent like painting. I just took a picture of what's there. You create."

- "We all have different talents Elaine. You use your eyes to see and capture beauty just like I do. You shouldn't undervalue yourself."
- "Don't hide your light under a bushel huh?" she laughed.
- "Exactly."
Our friendship was cemented that day. Rather than being the last, it was the first that really mattered. It was the day we went from being people who knew each other to being real true friends. Elaine liked my fairy pictures the best, and I sometimes wonder if that isn't the reason that I've painted so many since then.
Elaine became my model, and secretly my muse. She would sit for me whenever I needed to do a painting for class, or even if I just wanted to practice sketching features. One day when I was preparing to do an assignment, she said something that made the hair on my arms stand up.
- "Do you ever do- you know, nudes?" she asked quite shyly.
- "Sure, in class I've done a few," I told her trying to be nonchalant.
- "Would you want to- I mean, well. I think it would be a cool thing to have, you know, a once in a lifetime- Or do you think that would be too weird? You know since we know each other so well?"
- "No, not at all. I mean if you were ok with it. I know some tricks to help you if you're uncomfortable."
- "Tricks?"
- "Sure- like wearing a sheet, keeping the room warm, stuff like that."
- "Oh," did she blush?" "That's thoughtful."
- "All in the name of keeping the model happy," I told her with a smile. "And if you decide you're uncomfortable at any point, and don't want to continue- I just stop. I'll paint over whatever work I've

already done and re-use the canvas for something else. I don't want to do anything to make you uncomfortable."

- "I feel totally comfortable when I'm with you," she assured me.

There it was again. Something between us. What did she mean? Was it something more than the sum of the words spoken? I had just told her that I didn't want to make her uncomfortable, so I was afraid to ask, to pursue it further.

She mentioned the nude painting a few times again, but whenever I asked if she wanted to do it, she said she wasn't sure yet. I was patient. I tried not to let it show how eager I was to see her body naked, laid out for me to caress with my mind's eye and stroke over the canvas board with my brushes. How often I had imagined it and dreamed about it, hoping that somehow, she might feel the same way about me. Alone in the night I let the fantasy take me away, to heights of pleasure. But when she was in the room, standing so near me, I could feel her body heat and smell her shampoo, I would say nothing of the desires that burned within my heart.

Finally, the day came. "I'm ready," she told me resolutely. I didn't have to ask what she meant. It had been on my mind for so long, and I could see that she had steeled up her courage to take the plunge.

I led her to the room, turned up the heat to a comfortable temperature for the clothing-impaired and left to let her take off her clothes and cover with the sheet. "It's just like the doctor's office," she said, giggling nervously.

She called out when she was ready for me.

- "The doctor can see you now," I said with a chuckle. I could see she was tense, but relaxing. "The next thing we need to do is decide on a pose."

- "I thought I would just lay on a…" she looked around, realizing that there was no couch in the room. "Hmm, what do we do now?"
- "I could draw you standing or sitting. In fact, I have a couple of pose ideas of you sitting down under the windowsill. Would you like me to show you?"
- "Ok."
- "All right, you stand here, behind my easel where I would be. That way you can see how you'll appear from my point of view."

I went to the window and showed her several sitting positions, including one where her knees were over her breasts and her hands down by her feet. It's a good pose that looks fresh and sensual without showing too much detail. The one she chose had her legs together and bent so that the bottom half of her anatomy would be covered, but her breasts exposed. Then she leaned at a 50–60-degree angle on her hand and faced forward toward me.

Elaine seemed to have no problem shedding the cloth. It seemed to me that she had been building herself up to do this for a long time, and now she was determined to do so without showing any fear. It made me like her even more.

Now she sat in front of me, naked at last. "Breathtaking," I said, not even realizing that it was out loud. Her breasts were round and firm with large put pale areolas and pale pert nipples. I sketched her quicker than anything else I had ever drawn and when I reached for my brush, even she was surprised.
- "You've finished the sketch already?"

I stopped what I was doing and looked at her carefully. I searched her face and found no fear, I decided for myself to be brave as well. "It's like I was born to paint you like this."

The words fell into the air. There was no tension in the silence, only understanding. The room was infused with a soft kind of energy. A glow of mutual respect, caring, and something else. Dare I even call it love?

I painted like that, in silence. The sun moved down in the sky and the shadows in my painting moved too. They were fluid, almost surreal as if the viewer could hear them whispering. Something was different now. Elaine felt it, I felt it. She looked at me differently now. She was waiting. Waiting for me to finish; waiting for me to make my move.

When the last bush stroke was laid down, I nearly dropped my brush and pallet. I didn't run to her but moved with a fluid motion as though pulled by some force beyond my control. I stopped just in front of her without touching her. Now we looked into each other's eyes and calibrated our breaths to one another. The air was thick with anticipation, I could feel our souls being drawn toward one another.

I leaned toward her, taking her in my arms, wrapping myself around her. I didn't kiss her lips, but her cheek near her ear lobe. I kissed her neck and felt her melt into me. I nuzzled her neck, feeling filled with joy. I had painted her so many times, but I had never been able to touch her like this, to capture her in this way. She was like smoke in my arms, like a dream, only I knew this was real. I had dreamed this so many times and this was different. I heard her moan softly, accepting me as I slid my hand down between her legs.

She pressed into me as I massaged her moist outer lips. Her moans were like soft mewing, a beseeching sound begging me to take her but to take her gently. I knew instinctively that this was new for her, yet she was willing because she knew me, trusted me. I took my time covering her neck with kisses, blowing softly across her ear, and stroking her gently between her legs. I waited to go further until she was sure she wanted it, until she wanted it so badly that her body was begging. Her head was tipped back, her breaths long and steady.

- "Do you want me inside you?" I whispered; our cheeks pressed together.

- "Yes!" she moaned back. "Yes."

I pushed two fingers up past her external folds. Her body opened to me as I slid into the velvety flesh, and she cried out again. Very slowly I worded my fingers in and out of her, in time with her hard and steady breathing. In and out I slid past the sticky entrance to her cunny. Her breathing quickened and so did my thrusts. She moaned her pleasure as if in a dream, saying my name and calling yes, yes, and please.

- "Oh, God Tiffany- yes! Oh yes, please. Just like that, baby. Just like that." She was lost in the ecstasy of the moment. She seemed almost possessed some medieval spirit of sexual rapture, the way she rolled in my arms and pleaded for more.

I brought her up, all the way up so that she was so close- her moans deepened, her cries edged toward screams. My fingers flew in and out of her, bringing her close to the edge, but then backing off. I slowed and now she went back to the moans from before. I could tell she was wondering why I had not let her come, but what I was now doing felt so good that she quickly forgot to complain.

My arm was wrapped around her back, and I now leaned her back on top of the sheet on the floor and slipped out from underneath her. Continuing to work my fingers over her g-spot, I used my other hand to lift her knees and spread her thighs open. When I leaned down and reached my tongue out to touch her, she gasped in shock and pleasure.

I liked her inner lips evenly, tasting the condensed sweetness of her juices. Her pussy-juices continued flowing in response to the generous tongue bath I was providing and together we slicked up both her sweet nether regions and my mouth with a mix of our fluids. Her sweet taste was encouraging to me as I continued to stimulate her g-spot while I flicked teasingly at her clit off and on.

Elaine's head was now thrashing back and forth, and the words and moans that emanated from her mouth were all gibberish. But each time my tongue danced over her protruding little nub; a high-pitched squeal would escape amidst the lower earthy tones of lust. Each flick was followed by more attention to her lips and then another flick or series of flicks and then back between her lips. I used my hands to pull her inner labia apart, finally releasing her g-spot with some protest from her. That quickly died down when I pressed my tongue up inside of her, fucking her wet pussy with my driving thrusting organ.

Now I could feel her fluids gushing down my tongue and onto my chin as I searched for the tender g-spot with my bending stretching tongue. Her hands gripped the sheet on the floor and her body began to tense again. I jabbed at her frantically, hopping to bring her off in my mouth and catch a flood of sticky girl come to gobble down. She moaned, thrashed, and seemed so close, but just continued on like this rather than exploding in orgasm as I had intended. It didn't seem to bother her, although her moans grew more and more frantic, and she bucked her hips into my face almost violently. She felt she was close, but for some reason she just couldn't reach climax.

I decided that I would need to slow down again, to ease her into this process and seduce her body into letting go. I held her hips still and slid my tongue out of her gushing pussy, and pushed my wet fingers back in. "It's ok," I reassured her. "I want to try some other thing."

I brought her up in my arms again and looked into her beautiful face. I couldn't believe that I was so lucky to be here with her, holding her, fucking her on the floor of my studio. I wondered if she would accept her own juice on my lips as I moved in to kiss her.

She sucked my tongue hungrily, reveling in her own taste. I could feel another gush of excitement down below as my drenched tongue touched her own. She sucked my tongue into her mouth as though it were a man's cock, performing her oral delights with enthusiasm. My own pussy was drenched now and begging for attention.

I broke the kiss to tear off my clothes, wiggling out of a pair of overalls and a plain t-shirt. I had no bra on, as I sometimes feel more comfortable without one when I'm painting. My bikini cut underwear where simple and unglamorous, and I tossed them aside without much thought. As soon as my clothes were out of the way, Elaine pounced back onto my mouth with a ferociousness that took me by surprise.

I slid her inexperienced hand down between my legs and she quickly figured out what to do. She stroked my wet folds as I had stroked hers, encouraging my already copious flow of lubrication. I slid my hand back into her and we continued to manually stimulate each other for some time while she licked and sucked at my tongue.

- "Are you sure you've never done this before?" I asked her as she nuzzled my sensitive neck area.

- "How did you know!" she gasped. "Have I done something wrong?"

- "No, my dear, you've done everything right."

- "But I can't- what if I can't-" there was a tear and a catch in her voice. I knew I had to make it go away.

- "You will," I assured her, brushing her damp bangs from her face. "I am very patient. You just relax and it will happen. I want you to enjoy yourself, that's what's most important, ok?"

- "Oh, I am! I really am. Tiffany, you are amazing. I've been wanting this for so long. But I was afraid."

She had been wanting me too, all this time. The thought filled me with tenderness and deepened my desire. This amazing girl had wanted me. It was not my imagination or wishful thinking. I had not pushed her into anything she wasn't ready for, I hadn't influenced her to do something she didn't want. There was relief, there was pride, and there was determination. I would make her come if it took the rest of my life. In fact, I didn't mind spending the rest of my life like this, wrapped up in each other's arms, bringing untold pleasures to each other for all eternity. In fact, it sounded like heaven to me.

- "You don't need to be afraid anymore," I told her. "I'll take care of you."

- "Can I- I mean..."

- "What is it? You can ask me anything."

- "That taste of myself, on your lips. It was like nothing I've ever tasted before. It was such a turn on."

- "I know," I told her with a smile.

- "Could I- you know?" she asked nodding down at my lap.

- "Of course, darling. I would love that."

- "Love," she whispered with a hint of a shy smile."

- "We can talk about that later."

- "Of course, now lay back sweetheart."

She called me sweetheart, and she wanted to taste me, to lick my pussy like I had done to her. The girl could not stop amazing me, I thought as I did as she told me, and leaned back with a smile on my face.

- "Oooh!" I gasped as she licked me experimentally. I noticed she stopped exploring the taste.
- "You're sweeter than me," she told me.
- "You'll have to share with me later, so I can judge that for myself," I told her.
She laughed, "You naughty little vixen."
- "Yes, I a-A-A-AM!" I gasped as she descended on my disentrance. "Oh Go-od! Oh yeah, Oh, Oh, Oh!" It was my turn to thrash my head back and forth as she slid her wet tongue into my intimate folds. Her method was more exploratory than mine, tracing over my lips and burrowing into the valleys and folds of the inner and outer labia. She hit my clitoris by accident I think, for she seemed as surprised as I was. I howled and begged her to do it again.

"Among all types of sexual activity, masturbation is, however, the one in which the female most frequently reaches orgasm."
Alfred Charles Kinsey, *Sexual Behavior in the Human Female*

RUM AND COKE

We entered my house. I am immensely proud of it. I found it ten years ago after the owner passed away. I snapped it up before it went on the market. I have invested a lot in decorating and making it my little treasure. I collected many antiques, but I'm sure Rachel had no appreciation or understanding of them or the value of the Persian area rugs on my floors. She probably didn't care for my period furniture and Tiffany lamps. They were just colorful to her. The house had a front parlor with the living area behind pocket doors and the kitchen in the back. The two bedrooms were down the hall.

She looked around and said, "I like your little house; it's nicely decorated."

So maybe I was wrong; perhaps she did have some appreciation. "Thank you, I have worked hard to make it mine and filled it with things I like."

- "So, do you live here by yourself?"

- "Yes, I live by myself." Rachel was fishing.

Enough small talk: I was eager to 'break the sexual ice'! I decided to offer her a real drink. I suspected she would enjoy the sweet taste of a Rum and Coke.

- "Have a seat, and I'll get us a drink," Rachel looked around that sat on the sofa. I went to the kitchen to mix two drinks, brought them in, giving her one.

I joined her on the sofa, not sitting too close so I didn't scare her off. I held my glass in a toast, "Here's to an interesting day between new friends." We clicked our glasses together, looking into each other's eyes. Hers had this dreamy look, so I was sure we would have a wonderful time today.

I sat back and watched her take a sip of her drink. The smile that rose on her face was enough to tell me that she liked the Rum and Coke. She took another swallow and sat the glass down, turning toward me like she would say something. I leaned closer to her and boldly asked, "Have you had sex with an older woman before?"

Rachel looked at me, her big green eyes gleaming. She slowly shook her head, chewing on her lower lip, "No, I have only had sex with my friend."

- "Today, we are going to remedy that. I want you to enjoy everything about today, and I want you to learn what I can teach you. Since we will become close friends today, please call me Carol," I told her.

Rachel flashed me a big smile, her eyes opened wide, and she said, "OK!"

Hearing her agree made my pussy twitch, and my juices started flowing, wetting my panties. I slid closer to her and kissed her softly on the mouth. It was a simple kiss until she moaned and opened her mouth. I pressed my lips harder against hers. She accepted my tongue as it slithered across her lips, seeking hers.

I knew she wanted this, so I placed my hand on her small firm right breast and found no bra under her baggy shirt. I slipped my hand under the shirt up across the soft skin to her belly and chest, cupping her breast and massaging it. Rachel let out a low moan, then sighed, "Oh, Carol, that feels so good!" she leaned over, pressed her breast into my palm, and kissed me.

I pulled her shirt up over her chest, exposing her small breasts. My eyes glazed on her adorable breasts; they looked so delectable. My mouth watered, and I licked my lips as I pulled her shirt over her head, dropping it on the floor.

Her breasts were a little fuller than half-oranges and begged to be kissed. Her quarter-sized areolas were light pink, swollen mounds with hard, pointed nipples. They needed to be sucked, and I couldn't resist, so I bent over, licking each breast, then took her right nipple between my lips, sucking it.

- "Oh, Carol, that feels so good." Rachel moaned, sucking in her breath.

Her skin was soft on my tongue as I teased the little bumps on her areola, then sucked her nipple in my mouth. I played with her hard nipple flicking it, biting it lightly in my teeth,

- "Oh Gosh!" she chirped, reaching out and squeezing my left breast. Her hand squeezing me made me moan against her breast as my tongue teased her nipple more.

I switched to her other nipple, sucking on it until she started breathing hard and moaning louder. I pulled back and kissed her passionately as our bodies were rubbing together.

I moved back to her breasts, kissing and nibbling them, teasing her with my tongue while pinched her other nipple, making her moan.

- "Oh, Carol." She moaned as her hands squeezed my breasts and then pinched my nipples through my clothes.

I loved her breasts, sucking one then the other, but my pussy was telling me I needed to see and eat her pussy. I dropped my hand to her lap, cupping her pussy through her tight shorts. Her pussy was very hot, radiating heat through the linen material in my hand.

I pulled my mouth away from her breast; she gasped, begging, "Oh No, Carol, don't stop."

I squeezed her pussy through her shorts. She moaned and started to squirm, pushing her pussy in my hand. I felt her shorts growing wet in my palm. I moved my hand up and unbuttoned her shorts.

I moved to the floor so I could pull them off. First, I removed her shoes and socks, taking the opportunity to massage her feet; Rachel moaned with her enjoyment. I looked up at her smiling. She was chewing her lips as I ran my hands up her legs. Her eyes were a little glazed as sexual pleasure overtook her.

I finished unzipping her shorts and pulled them down. Rachel arched her back, lifting her cute little ass enough for me to slip her shorts over her hips. The shorts were like her skin as I peeled them down her legs and off her feet. I sat back and looked at her.

Her legs were smooth and sleek. My eye moved up as my hands slid over the soft skin on her thighs. This young girl is trembling under my hands, telling me she wanted it badly.

My eyes reached the top of her thighs, focusing on the little blue patch of wet fabric covering her pussy. It was a little lacey thong with a big wet spot in the front. I could smell her scent; she was intoxicating and filled my head. My pussy was wet, and my mouth was dry. God, I wanted to fuck this girl!

She was looking down at me with lust in her eyes. I smiled at her and asked, "Rachel, how old are you, baby?" I asked.

She looked at me straight in the eyes and said, "Eighteen, last week."

'Jesus, such a sweet, tender young thing,' I thought, as my pussy gushed warm juice into my already soaked panties.

I thought whatever I would do with this sweet young thing had to be done right and in the right place, so I held my hand out. "Rachel, come with me, baby. We need to go to my playroom."

Rachel looked at me; her eyes were on fire. She took my hand, squeezing it as she stood on wobbly legs and shuffled down the hall, following me to my bedroom. She had not seen my room yet, so she was impressed.

- "Oh My, your bedroom is beautiful."

I have a beautiful room far different from the rest of the house. It is lesbian, my playground is designed for exquisite female pleasure.

Rachel walked in, looking around. "Wow, this is amazing," letting go of my hand and looking at herself in the wall-to-wall mirror, showing my full California king bed. She looked beautiful standing there, almost naked. She captivated me.

I walked up behind Rachel, cupping her breasts and pinching her nipples. She whimpered and pushed her smooth bottom back against me. Her eyes were looking into mine in the mirror. We were almost the same height, with me being an inch or so taller due to still having my wedges on.

Rachel moved away from me to the bed, looking at the massive four-poster bed. She crawled up on the bed and rolled on her back, looking at the ceiling above.

- "OH WOW, you have a mirror over the bed; I have heard of that but never seen one."

The little girl in her took over, and she spread out, lying spread eagle, looking up at her near-naked self except for her blue thong, with a big wet spot in the front.

I knew what she would experience today would be like a visit to Lesbian Disneyland, an adventure she would never forget. I hoped she would want to come back and play often and even bring her little friend Bec.

Rachel rolled on her side and watched as I slowly undressed for her. She looked straight at me and at the mirror for my other side. Her tongue was busy licking in and out of her mouth, and she chewed her lower lip. I placed my clothes on the chaise lounge in the corner and turned to her.

Rachel was so thrilled looking at her body in the mirror that she wasn't paying much attention to me. My eyes never left her as she rolled side to side, squeezing her breasts and pinching her nipples. She reached down, quickly skinned off her little thong, and laid it on the bed. Her hands slipped down her tight belly, between her legs.

As I watched her, as sexy as it was, making me wet, I knew I had to stop her. She would cum too fast on her fingers. I could not let that happen. I was the only one that would make her cum today, and I would make that happen many, many times.

I was naked now with my soaked panties in my hand. I slowly slipped onto the bed, crawling up on the bed. I have a memory foam mattress, so Rachel never felt the bed move but finally did see me in the mirror. Rachel rolled her head back, looking at me.

God, she looked adorable. I kissed her mouth, pushing my tongue between her lips. Then I laid my soaked panties over Rachel's face with the soaked panel over her mouth. I kissed Rachel softly through silk on the wettest spot so she could taste me for the first time.

Rachel moaned and kissed me back through my panties. I let my hand slide over her chest, teasing her breasts and tweaking her nipples. Again, Rachel moaned through my panties.

Then I moved the panties and kissed her hard on her sweet lips as I watched her as her hands roamed over her body. Her breathing became more labored. I moved around to her, lying down beside her. Rachel rolled on her side, facing me. I kissed her hard, picked up her little wet thong, and inhaled its aroma.

I moaned, "Rachel, you smell so good I bet you taste even better. Rachel smiled and pushed me over on my back. She sat up, looking at my nakedness. Her mouth was open, and her tongue was licking her lips. "My God, Caroline, you are so beautiful," and leaned down, kissing me, taking control for the first time.

I thought about what she said. It made my pussy tingle. I am attractive; at least, I am told I am. We are always much too critical of ourselves, so I have learned that the perception of beauty is in the eye of the beholder, so I accept every comment willingly.

I am thirty-two years old, and I work out every day. I take yoga classes and a women's martial arts course every week. I am in great shape and have always ensured I have great stamina in all parts of my life, especially so I pleasure my lovers far beyond their expectations.

I am proud of my body. It is tight. My breasts are natural 36D cups with small areolas but big, long nipples that love to be sucked. I always thought that if I had children, I would have been cumming all the time while I breastfed them and would never want to stop.

My hair is strawberry blonde, but I color it redder to compliment my green eyes. I have had all the hair Laser removed from my underarms, legs, arms, and face through electrolysis. I left my light blonde pussy hair covering my mons, so if I have a lover who likes pussy hair, I can make that happen, but otherwise, I have it waxed every two weeks.

The girl that waxes me is a dream. She has an almost painless technique, and she makes me cum so hard after she finishes each time; I am hooked on her and can't wait to go back for my next treatment. I have always wanted to see her outside her job, but she is married and loves her husband.

I have never been with a man, so no Carole hands have ever intimately touched my body. I love men and have many great Carole friends, but I am a pure lesbian and proud to be one. I truly love women, especially young women, and I have one here before me I need to attend to.

Now that I got all that out, you can understand my desire to love this nubile young girl lying beside me on my bed.

I looked up at Rachel. No words were exchanged or necessary. Her eyes were glued to the mirror above us. Her right hand was between her legs, and her left hand was massaging her left breast and pinching her nipple. She was so caught up in watching herself that it was like she was watching a real porn movie starring 'Rachel.'

I slowly rose to my knees. Rachel's eyes shifted to me, locking eyes. We were face-to-face for the first time. I cupped Rachel's face and kissed her sweetly with my soft lips on hers. She moaned and kissed me more aggressively, but I held back, wanting our first loving session to be gentle and caring. The real fucking would cum later, and Rachel had no idea what I had in mind for her, but she would never forget the fucking she would receive today.

I gripped her by the wrists, placing her hand on my breasts. Rachel got the message and started to massage them and play with my hard nipples. Rachel raised her head, and I lowered my breasts to her lips. Our eyes never broke as she kissed each of my breasts, then took one nipple between her lips and sucked it, sending sweet sensations through my body to my core.

Something very sensual about this girl's mouth on my breasts made a low moan roll out of my mouth, "OOHH!"

Rachel smiled and switched nipples, taking it into my mouth, sucking it. I moaned again, and my pussy started leaking. The sacred juice slowly rolled down my inner thighs. So, I squeezed my thighs together, increasing the sensation. I laced my fingers through her silky blonde hair holding her against my breasts as her tongue battered my nipple.

I felt Rachel's hands on me, sliding across my tight belly to my hips. She pulled them to her making me shuffle closer on my knees. Rachel slid her hands back, cupping my ass cheeks, squeezing them as she moved her mouth from my breasts and kissed me harder. Then she pulled my hips tight against her pressing our pussy together as we tribbed, our wet lips and clits together.

It quickly became clear that Rachel was far more experienced than she was on, and I was probably really going to enjoy our time together. I was getting excited now, and it was clear that Rachel was prepared to give back and receive.

Rachel looked at me as she pushed her thigh between my legs, pressing against my wet pussy. She pulled my hips forward, making my pussy slide against her thigh, wetting as strip un her thigh. The feeling was amazing. Rachel wanted me to ride her thigh, so I did. I fucked her leg, soaking her with my juice. Once, we were in a rhythm, and her hand slid down to my clit and played with it.

I groaned as Rachel flicked my clit for the first time. Her eyes shot open as she discovered one of my secrets, and she moaned, "Oh Carol, your clit, it's so big!"

Yes, I have a large clit, and when it gets direct attention can grow to over an inch long and swell pretty fat. It's like a little cock and likes to be kissed, sucked, stroked, and pinched, just like a real cock. Rachel was surprised at how it had grown so big as she played with it, tweaked it, and stroked it.

I moaned and rolled onto my back and whispered, "Rachel baby, please, you need to suck my clit, and I will cum for you quickly."

I reached up and put light pressure on her shoulders, urging her down. Rachel dropped down on her belly between my legs. I rolled my hips forward. I could feel her hot breath on my pussy, making me shiver. This girl was having a strong effect on me; my body was responding like she was playing me like a violin string waiting to be plucked.

Rachel closed her lips over my clit, giving it a sweet kiss. My hips buckled, and I moaned as her tongue licked around its little crown for the first time.

- "Oh God, yes, suck it, baby, suck it!" I gasped as sheer pleasure spread through me.

My legs started to shake as Rachel sucked my clit and flicked it with her tongue. It felt amazing, and my hips bucked up against her mouth as my body shuddered. Then just like that, I edged toward my first orgasm closer and closer, building fast, and Rachel knew it. Rachel continued to make love to my clit as she crawled forward between my legs, pushing my legs open and back, spreading my pussy open. She covered my whole pussy and seriously started eating me. She was experienced for sure and got busy devouring me. Her finger slipped into my hole, slowly fucking me in and out as her mouth sucked my clit. Her lips took the little shaft between them and sucked it like a little cock. I was so into her mouth I couldn't hold back any longer, and my pussy exploded, spewing cum into her mouth and over her face, "Oh my God, yes, baby, eat me, Rachel, make me cum again!"

The power of my orgasm made me shake violently. I ran my fingers through Rachel's hair, holding her mouth as if glued to my cunt. My hips were fucking her mouth as I was squirting cum in her mouth. I thrashed around on the bed and moaned, "Oh Fuck, Rachel baby eat me. I'm cumming so fucking hard!!"

Rachel held on like I was a Bronco rider. Her hands slid under my ass, squeezing my cheeks, kneading them, and eating me with youthful abandon. I was moaning loudly; she was moaning into my pussy. We finally collapsed on the bed, gasping for air, and wailing loudly. Our sweaty bodies clung to each other, her head on my quivering belly.

I was exhausted, lying there in a sexual fog. This girl had fucked me well. I finally came to my senses enough to pull Rachel up, holding her to my body. I pulled the coverlet over us, creating a love cocoon. We lay this way for a good while, holding each other. I kissed her head and stroked her back. She felt warm and comfortable next to me.

After we recovered, we slowly separated. Rachel looked at me with lust in her eyes. I didn't think she knew what to say, so she kissed me softly, whispering, "You are amazing!"

- "Oh no, Rachel, you are the amazing one. You are eighteen years old and made me cum faster and harder than anyone has in a very long time." I hugged her closely and kissed her hard, letting our tongues play together.

I broke the kiss before we couldn't stop. "Your fucking made me hungry; how about you?" She nodded her head and smiled. I rolled off the bed, pulling Rachel into the bathroom to clean up. We washed up and combed out our hair. I gave her a short robe, and I wore my lounging gown.

We headed to the kitchen for some sex fuel preparing for our next session. I wanted Rachel's strength to be revitalized for what I had planned for her next. We had a nice Caesar Salad with some rotisserie chicken. I opened a nice white wine and introduced Rachel to an after-sex lunch. We chatted about her life and family.

I learned that her dad left them for another woman seven years ago, and Rachel had not seen him since. She seemed OK with that. Her Mom is an independent accountant and works for many small companies. She has mostly women friends and spends most of her time with Rachel and her brother Edwin. Socially she goes on 'Girls' Night Out' with her friends several times a month. She has a best friend, Beth, who is around a lot.

Her Mom is a closet lesbian; maybe I will find that out later.

- "So, Rachel, what time must you be home, baby?" I asked.

- "I don't have to go home. Mom is gone for the weekend with Beth and a couple of other women, so I was staying with my friend or going back to my house one or the other." She explained.

Wow, that opened up several opportunities I had not expected. Rachel knew that, too, and hoped we could spend the weekend together.

I cleaned up the kitchen while Rachel watched TV for a while. I joined her, and we cuddled, watching some soap opera. She fell asleep in my arms. I held her close and stroked her back as she slept. My heart was beating fast. I was anxious to get her in bed again.

Rachel stirred. I stroked her face and kissed the top of her head. She looked up at me. I leaned down and kissed her. She put her hand behind my head, pressing my lips to hers. Her tongue painted my lips, making my pussy twitch. We broke the kiss, and Rachel stood, pulling me up and leading me back into the bedroom. She untied my sash and pushed my gown off my shoulders, letting it float to the floor. I undid hers, and the silk slipped off her shoulder, fluttering to the floor. We stood looking at each other's naked bodies. My mouth watered as I looked down at her blonde pussy. I wanted it to be smooth, so I asked, "Rachel do you want me to shave your pussy hair off, baby? You will love how it feels and how sex feels. You will never want it to grow back."

Rachel looked at me and ran her fingers through her thin hair thatch on her pussy. She slid her finger into her slit and pulled it out wet with her juice. She licked it clean and smiled, saying, "Please shave me. Make me smooth like you."

I smiled at her and went into the bathroom. I tossed a towel to her and said, "Hop up on the bed and lay on the towel." I gathered all my supplies and went back into the bedroom.

Rachel was lying on the towel, leaning up on her elbows. Her legs were spread wide, and she watched me walk toward her. Her hand went to her pussy. She dipped her fingers inside, bringing them out covered with her juice. She held them up to me as I reached the bed. I leaned over my mouth with my tongue sticking out. Rachel smiled, laying her fingers on my tongue. I closed my lips, and my tongue swirled around her fingers, tasting her sweetness.

I gave her my scissors, "Trim your hair short, please, then I will finish."

I shaved her pussy and all the little hairs around her asshole. Rachel was so turned on that she had been struggling to stay still. She was near cumming the whole time leaking her juice. Her pussy looked so delicious, but her asshole looked even better. I have a weakness for girls' assholes, and I couldn't wait to eat hers. I put Witch Hazel all over the shaved area, and I gave Rachel some Aloe lotion, "Rachel, be sure to put this all over your pussy and asshole."

- "It's so smooth; touch me and see."

- "I will touch you soon enough, you play for a while, but now you need to put on the Aloe lotion."

I went into the bathroom and cleaned up the shaving gear, then stood in the doorway watching Rachel play with her freshly shaved pussy. I knew it was so sensitive now that she would make herself cum with her fingers very fast. Rachel came once, then again very quickly. She withered all over the bed; it was a beautiful sight.

As I watched her, my fingers drifted to my smooth pussy and played with my soft wet lips and clit. I imagined my fingers were hers and they had keyed me up for the main event that was coming shortly. I had to stop touching myself, or I would cum, and I wanted Rachel to make me cum, not me.

Rachel was watching herself in the overhead mirror, not paying attention to me, so I quietly moved into my closet and toy cabinet. I have a wide assortment of toys, strap-on cocks, butt plugs, vibrators, dildos, and many more; plus, I keep a variety of lube, stimulant gels, and massage oils to enhance my love sessions and my lover's sexual experiences.

I looked over my collection for the right items to help take Rachel to sexual heaven. I would make love to her and then fuck her like she had never been fucked. As we are enjoying these toys, I will teach her how to pleasure anyone she sleeps with. I hoped she would leave here wanting me again soon, but she would also have more control of her sex life. I would also give her a toy or two to remember me by and use with her little friend.

As I looked out of the closet, I could hear Rachel panting. I looked out, and she was still watching herself in the mirror and her hands running all over her body, covered with a light layer of sweat that made her body shine in the low light in the room.

I picked up my favorite emerald butt plug and dribbled some lube on it. I spread my legs and squatted, sliding a lubed finger up my ass, making my pussy pulse. I slowly pushed the plug against my pulsing star, letting it slip in as my ass opened up. It pops into place, sending a hard pulse to my pussy. My body shuddered as I spun it around and pressed on it to ensure it was seated. I slid a finger through my pussy furrow and across my hard clit, letting out a low moan.

I walked to the side of the bed. I was ready to fuck Rachel now. "You like your new smooth pussy, baby?" in a sexy voice.

Rachel looked up at me. Her face was flushed with lust. It was time!!

I slowly crawled onto the bed. I gently pulled Rachel's legs apart, almost in slow motion. I moved between her legs. Rachel rose on her elbows and looked at me. Her eyes dropped down on my body, and she gasped. Rachel's eyes grew wide and shot up to mine, then back down to the long black strap-on cock hanging from the harness strapped to my hips. Her mouth dropped open, but no words came out.

- "I promised to love you as you have never been loved before and to teach you lesbian love. I am prepared to start now. Are you ready to change your life forever, Rachel?" I asked with a sexy grin on my face.

My eyes never left Rachel's. My hands stroked the soft skin of her inner thighs, making her legs spread wider. Rachel's eyes were darting up and down my body, finally stopping on my eyes. She couldn't answer, only able to nod her head, 'YES,' as she was chewing her lower lip.

- "Rachel, I want to relax, enjoy everything that will happen between us, and learn all you can retain. I promise not to hurt you in any way. Let me know if you are uncomfortable with anything we do, and we will stop. I want to love you, Rachel, and I want you to love me. Everything I do to you, please do to me. If you are ready, we can start now."

Rachel's eyes were wide open, and her breathing was shallow. She nodded her head and lay back, surrendering to me. I am going to fuck you, baby. Have you ever been fucked before?"

Rachel shook her head as she took a deep breath.

- "We will take a break in a few hours for dinner. When we start again will be determined by our desire for each other. From now on, things will be spontaneous, so you can do anything when the feeling comes to you.

Rachel sat up and pulled me to her kissing me hard, pushing her tongue into my mouth, holding our kiss, and she squeezed my breasts, making my nipples harder. I moaned into her mouth; my pussy tingled and started leaking more juice.

I broke the kiss and laid her back on the bed. I kissed her softly, then moved down to her chest, kissing her sweaty skin along the way. Her breasts were flush pink, and her nipples were long and hard. I kissed around her areolas and did not touch them, teasing her skin. They started to swell into puffy little mounds pushing her nipples out further.

Rachel squirmed under me, moaning. My knee was pushed tight against her freshly shaved pussy. Rachel moaned and started humping my knee, making it wet with her juice. I could smell Rachel's pussy which was intoxicating to me. She started moaning continuously, panting for air. My teasing had the correct effect. Rachel was definitely, 'completely mine now!'

I just had to suck her areolas and nipples, so I covered the whole areola and nipple of her right breast with my mouth. I lashed her hard nipple with my tongue and pinched her left nipple in my fingers. Rachel started to tremble and whimper. "Oh God, Carol, I am so close to cumming, as her hands gripped the rumpled bed sheets in her fists, squeezing them tight. Her pussy was on fire, almost burning my knee.

Then Rachel whimpered, begging me, "Oh Carol, you're killing me; I need to cum, please, please, please, make me cum!"

I decided to give her a little relief and smiled down at her. Rachel must have been reading my mind. She pulled her legs, upholding them back behind her knees. Her sweet pussy slowly opened, letting her delicate inner lips open like a little flower blooming just for me. Her rich pink center showed as her lips opened, glistening with her juice. My eyes locked on her pussy, and my mouth watered as my eyes watched her young bald pussy lips spread open for me.

- "Oh God, Rachel, your pussy is so beautiful!"

Her face glowed with lust as she smiled at me. I knew that she needed this as badly as I did! So, I licked my lips and leaned in, running my tongue through her slit from the bottom to the top. I am gathering her sweet juice on my tongue and letting it drip off on her belly, leaving a little puddle of her liquid in her navel.

I took her clit in my lips, and Rachel gasped, "Oh Fuck, Carol!"

Then I let it go, licking around her clit without touching it, lathing her freshly shaved mons. Rachel gasped and screamed, "Oh fuck, yea, eat my cunt, Carol, make me cum, oh fuck!" approving my tongue actions.

I slid my hands under her bottom, cupping her cheeks, and lifted her ass so my mouth could access her little brown asshole and pussy. I started licking her asshole. I wanted it to be nice and wet. Rachel began to pant, and she repeatedly moaned, "Oh God, Oh God," so I knew she loved what I was doing.

My tongue wiggled all over her asshole, rimming it and pressing into its center. Rachel was squirming all over the bed, so I had to hold on to her as I ate her ass. I pushed my tongue hard against her crinkled hole. It slowly opened slightly. My tongue pushed harder until it eased inside her asshole. At the same time, I thrust two fingers into her pussy and fingered her fast and hard, rubbing her clit with my thumb.

Rachel exploded, "My God, Carol... I'm cummmiiinnng!!!" she screamed as a strong orgasm crashed through her body. She was moaning and twitching as white pussy juice flowed into my mouth. She suddenly went limp, but I ate her like a hungry animal. I finally lifted my face to see her lying lifeless on the bed. Her eyes were closed tight. She had cum so hard she fainted.

I kissed her body, sucking each nipple and kissing her as she slowly awoke. Her body was still trembling as her orgasm slowly subsided. Rachel calmed slightly, saying, "Carol, that felt so amazing; my girlfriend has never eaten my pussy as good as you did, thank you!"

"Well, thank you, but that was only the beginning, Rachel; I'm not done yet." I held her for a minute and told her. "I need you lying on your front," as I rolled her onto her front, pulled a pillow under her hips, and raised her ass. I moved behind her, rubbing her hot ass cheeks, patting, and squeezing them.

We had some playing to do before the main event, so I unbuckled my strap-on and let it fall to the bed and moved it to the side.

I loved her pert little bottom. It was so enticing to me. I put a hand on each cheek, giggling at them, then spreading them apart, showing me her sweet asshole and young pussy. I was so horny that seeing her special hole made my pussy spasm.

I made sure the butt plug, and lube were beside me when I kneeled between her spread legs. "Rachel, spread your ass cheeks for me. Her hands moved back and opened them, offering me a beautiful sight. "I want you to relax now and don't tense up at all, OK?" I told her. She moaned in agreement as my hand roamed her smooth, warm, young ass cheeks.

I leaned down and kissed each cheek, then ran my tongue up her crack from her pussy to her asshole. Rachel moaned and lifted her hip, spreading her legs more and opening her ass cheeks completely. God, she looked amazing. Her little pink virgin asshole was winking at me, not knowing what was coming next.

I rimmed her hole, pushing my tongue against the center, teasing, and wetting her hole. I sat back and put some drop lube on my middle finger. I rubbed it lightly around her hole and then pressed it in the center. Rachel groaned and pushed her ass up against my finger. Her asshole opened, and the lubed tip of my finger slipped past the muscle ring.

Rachel gasped as my finger pushed deeper inside her ass, lubing her up. I fucked her hole a few strokes, then removed my finger, to Rachel's disappointment, "No, it feels so good, don't stop."

I lubed up the pink stone butt plug, making sure it was slick so it would slide smoothly into her ass. "Now, Rachel, relax your ass, and you will love his. I rubbed my hand all over her bottom cheeks. They were shaking under my hand, pushing back as I stroked her.

I pushed my middle finger back up her asshole, sliding it in and out and lubing her more. As I pulled my finger out, I slowly pushed the butt plug into her ass. She groaned, "Oh God, what are you doing? She said with fear in her voice.

- "Relax, baby; I would never hurt you; just relax and enjoy the pleasure," I whispered as I pushed the plug against her tight muscle. It slowly popped in, giving her an amazing sensation she had never felt before.

- "Oh God, Carol, what is it? It feels so smooth?" she asked in a choking voice, then moaning again.'

I pushed harder, and Rachel shrieked, "Oh Fuck, it's too big!"

I spun it in my fingers and slapped her ass cheek hard as I pushed the plug past her muscle, and her asshole clamped shut on the plug stem.

She pushed her ass up and moaned onto the pillow under her face. 'God, Carol, it feels so strange but really good. Her fingers reached back between her legs, touching her butt plug for the first time. "Oh wow, that feels amazing," Rachel moaned as she pushed back against it.

- "Role over, baby," I told her as I moved into a sixty-nine position. She looked at my pussy and the emerald, green butt plug in my ass.
- "Carol, you have one too!" she gushed.
- "Yeah, we are twins. Only mine is green, and yours is pink." I moaned as she pressed on my plug, making me moan.

Her hands we are smoothing my ass cheeks as she blew warm breath on my wet pussy. It was such an erotic feeling I shivered. I looked down at her sweet young virgin pussy. It was pink and swollen, wet with her juice. Rachel was so turned on that her hard clit appeared like a trigger.

I blew on Rachel's pussy up to clit; she let out a soft low moan raised her head and pulled a pillow under it. She gripped my warm cheeks and pulled my hips down, pressing her lips against my wet pussy, and her tongue slipped through my slit, licking around my green jeweled plug. My hips humped down on her mouth, and I groaned, "Oh Yes!"

I lowered my mouth, pressing my lips softly against Rachel's sweet lips. Her pussy was so wet with her juice that it was leaking out and running down, covering her plug. I slid my tongue down through Rachel's slit over her taint and rimmed around her plug, lapping her sweet juice.

This was only the appetizer, but now I was ready for the main course.

I moved off her and slipped my big black strap-on back on. I buckled it and ensured my pussy plug was nestled against my G-spot and the pad pressing against my clit. It felt so good, buckled tight in place. It was designed to give mutual pleasure to both lovers. As I fuck Rachel, she will benefit from my fucking skills, and I will benefit from the pussy plug moving against my G-spot with every stroke. My clit was constantly teased with every move I made.

I rolled her over, moved between her legs, and pulled the pillow under her hips again. Her hips were high now at the perfect position. I let my cock drag over her sweet cheeks, making her gasp. I gently kissed her shoulders, up her neck, and behind her ear, bringing out a low moan. Her skin was hot with a light sheen of sweat.

I whispered into her ear, "Rachel baby, are you ready for a wonderful new experience?

- "Oh, Yesss," she moaned.

- "Do you trust me, baby,"

All Rachel could muster was a low moan, "Yesss."

- "OK, baby, just relax and let me take you to sexual heaven," I said as I leaned back and rubbed my cock over her ass cheeks.

Rachel started to shake as I played with her ass, spinning her jeweled plug, and running my fingers through her wet furrow. Rachel's hips were wiggling, and her pussy was dripping wet as Rachel moaned constantly.

I put my hands on Rachel's hips, lifting them as I slipped a second pillow under her raising her hips to an even better position. I reached under her and pinched her clit hard. Her hips pushed against my fingers, and she cried, "Oh Fuck, I need to cum!"

- "Shush, baby, I know you are about to explode, and that's the way I want you. Rachel, you are about to have the greatest sexual experience of your young life. You will never forget this day. You will cum more times than you can count, and you will be exhausted when we sleep tonight."

The smell of Rachel's scent was strong, wafting through the air. I loved her scent and mine as they mixed and made my pussy quiver.

I slipped two fingers into Rachel's pussy. She was wet and tight, gripping my fingers as they slid deep into her cunt. I finger fucked Rachel as her hips worked back against my fingers. I added a third finger stretching her and making her moan louder. I pressed against her jeweled plug, making her moan again, "Oh Fuck, I need to cum so bad!"

I dripped some lube on my lack cock and slid my lubed fingers into her pussy, spreading it all along her hot walls. Once I lubed her, I wiped my fingers on the sheets and gripped her hips. I felt her tense and holding her breath.

- "Relax, Rachel baby; you are about to get the first real fucking of your life. I promise you will love it." I comforted her.

I rubbed the head of my cock along Rachel's wet slit, teasing her and making her moan and shake with anticipation. My pussy was on fire, and I needed to cum as badly as Rachel did. I yanked on the cock, making the pussy plug hit my G-spot. I groaned, "So good."

I lined up the big black cock head with Rachel's flowered lips and slowly pushed my cock between them, seating my cockhead in her tight hole, then stopped holding still as she adjusted to the size.

- "Oh God, Carol, it is so big!" she groaned. "You are going to split me open."

I pushed forward an inch at a time. Rachel's pussy was so tight it gripped my cock as it slid in. My pussy loved it as my pussy plug rubbed against my G-spot. I started to pinch my nipples, making me start to climb the orgasm ladder too.

It was time for some serious fucking. Rachel was up on her hands, now pushing back on my cock, helping it slide deeper in her cunt. I was about four inches deep when I slowly pulled out.

Rachel gasped, "Oh No, Don't Pull Out,'

I answered Rachel quickly, pushing my cock in harder, pushing in a couple of more inches deeper. Her head snapped back, and she groaned loudly, "Oh yeah, fuck me, Carol, fuck me hard."

That was all I wanted to hear. "Rachel, brace yourself, baby; you'll get all ten inches of big black cock, fucked deep in your pussy for the next thirty minutes. We will cum and cum together until we collapse together from sexual exhaustion."

I gripped Rachel's hips and pushed the remaining four inches of the big cock into her pussy. It finally hit her cervix, and she screamed, "Oh Fuck Yes!!"

Rachel took nine inches in her young eighteen-year-old pussy, groaning as every inch slid in deeper. I was amazed that she could take that much, but I knew she was a special girl from the start.

We settled into a steady rhythm, and I fucked Rachel hard, then soft, but we fucked. Rachel came over and over. I reached under her and played with her clit making her cry out. "OH MY GOD, I'M CUUUMMMIIINNNG!!!" her orgasms started to take over her body.

After about three hard orgasms, Rachel's body convulsed hard. When she came, it sent vibrations up my cock through my pussy plug, making my pussy tingle, and I started cum with Rachel. I was all about fucking Rachel, making her cum, and giving her an unbelievable experience. But now, this was so erotic I was cumming almost as often as Rachel was.

We fucked for almost 30 minutes when Rachel had a massive orgasm, shaking us both to the core. She buried her face in the pillow as she came hard; I spanked her ass, making her cry. "Oh, Fuck Yes, I am cumming so hard!" My body shook along with her as my pussy finally exploded in a massive orgasm.

I held on to Rachel's hips with my hog black buries in her pulsing pussy. I came so hard. This was something I had been missing, and now I had it again. Tears were running down my cheeks.

I moved to stand up, not letting the cock leave Rachel's pussy. I moved over her hips, straddling her, and started fucking down into her stretched pussy. I stroked deep into Rachel as I played with her butt plug, spinning, and pulling on it is stretching her asshole and then letting it snap back into place. Rachel groaned as I did this repeatedly; there were no words, just grunting and moaning. Rachel was in the sexual state I wanted her in. I was ready to fuck her ass!

- "Rachel baby, it's time for your new experience, so relax and enjoy."

I knew she didn't hear me because she was still constantly moaning.

I twirled her plug and quickly popped it out. Her asshole was gaping open, waiting for the head of my cock. I quickly slid my big black cock from her pussy, dripping with her juice. I slowly pushed the charge against her gaping asshole, popping the head inside.

- "Oh Fuck, you will split me open!" and Rachel tried to slip away. I was holding her just above her hips so she could not escape. I pushed down harder, and my cockhead pushed past Rachel's muscle ring and slid two inches into her ass.

- "Oh Fuck, God Damn!" Rachel screamed as she rose on her hands, and she pushed back on my cock, taking in two more inches. Her hand slid between her legs and started to finger fuck her pussy. Rachel was now in a sexual frenzy, totally out of control, acting on animal instinct.

I was seated deep in Rachel's ass, so I started fucking her fast. I was buried deep in her ass, and she was furiously finger fucking her pussy, moaning. I loved this more than any other fucking I had ever given. Rachel was such a good sport, and she was so sexual. I really could not wait for her to fuck me.

I was furiously fucking Rachel's now, hammering her ass. She was withering and begging for more, cumming again. I lost count; Rachel came so often.

I was tired and needed to rest, so I quickly pulled out and rolled over on my back, pulling Rachel over. "Ride my cock in your ass, baby, and let me play with your pussy."

Rachel scrambled up on me, rolled her hips forward, and reached back, gripping the big black cock. Rachel pushed it in her gaping asshole. Her eyes widened as it slowly impaled her ass. She groaned, "Jesus, your cock is so fucking big in my ass, but God, it feels so good." Rachel fucked herself on my big dildo taking all of it deep in her ass, as I played with her pussy fingering her until she exploded. As her body convulsed, she fell forward on my chest, laying down on me. I held her and fucked her steadily until we both came together. I held Rachel tight to me as a beautiful feeling that I had missed for a long time suddenly swept over me.

That was the day I met Rachel, and our lesbian affair began.

"We deserve to experience love fully, equally, without shame and without compromise."
Elliot Page

INTIMATE DINNER

Patty's hands were tied to the brass bedposts by some colorful scarves. She shook her body impatiently, willing her friend to hurry up in the next room. Her eyes shifted from the door to the ceiling, to the frosted glass on the window and then down to her own naked body. Beads of sweat glistened all over her breasts and torso from the seemingly endless number of orgasms she had been through over the last few hours.
- "How long has it been?" she wondered, desperate to see the alarm clock on the other dresser. Try as she might, she could not twist her neck enough.
- "Damn," she muttered. "Why did I let myself get into this?"
The answer was on a coffee table a few feet to her right. Two goblets and an empty bottle of Pinot Gris had culminated in her allowing Kel to put those scarves to good use.
- "She's crazy," Patty thought, adding. "...and I love her for it."
Her mind flashed back to the special romantic dinner that Kelly made for her. She could not take her eyes off Patty even as they ate. The food was a mere impediment to what lay after. Kelly used the wine to get her in the mood for something she had never experienced before. Then she took out the scarves.
After getting her tied up, Kelly parted her legs and dove into her. Her tongue drove Patty off the edge of sanity into delirium and back again. That tongue was as relentless as it was skillful. It started teasing her tantalizingly, paying a special degree of attention to her calves and thighs. Just the tip of Kel's tongue delicately teased her inner thighs, making her squirm. Kelly took her sweet time making her way from the left thigh all the way to her inflamed orifice and down the right

thigh. Each time, her tongue would come within millimeters of Patty's engorged nub but would divert at the last moment. Kelly's brown hair splayed all over Patty's abdomen, tickling her when they scraped over her skin.

Patty screamed in frustration. She tried to raise her hips into Kelly's face, but her thighs were pinned down by the entire weight of her devilish roommate. Her head rose painfully off the bed so she could look down at the face which she loved to see so much. The sex was feral, bordering on painful, but they never forgot that they were in love. They had been hopelessly in love right from their freshman year.

Just when she thought she would rip the scarves out from frustration, it happened. The rough layer of tastebuds of Kelly's tongue rested against her clit. The sheer exhilaration of the first contact almost made her cum on the spot. The deviant tongue then wrapped around her erect clit, scrubbing it. Also, two fingers slipped into her damp orifice, hooking themselves inside her.

- "Oh FUCK!" she screamed.

The two fingers became three. They moved in and out of her with a piston's rhythm. The fingertips made contact with her G spot at the end of every in-stroke, making a small shudder go through her loins. Her sex was a cauldron of seething desire which Kelly wantonly stirred with her fingers and tongue. The fingers and tongue interchanged places. Now the tongue plunged deep within her drenched orifice, and she tweaked the throbbing clit between her thumb and forefinger.

The sudden stretching of her clit made Patty feel a unique cocktail of pleasure and pain spread through her being. Her pheromones went on overdrive sending her arousal through the roof. She exuded the unique fragrance of sex from every pore of her body. Patty gasped and lifted her hips into her lover's face.

Kelly lifted her face for an instant to see Patty's eyes pleading with her to return her attentions to her hungry pussy. She smiled and lowered her face to the clit. This time, she planted her lips around the clit and took the very tip of it between her teeth. She pulled back with a sharp tug and simultaneously impaled the sopping vulva underneath with three fingers.

Patty was shocked. Her senses were reeling under the overwhelming rush of pleasure. She screamed in several short yelps and thrashed against the bed, a massive orgasm erupting inside. Kelly knew from experience what was about to follow. She eagerly propped her face up on her elbows in front of the gaping opening and waited for the moment.

A clear liquid squirted out and splashed against the expectant face. More followed in spasmodic bursts, each burst ejecting her liquids onto her face and lips, dripping off her chin. Kelly opened her mouth and captured the last few sprays.

Patty took several deep breaths, her bosom heaving with each one. An incandescent flare danced before her eyes, dazzling her with a psychedelic whirl of color. The riptide of orgasm had left her feeling distinctly woozy in its aftermath. Her body descended from the fluffy clouds as she felt a tongue lick its way up her sweaty torso. It planted a soft peck on each nipple and finally a pair of lips pressed against hers.

Kelly's tongue parted her roommate's lips and fiercely kissed her tongue, letting her have a taste of her own squirt. They lip-locked passionately, tonguing with gusto for several minutes before Kelly drew her face back. There was no sight on Earth better than the peaceful post-orgasmic pallor on Patty's face.

- "Did you like it?" Kelly asked playfully, her fingers fiddling with her roommate's spent sex.
- "It was... oh my god!" Patty managed to squeeze out between gasps.
- "Well, I hope it inspires you," Kelly said, swinging her legs around and straddling her sweaty face. She was also leaking from the raw lust of what had transpired. Leaning forward, Kelly parted those rosy nether lips which she loved to make love to.
- "Kelly. No. I'm too sensitive right now..." the rest of Patty's words were cut off by a delicious labium being lowered onto her face.
- "Put your tongue to better use than talking," snapped Kelly.

Patty was helpless. Part of her got stuck into the enviable task of eating out the woman she had come to love more than she thought possible. Another part prayed she could withstand the onslaught of one more shattering climax.
- "One more..." she muttered, snapping back to the present. "Then one more after that, then one more... then another one... then..."

After a bit she gave up trying to count how many orgasms she had been through. It was probably in double digits. Not bad considering they had come one after another with no respite. There had come a time when she was no longer aware of herself or her surroundings. All her senses had succumbed to a continuous orgasmic fugue. The orgasmic haze persisted as her roommate churned out more from her body than she thought humanly possible.

Her thoughts were broken when the door opened. Kelly stood in the doorway, completely naked except for a wicked grin on her lips and a ribbed dildo strapped onto a harness around her waist. She held a box under her arm, the contents of which were currently left for

Patty's imagination, although she was sure she would be very intimately acquainted with every implement inside that box.

Kelly took a deep breath and smiled.

- "I love the smell of fresh sex in the morning."

She laid the box down beside the bed and procured a Gatorade from the fridge. Undoing the cap, she brought the tip near Patty's lips.

- "Drink this," she said. "Don't want you dehydrating on me now."

Patty obeyed and replenished the fluids in her system. The size of the box told her she would be needing all the energy this energy drink could provide. Her lower lips were sore, and her clit hurt from the streak of orgasms she had been through. Yet, the prospect of even more made her tingle with excitement.

Kelly tossed the empty bottle away and laid Patty flat on the bed. Her hands grasped her roommate's shoulders, and her legs pinned down her knees. The head of the dildo rested along her slit. Kelly flicked a remote switch in her hand and the mass of plastic and rubber began to vibrate. The vibrations sent ripples through Patty's body, promising a new vista of pleasures up ahead.

- "Happy Birthday, Patty," she said with a smile and drew back for the first thrust.

Patty braced for impact. The first push itself embedded the entire eight inches inside her. She gasped and looked up to see a wicked gleam in Kelly's eyes. Those eyes came closer to her. Soon, Patty could feel her roommate's warm breath on her skin and could see those haunting eyes inches from her own.

Their faces were close, so close. Patty was barely aware of the dildo inside her. All her senses focused on that face. Her gaze roamed over Kelly's face, resting on every beautiful feature. It started in her eyes of course, then went along her pale cheek. It lingered on her sumptuous lips for a small eternity.

Those lips were even closer now. So close that every exhaled breath caressed Patty's skin. They raised themselves to Patty's forehead and kissed her. The kiss moved from her forehead, leaving her skin intermittently to leave trail of lip-marks down her cheek and neck. Sweat glistened on her skin, flushed crimson.

Kelly continued to pepper her with a multitude of kisses. For a time, the raging sexuality had given way to a tender love. Those lips eventually sought out hers and they kissed. Patty surrendered to the sweet sensuality of the simple kiss. Her interactions with Kelly may have become a kink-riddled carnival, but it was the underlying love which they never forgot.

Their tongues did not force the issue, rather made love to each other. Kelly let her taste buds wander to various corners of Patty's mouth, savoring the intimacy. It was a slow and studied kiss, a perfect interlude.

Kelly broke the kiss and sat back. Patty looked at her dreamily, still barely aware of the plastic contraption inside her.

- "She looks so beautiful," thought Kelly. "So... vulnerable."

The beautiful blonde hair lay strewn on the pillows. Patty took deep breaths, her breasts inflating and subsiding with each one. Her nipples stuck out hard atop them. Her face was exhausted, almost stationary after their exertions. She opened her eyes a sliver and smiled at Kelly, telling her she was okay.

- "I won't let anything come between us," a private voice echoed deep in the recesses of Kelly's mind.

"Masturbation: the primary sexual activity of mankind. In the nineteenth century it was a disease; in the twentieth, it's a cure."
Thomas Szasz, *fellow of the American Psychiatric Association*

EASTER PRESENT

A letter from Elizabeth to her best friend, Melany.
"Dear Melany,
Melany my love, I told you I had an idea for an Easter Bunny costume to wear for Freddy when he comes home on leave at Easter. Well, here is how our dear friend Tatyanna helped me create something. I will save it 'til he has been at home for several days, and when I think he might best appreciate it!!!!!
If you remember I wanted to create a sensuous bunny costume that I could surprise him with and had definite ideas about it. I wanted something diaphanous to cover but not conceal all my girly bits, be easy to slip into and easy for me to adjust to get the visual effect I wanted. There had to be two pretty, floppy, bunny ears and finally I wanted a bunny tail. Ideally the back would be minimal and only something sufficient to hold the costume in front of me quite securely as I moved. The rear (as in rear-end) I wanted to be thong-like in nature, so there would be an illusion of me wearing nothing except a fluffy tail, as the material would disappear between my bum cheeks.
To Tatyanna I had suggested using a piece of sheer pure silk that I had had for absolute ages and that Freddy had brought back for me from the Far East, but she was horrified. As you know she is an enthusiastic and very proficient amateur dramatic person who has incredibly good needle skills (quite unlike me – a sail maker's needle I can handle but that's about it).
I arranged for her to come over the day before yesterday, during the early afternoon; she had organized things very well because it coincided with her husband being away from home and she had plenty of time. So, when she came, she had already made the ears, and they were exactly what I wanted. She had

arranged them on a sort of springy theatrical metal (a bit like headphones) that fitted into my hair so that the ears popped up quite realistically. They were Delightful and amusingly floppy too.

Then she showed me the material ... Again, it was theatrical and gossamer like but cheaply made ... quite strong. Her approach to the design was that she would start with the material around the back of my neck like a scarf, equally on both sides, so that the two "tails" hung down my front. She brought the tails over my breasts, down between my legs and cut the tails so that they finished slightly higher up my back than my anus. At this point she sewed on the fluffy tail and a length of flesh colored ribbon. She took the ribbon up my spine and formed it in a loop around the neck of the "scarf" and sewed it. So that was the design that she discussed with me, and she had brought everything to complete it.

- "GREAT," I said, and stood there in bra and panties so that she could do the fitting. She went behind me and 'snip' the 'tails' were right. She quickly attached the fluffy tail and ribbon then stood behind me again so that she could get it fixed at the neck. Presto! It was done.... About 10 minutes if that.

I paraded in front of my bedroom mirror. Tati held a large hand mirror behind me so that I could see the effect at the back, then I slipped it off. Absolutely delighted and exactly what I wanted.

Then Tati said, "Here wear these as well," and she gave me a pair of white silken gloves! They absolutely were the perfect finish to my costume. I carefully laid my new costume on the bed and reached for my skirt.

- "Oh no you do not. Dress Rehearsal time. We are going to make sure that it LOOKS right as Freddy will see you on that morning, after you must put it on for yourself without any help."

How stupid of me ... of course I should wear it, do a dress rehearsal, and make sure I could get into it. So, I quickly slipped out of my bra and panties and picked up the costume. Well of course I was clumsy trying to get it on for the first time and getting the ribbon to feel right on my back and fumbling for the bunny tail. Then getting the material so that it parted nicely over my shoulders and was just the right tension over my breasts to both reveal the shape and hint at the color of my nipples and be held in place by the tension. It then had to come together to pass between my legs and it needed a lot of fidgeting about to get the material looking neat as it disappeared down there. I also wanted despite two thicknesses of material for there to be no visual doubt of my bushy front hair, my girl's hair. Finally, I got it right, but she made me take it off and put it on about a dozen times until I knew I could get it how I wanted it.

Finally, I was happy that I could quickly get it on and look right without Freddy becoming suspicious at my being gone from him. So, I gave her a quick kiss and said, "Cup of tea?"

Tati said, "Just turn round for me," and she sat on my bedroom chair as I turned and 'displayed' in front of her. "Mmmmm I'm not just sure..." She said. "Come here."

So, I came from the middle of the room and stood about three feet from her.

- "Closer" she said. I stood about two feet from her.

- "Elizabeth, I'm not just sure that there isn't something here that I need to work on just hold still."

I stood like an idiot not seeing it coming at all. She reached out as she had a dozen or more times and seemed to adjust the folds of gauze between my legs. Then the sides of her fingers were brushing MY folds and were easing forward and back, forward, and back under the material. I felt that familiar flush through my body. My knees seemed to weaken. I put my hands on her shoulders to steady myself. Her other hand reached out and she eased the gauze away from my right breast exposing my hardening nipple.

- "Closer Elizabeth" she said, and I inched closer to her. She raised her head and looked at my face, then she pursed her lips and blew softly on my bared nipple. I shivered and heard myself whimper "Ohhh."

Her right hand had pulled the material to one side, and she was now easing my lips apart. She held it to one side with her thumb and crooked her finger to find my hole. I knew I was leaking onto her fingers as she circled my muscle there with her fingertip.

She lifted her head again and her lips found my hard nipple. I felt the softness of her lips, my nipple slipped between her lips, and she suckled on me. She took my arm and pulled the material so that I was free of it, then the other side. I bowed my head, and she slipped it over my head and across my shoulder and it drifted to the floor like a rose shedding its petals.

I was naked. She started to kiss my lips, softly, gently. Her lips were soft on mine, a woman's lips not the hardness of a man's. I found myself stumbling backwards as she pushed against me; I felt the bed against my thighs and collapsed backwards onto it. I lay spread before her, gasping, breasts heaving, my wets running from me. My eyes felt puffy, my cheeks glowing, and every part of me tingled.

Through half closed eyes I saw her take off her blouse, unclip her bra and let it slowly tantalizingly fall forward. I saw her glorious breasts, tiny nipples, rosy pink and thrusting proudly at me. I saw her hands fall to her skirt, unfasten, unzip, puddle to the floor around her feet. Her panties that day were pure white, open laced, high hipped and between the lace designs I saw the tantalizing shadow of her female hair.

She hooked her thumbs in the waistband, slowly moved then down knowing I was watching her reveal it to me.

I saw her naked. I heard her soft voice. I closed my eyes.

- "Middle of the bed, Elizabeth" I shuffled into the middle and felt the bed dip as she knelt beside me. Then, then she said.

- "This is a FULL undress rehearsal, darling, open your eyes."

I looked at her kneeling beside me. She put her hands on the bed and leant down. I saw her pendulous breasts getting closer and closer and I opened my lips. Her nipple slipped into them, and I licked it with the tip of my tongue. Then I drew it in and sucked it with my lips only. Her hand touched my tummy and circled it. For a moment it tickled, and I giggled. Her fingers were in my hair, just the tips, her nails just able to reach the skin of my mound. She put the palm of her hand over my hair. It did not touch my skin. It did not press on me. Her palm caressed the surface of my hairs 'against the grain' and I felt them rise like the hackles on a dog. Her hand went to my knee. She seemed not to touch. She seemed able to move her hand so close to me that it was the movement of the air between her skin and mine that gave me this wonderfully exciting soft sensation. A fingertip touched the softness of my inner thigh close to my joining. It withdrew and I wanted it back. She went back just as gently to my knee and then back to my joining, but she would not touch it. She would not touch me there. God, I needed her touch.

I reached out to feel between her legs. She said "NO."

I said "Please, Taty, please."

- "Elizabeth, this is payback time for your costume. Lie still my darling. I want you. I want to be your first in that costume. When he touches you, wearing that, I will have touched you first. You owe me darling. Just lie still for me."

My arm collapsed on the bed. She was still drifting her hand up and down my inner thigh. Then OH GOD, she touched IT for me, and my hips arched off the bed. I tried to find her fingers with my cleft, but she had taken them away. She moved and straddled my upper thighs with her own. Her cleft was on my thigh, I could feel it on me. She bent forward and licked my belly button. Around my tummy, moving higher and higher...my nipples each in its turn. A deep suck of my breast into her mouth ... her lips on my shoulders.... I felt her tongue – just the very tip – touch, lick at the base of the side of my neck and I shuddered.

I heard myself whimper and say "Please."

Her tongue found my ear and again I shuddered as a flash of lightning flicked to my clit. I was conscious of it hard, needful. She slowly retreated, her tongue and her kisses and her breath teasing me every millimeter of the way down, down, down to my hairs. She slid back down the bed, off me; her gentle hands parted me. She knelt in between. She kissed my knees, trailed her tongue higher and higher.

Oh God she was nearly there. Please do not stop Taty. I will die if you stop. I felt her breath as she blew on my heated clit. My hips rose and tried to find her lips. She blew on it again and again I reached out to her.

- "Naughty, naughty Elizabeth, now be a good girl and lie still."

LIE STILL!! I could have screamed. How IN HELL COULD I LIE STILL? She was cruel. She would not let me, and I HAD GOT TO.

I felt her hands tipping onto my tummy. I was helpless and rolled her hands. I was on my tummy. Her tongue ran lightly down my spine and again I almost screamed out. My back was arched. She was kissing my shoulders, my shoulder blades, my sides. She was working lower and lower. She kissed my cheeks down there. I felt her gentle fingers open them. I knew she was looking at my most secret place. I waited. I felt her move. Then oh God I felt her breath as she pursed her lips and blew on my anus. I clenched spasmodically there, and she blew again and again after each clenching. As I clenched, I could feel my wet leaking out of me onto my bed. She licked and kissed me behind my knees. I was breathing heavily, my breath harsh. My heart boomed in my ears.

She turned to me again. Please, please let her touch it for me. She raised my arms and told me to grip the bars of the headboard. I did as she told me. She lay on my body; her beautiful passionate body lay nakedly on mine. She was kissing me with her gentle soft kisses all over my cheeks, my eyes, my neck ... ohhhhhh then she kissed in my armpits. She licked me there. She lifted her chest, her tight breasts. I could feel her bush on my thigh as she rubbed herself on me there. I felt the heat of her wetness and then the cool as it dried on me. She moved down, down, down and rubbed her nose in my female hairs, smelling me. My legs were spread. I was looking at her, my eyes swollen, my breath heavy and my mouth slack.

I tried to say "Tatyanna," but it was a dry croak. I swallowed and said "Tatyanna??...Please, Tatyanna, please let me.

I lurched, I lifted, I yelled as the tip of her tongue touched my swollen clit. I wailed. She knew she was tipping me over. Her fingers reached to find me. Enter me. She let her fingers be a man for me and she touched my clit. She glided her fingers each side and masturbated my clitoris inside her little nest.

I began filling up. The funnel low in my tummy was filling me. It could not take any more. It was too full for me. I was conscious of writhing on the bed as I exploded. Tati tried to keep her fingers in me as I bucked wildly onto them, and I called her name again and again and again "

OHH TATTTYYYYY, TATTYY, TATY, Taty, Tat? Oh Tat. Oh Tat."

Her fingers slipped out of me. She lay beside me and held me in her arms. She kissed my eyes.

I heard her whisper "Elizabeth, I love you." And tears ran from my eyes. She kissed my tears away. I felt water drop on my face and I looked at her. Her tears were falling too.

And then my butterflies came to me, fluttering in my tummy, between my legs, and I was slowly, slowly returning to peace in her arms.

After I had come down, after I had recovered. I loved her too.

As she left to return home, she said "Christ Elizabeth, wearing that, if you come out of battle with your sailorman in only one piece I will be amazed. But if you do not survive, will you leave me that bloody costume in your will. It will kill my old feller if I wear it for him. But what a way to die, hey?"

So, my Darling Melany, there we are lol. I can never wait for Freddy to be home. But I really am dying to wear my bunny costume for him when he is not expecting it!

Let me know when we can meet. Would you like me to put it on for you too? Hee hee hee

Or you can wear it for me. Yummy!

Kisses my angel.

Elizabeth"

I had finished her letter, caught up in the emotion of what she had confided to me. My cheeks were glowing,

my heart thudding, my body responding to the picture in my mind of her and our friend Tatyanna. Loving as we three had done so many times at university.
Unconsciously my hand had strayed inside my dressing gown as I sat at the breakfast table, pulled it wide. My fingers caressed my flushed and needful body, wakened by Elizabeth's letter.

"Love is the master key that opens the gates of happiness."

Oliver Wendell Holmes Sr.

INTERNSHIP

It had been one let-down after another for Ericka. She was in college and dying to do an internship before she graduated, but it did not look like it was ever going to happen.
Most companies were being too picky. She had been to a lot of interviews, and none had called her back, which she found insulting considering it was free labor.
She had spent a lot of nights crying, but not just because of that. Her whole life was going straight to shit.
She had recently broken up with her boyfriend because she had gone on a trip to Las Vegas without him. He had been accusing her of cheating since the day she got back because she did not call him while she was there.
She explained that she was planning to, but every time she had time to call, something would come up and she could not do it. He did not believe her, and they had argued about it so much that it eventually led to their breaking up.
On top of that, her closest friend was moving to Australia. She and this guy were as close as two people could be. It was like losing one of her sisters (he was gay). She was having a hard time getting used to the thought of him not being around.
It seemed like every possible problem that one person could have been coming at her all at once. She spent a lot of time watching comedies to try and keep her spirits up. She did not want to look too sad in her interview.
The day of the interview arrived. Ericka felt like shit, but she went anyway and tried to keep a fake smile throughout their conversation.
It had been going well despite the intense nervousness she felt inside. It was like all the mistakes that she had

made in her previous interviews were helping her now. She could speak more fluently and answer without hesitation because she had heard all the questions a dozen times before.

Monique was the woman doing the interview. She was the sexiest older lady that Ericka had ever seen. Monique was blonde, had a distinguished face, and was confident. She wore a sexy form-fitting outfit that hugged every curve, and Monique had plenty of them, especially her big, round ass. Ericka could only hope to look that good when she was Monique's age.

At the end of the interview, Monique said, "I like to keep a nice, warm working relationship with all my employees."

Ericka leaned over and picked up her portfolio. She said, "I've got some papers here, actually, if you want to go over them with—"

- "There'll be plenty of time for that later," Monique interrupted. "I think a little conversation will be just fine right now."

Ericka's heart skipped a beat. Did Monique just say the word, later?

- LATER

- As in, 'I'm going to hire you, so there's no need to talk now because we can talk later?'

Ericka was having a difficult time trying not to shout for joy as Monique stood and asked if she would like some coffee. "Yes, please," said Ericka.

- "How do you take it?"

- "Black, two sugars, please."

Monique excused herself to get the coffee. Ericka took a deep breath of relief. Her persistence was finally going to pay off.

She started looking around Monique's house, which was where the interview was being held. It looked good. It was nicely decorated.

A smile surfaced on Ericka's face as Monique was handing her the coffee. Maybe one day she would own something like this. Maybe one day she would be the sexy older woman welcoming a struggling younger version of herself into her empire.

There was a brief moment of silence. Ericka took a sip of coffee. Monique was staring at her up and down.

As soon as Ericka removed the cup from her lips, Monique said, "So, do you have a boyfriend?"

She almost said yes, but then she remembered that she and her boyfriend were not together anymore. "No, I do not. Not now," she replied.

- "A girlfriend perhaps?"

Ericka giggled. "No, I haven't got a girlfriend."

Monique let some thoughts run through her mind as she watched her sipping her coffee.

- "Have you ever been with a woman?" Monique asked.

- "I haven't really thought of it, actually," Ericka lied.

The lie was very unconvincing, of course, so Monique's next question came as quick as the smirk on her face.

- "Would you like to see my Rumpus Room?"

- "Your...rumpus room?"

Monique led her to a room on the same floor at the rear of the house. It was a large room with white walls and a king-sized bed. The bed was made up in black and white bedspreads and a zebra-striped comforter. It was a nice-looking room, but Ericka did not understand why she was showing it to her.

It is very nice, Mrs. Hartley," she said.

- "Yeah, I've had a lot of good times here," said Monique as she took her suit jacket off. "It's my favorite place to relax and get rid of the stress of the day."

Monique climbed onto the bed, tapped the space on the other side, and said, "Sit next to me."

Ericka was dumbfounded, but she obeyed. When she was in a comfortable sitting position, Monique asked, "So you've never been with a woman?"

That is when Ericka figured out why she wanted to show her the room.

Monique wanted to fuck her.

She had leaned in closer and was rubbing Ericka's thigh. She looked her up and down like she was a piece of meat, but she was sensual and made sure not to move too fast so not to scare Ericka off.

Ericka smiled at her and started blushing. Answering Monique's question, she said, "No."

Monique kissed her hand and said, "Well, welcome to the firm."

- "Thank you, Mrs. Hartley."

Monique grinned as she kissed her hand a second time, then turned it over and kissed her wrist. She slowly started kissing her way down Ericka's arm until her mouth touched the cotton of her sleeve.

She gently grabbed the back of Ericka's head and pulled her in for her first girl-to-girl kiss. Ericka felt awkward at first and her lips were tense because of it, so Monique slid her mouth around to the left side of her neck and started sucking and gently biting it. Monique heard a low moan come from Ericka's mouth, so she bit her again and allowed her warm breath to pass over the moisture on her neck.

Ericka's pussy was almost as wet as Monique's now. She was happy about the job. She was flattered that another woman would take such an interest in her.

She looked at her with genuine desire and admiration and leaned in for another kiss. This time it was longer, more passionate, deeper, hungrier.

Ericka's legs began to separate as Monique helped her get her blouse off. Then she took her own blouse off.

They took their skirts off next, leaving them in bras, panties, and stockings. In between some affectionate touching and passionate kissing, they took everything else off, leaving them naked.

There was not an ounce of fat on Monique's body. Monique's breasts were firm and perky, sitting upright. Her hips were slender. Her ass was shapely and toned. It was like Ericka was looking at herself, only older, but the same body.

Once Ericka was on her back and out of her panties, Monique lowered her head between her luscious thighs. Ericka felt a rush of excitement. She loved having her pussy eaten, but her ex-boyfriend never wanted to do it. She raised her legs high and wide. She let out a sigh of relief as she felt Monique's long tongue slip between her wet pussy lips.

She licked the hole for a while just to tease Ericka. She knew where the most pleasure from licking the pussy came from, and after a few seconds, her tongue found its way up to the protruding nub.

Monique got it wet with her tongue and lapped up pussy juice to spread over it. Once it was soaking wet, she closed her mouth around the clit and started sucking it while letting her tongue slither all around it. Ericka was quiet so far, but Monique could see her legs trembling slightly out of the corners of her eyes.

Her young apprentice was enjoying her first lesbian sex thus far.

Ericka's mouth was wide open, and she was quietly gasping for breath. She was gently squeezing the pillow and sometimes fondling her own breasts. She clenched her teeth from time to time.

This let Monique know that Ericka was the type who was too insecure to let herself go during sex. She was intentionally trying to keep quiet.

She wanted to see Ericka really cut loose. She wanted to bring the wild slut out of her, and she was not going to stop until she did it. Her pussy was tingling more just from imagining it in her head.

She slipped a finger into Ericka's wet cunt, then two more and started masturbating her. Ericka started playing with her clit. She worked her fingers deeper until they were buried to the hilt.

- "Oh, god," whispered Ericka.

Monique smiled on the inside and started working her pussy a little faster. Ericka's legs were trembling more, and her breathing was getting faster all the time.

- "Ooh," Ericka said, still just a shade above a whisper.

- "Yeah," replied Monique.

- "Oh...oh...ohhh" whispered Ericka.

Monique stopped fingering her after a couple more minutes and held her fingers upwards while they were still in Ericka's cunt. Ericka was still stroking her clit, and since Monique was holding it in place (from the inside), the tingles felt a lot more intense.

Leg spasms were coming more frequently. Moans were getting louder.

- "Oh, oh!" moaned Ericka. Her vaginal walls spasmed. Her body convulsed as warm pussy juice started squeezing through Monique's fingers.

- "Ohhh, god!" continued Ericka when she felt Monique's soft lips touch her pussy. Monique licked and tongued her clit, then came up and started kissing and sucking her mouth and neck.

Ericka's body was really alive now. "Oh, it's so good," she said.

She wrapped her arms and legs around Monique and held her close. She loved the feel of female flesh, the way her breasts pressed against her own.

Now it was her turn to try eating pussy. They both sat up. They kissed and gazed into each other's eyes like animals in heat.

Their lips separated. Monique moved to the side. She slowly bent over so far that her head touched the bedspread. Ericka was left with the sight of Monique's round ass sticking up in the air with her puffy pussy lips poking out in between them.

Ericka touched her ass softly and stared at Monique's glowing wet pussy lips. She leaned forward with her tongue sticking out and placed it directly on her asshole.

- "Oh!" said Monique, partly because it felt good, but mainly because she was not expecting it.

Ericka was not expecting it either. She was planning to lick her pussy, but for some reason that she did not know, she went straight to her asshole and started licking that.

Then she flicked her tongue on Monique's pussy and slid her tongue from clit to asshole. She kept repeating this process but every now and then she would stop at the pussy hole and suck at its nectar as she listened to Monique screaming and moaning her approval.

- "Oh, that's very good," whispered Monique. "Oh, ooh, oh, that feels good. Do not stop."

For somebody who had never been with a woman, Ericka could eat pussy really well. Monique was beginning to wonder if she was being honest about her sexuality.

She started fingering her cunt so she could focus more of her tongue action on Monique's asshole. Monique was shouting out like crazy, and she jerked and squirmed around as one intense orgasm after another shot through her.

She lost all the strength in her body and her pelvis fell to the bed. She was seeing stars. When she could not handle anymore, she rolled over and kissed Ericka's hand. She was happy to see that she was satisfying her new boss.

Monique giggled loudly, grabbed hold of Ericka's face, and gave her a playful kiss. "Ummm," moaned Monique, and the kiss got slower and deeper with every passing second.

Monique got off the bed and pulled a strap-on from the closet. She put it on.

Ericka thought it looked odd. There was a pretty woman with huge breasts and big red cock standing in front of her making lovey-dovey eyes at her. It looked kind of silly at first, but it did not feel silly once Monique put it inside of her.

It was long and thick, and it felt just like a real cock but without the heat. Monique fucked her with long, circular strokes, pulling the cock back so far that just the head was left inside of her and then slowly, but forcefully, grinding it back in.

The strap-on had a center strap that fit between Monique's pussy lips and rubbed her clit as she moved. It was just as stimulating for her as it was for Ericka.

She started pounding Ericka's cunt. She had the whole bed rocking.

- "Ooh, oh!" Ericka screamed. It was so good, almost like having a man in her sweet hole.

Monique pulled her up and lay down so Ericka could ride her. She noticed the expression on Ericka's face had changed. She was really into it now. She was not as nervous, and she was not trying to keep quiet anymore. She arched her back started bouncing her sweet pussy on the strap-on. "Oh, that's good," she hissed. "Fuck, yeah!"

Ericka got up. Monique asked her to suck it. She tried but it was not real. She could not get into sucking a fake cock, so Monique turned her around, licked her asshole and shoved it in her from behind while she circled her asshole with her thumb.

There is no sight so pretty as the back of a woman's head while you are drilling with a strap-on, Monique thought with a wry smirk.

- "You like my finger in your butt?" she asked.

- "Uh-huh," responded Ericka.

She let it slip halfway in. Ericka moaned and arched her back. Then Monique started fucking her hard and fast. This was new to Ericka too. There had never been anything in her ass. She had seen it in porn movies, but it did not seem like anything she would want to try.

Having something in her ass and pussy at the same time was giving her pleasure galore. Cum was splattering from her cunt all over the strap-on and Monique's pelvis.

- "Oh, yeah!" hissed Ericka. "Fuck me! Yeah!" Ericka looked over her shoulder and said, "I'm really starting to like this job."

Monique grinned but did not respond. She was too caught up in her role as the man. She liked fucking women with the strap-on. It gave her a taste of what it was like to be her husband when he was fucking her. The power was a hell of a rush. She even had her shoulders squared like a man.

- "Oh, god, that feels so fucking good," screamed Ericka.

- "How good?"

- "I'm about to cum."

Ericka closed her eyes. Her face twisted into an enthusiastic grimace. The tingles in her cunt were building with every thrust into her. Her head was bucking, and her breasts were jiggling like mad.

- "Yeah!" she screamed. "Ooooohhhhhh!"

Ericka's body shook. Cum was spilling from her pussy. Her vaginal walls were spasming. Her legs were jerking. Her eyes had rolled into her head.

- "Oh, fuck. Oh, shit," she moaned.

Monique was kissing her back and holding her closely throughout it all. She waited patiently for Ericka's orgasm to subside.

When it did, Ericka said:

- "It was so hot that you made me cum twice."

Monique started licking her ass again. Then she sat up and said, "Just wait 'til the Christmas party." She kissed her new intern one more time and they got dressed.

Ericka had needed guidance for her career, a new lover to take her mind off the old one, a new friend to replace the one who was moving out of town. In a matter of 30 minutes, this woman had managed to give her everything she needed to make her life happy again.

For the first time in a long while, Ericka felt something that had been evading her for months. Joy.

*"Love is not only something you feel,
it is something you do."*
David Wilkerson

SURPRISE IN THE BATHTUB

I had the house to myself. My friend, Helen, was home alone too.

I guess she had never been alone in her house before because I got a call from her, and she said she was lonely and scared. So, I invited her over to my house.

When she got there, she was wearing a tight, white shirt and a noticeably short miniskirt. She came in and hugged me. When she did her mouth brushed my neck. I did not really think anything of it.

We watched TV for a little while, and then she told me she was hungry. So, I went into the kitchen and opened the Refrigerator. I bend over to get some jelly from the bottom drawer. When I did, I felt something touch my butt. I grabbed the jelly and bent up quickly to see her standing right behind me. I looked at her and she was staring at me. I quickly made her a PBJ Sandwich and told her I was going upstairs to take a shower.

I got to my bathroom and locked the door. I could not believe I was locking the door from my best friend. So, I unlocked it and started the bathtub water. I stripped off my clothes and got into the warm water. The sound of running water really soothes me. I closed my eyes and took a deep breath. Suddenly I feel something on top of me. I open my eyes, and Helen is on top of me smiling.

I get ready to say, Get the hell off me! when she presses her lips against mine. Her tongue explores into my mouth and wraps around mine as it tries to escape. One of her arms is around my body, rubbing my back. Her other hand is tenderly toying in my pussy. I was still thinking, what the hell, when I realized it felt kind of good.

I relaxed my body and surrendered it to her. She pulled her head back and smiled. I smiled back and wrapped my arms around her. She scooted down to suck my breasts when it occurred to me, we were still in the bathtub. She sweetly said, "Let's get to your room." I nodded and we got out of the tub, not caring that we were soaking wet and had bubbles all over us.

We quickly headed to my room, and I jumped on the bed. Helen jumped on top of me, her legs straddling my thighs. Her tits pressed against mine, a feeling I cannot describe. She started to kiss me, and I kissed back like I was going to suck her tongue out. Her hands were rubbing up and down my body, pushing the bubbles around. She moved down to suck my breast. Her tongue went in circles around the tip. While she was sucking the hell out of my breasts all I could do was moan and stroke her hair. I guess she did not like my breasts because she did not suck them for very long.

But she got up and left the room. I was so confused! I heard her go downstairs and come back up. When she walked back into my room, she had a bottle of oil. I understand now. She opened it and squirted it all over me. Then she just dropped it and started rubbing and squeezing me. I loved the feeling of her hands gently rubbing my body with no friction. My legs hang off the end of the bed and she sat and stuck her head into my pussy. Her tongue reached in and out of it and it tickled me.

I giggled. She shook her head from side to side as she grabbed my pussy with her tongue. I just sat there limp, sighing and moaning. I sat there for about 7 or 8 minutes just limp. She is licking me in and out. Then she got up and told me to do her. I had never licked pussy or sucked tit before, so I was kind of nervous. I got up and laid her down on the bed. I wanted to do the oil rubbing just to waste some time. She must have known I was stalling because she said, "Come on baby! Give me some action!" I crawled on top of her and placed my mouth on top of her right breast. I licked the tip, and it got hard under my tongue. I loved that feeling! Before I knew that I was playing and jiggling them! I continued to lick down her body to her pussy. I stuck my tongue in and pulled out some juice on my tongue. I tasted it and it pleased me like no other! I violently started to push my face into her pussy. My hands were on her hips pulling toward my face. Helen noticed the change in my attitude and started to moan loudly. She arched her back, which is very sexy, and I started to jiggle my face into her pussy. I could not hear her moaning as much as I could hear me slurping up her juices.

When I was out of breath I got up and sat next to her. I was tired and pleased. She was not tired. She grabbed my face and stuck it back down into her pussy. I told her I was tired, and she said she did not care. So here I was, my head stuck in my friend's pussy and what I enjoyed about a minute ago was now pure torture. She pushed me around for about another hour. T

hen let me go to sleep. When I woke, I was chained to the bed-my arms and legs- and it was daylight outside. I asked what time it was, and she said 12:30. I was surprised I had slept that long, and that I had not woken when she chained me to my bed. I was asking her so many questions that she taped my mouth shut! I was like, OH MY GOD WHAT ARE YOU DOING??!! She had something strapped around her waist. I could not tell what it was because my foot was in the way. She scooted closer toward me, and it was some kind of strap on.

She stuck the end inside me, and I screamed within my taped mouth. Her hips thrust back and forward. Her breasts were flopping up and down. Mine were too.

I think I feinted because when I woke up- again- I was in my bed, unchained, and snuggled. I was soooo confused. I got up like normal and took a shower- with the door locked-. When I got to school, I saw Helen. She was sitting next to my seat. I sat down scared. She winked at me, and I was really scared! Later I went to the bathroom and there she comes following me. From then on, we had sweet, tender sex. I'm actually kind of glad that night happened. It has changed me- in a good way- forever.

*"Love is an irresistible desire
to be irresistibly desired."*
Robert Frost

THE COTTAGE

My name is Veronica, I'm 18, I stand 5' 3 and weigh 95lbs. I have small breasts, but they are full and very round for my size. I have a small waist and very sexy legs and tush. This story is about sex education. I am not a virgin, and I have been with 2 boys. One shot his cum on my face when I was 16 and then it was over, and the other I had protected intercourse with last year and it lasted about 6 strokes, and he was done. After those 2-events I decided that sex was not all it was made out to be and concentrated on my education.

I am very attractive, and I have let my hair grow down to my waist. I graduated high school with honors, and I have enrolled in a provincial University for September. My education is very important to me and that is why I do not have a job. My mom and Dad are covering everything from tuition to books to accommodation and living expenses. They were so proud of my school years, and this made me proud.

Well now that I was set up for school and I will be staying at residence I have 4 months off doing nothing. I saw an ad in the local paper of a lady looking for a sitter for twin boys for 6 weeks. I was excited because babysitting would give me time to read through some of my class books that we had gotten for me. The real test was to sell my dad on the concept of me working. I do like to shop also, and this would give me some spending money.

Dad was all for it, and he basically had so much faith and trust in me that he was never very strict. He liked to come across that way though and I could play dad like a fiddle. I was his pet and the youngest of 3. I have two older brothers.

I phoned the ad and went the next morning to the huge house in a ritzy part of the city. Mom drove me but she stayed in the car and was there if the lady needed any reference.

I rang the doorbell, and this very attractive lady answered the door. Good morning sweetie, you must be Veronica. She reached out and shook my hand.

I followed her to a large den, and she led me to a couch. She sat in a recliner. We talked about my schooling and what my parents did for a living and about my excitement about being a freshman at university.

She asked where I lived, and I told her about the other end of the city, but transportation would not be a problem. I told her that my mom was a stay-at-home Mom, and that dad owned a Car dealership which she was quite familiar with.

I told her that I had never worked before, but I looked after my niece a lot and she was 4.

She really liked my enthusiasm and would like to speak with my parents first. I told her that mom was out in the car and that I could go and get her. She laughed and said that would be wonderful.

I jumped up really excited and went out to the car. Mom was feeling my excitement too because I was doing this on my own. Mom got out of the car and came up the walk with me and she asked, what is her name Veronica?

I stopped in my tracks and was getting ready to cry. I don't know.

Mom swatted my ass and said, that is ok silly I will find out. Mom always had a way of making me realize that there are never problems in this world, only solutions.

We entered the den, and my mom reached out her hand and said good morning my name is Gaby.

- Hi Gaby, my name is Bec.

- Bec Connor

Mom looked at me and winked and then we all sat down.

\- You have a beautiful home here.

\- Thank you, all this for just me, and Mrs. C laughed. She had such a wonderful voice, and her beauty was electric. She had such elegance and poise about her.

\- I lost my husband in a car accident about 15 years ago and I never re-married. I am a 48-year-old grandmother, and I work a lot being an attorney and all. - I went back to university when Don was killed in a car accident. My daughter and I went together, which was a rush. I was 37 and she was 18 like you Veronica. I graduated and went to law school and my daughter graduated and never worked a day in her life. She met an investment banker and had these two wonderful twin boys. They are 8 now and very busy.

\- My daughter and her husband are going away for 6 weeks cycling through Europe. This is their first holiday since they were married, and I told them that I would be glad to look after them and arrange for a qualified sitter. This is the catch. Some days I work long hours, and I will never work on weekends as a matter of fact I will only be working 4-day weeks so I can spend more time with them. At the weekends I go to my cottage about an hour away so I will only need someone for 4 days a week. I would prefer someone to live with for three nights though because like I said I work long hours, and I start early. Does this sound like something that you would be comfortable with Veronica and Gaby?

My eyes were like saucers, and I was ready to jump at this opportunity, but Mom was the conservative one.

\- Well Mrs. Connor

\- Call me Bec

\- Ok Bec, I do have my reservations because this is a huge responsibility for Veronica being her first real job and everything Don and I have so much faith in her and her judgement that this decision will be all left up to her.

- Wow, Mom you are the best.

Mrs. C laughed and said: Just a second though, I have not offered you the job.

- This part was the formal guideline section and now I must ask you some personal questions and I am glad that your mother is here for them.

- Oh,..OK

- Are you married, and she laughed, not seriously, do you have a boyfriend?

- No

- When was your last boyfriend?

I blushed and said 7 months ago.

- Do you like to talk on the phone?

- Yes, I have a large group of friends, and I guess you could say that I am popular, but this is my job, and I would never have any of my friends over or speak to them at all while I am working. I will reserve my friend's time to working hours only.

- Good answer and she laughed again.

- Do you smoke or do drugs?

I blushed again and said that I do not do drugs, and I have tried smoking but did not like it. My boyfriend tried to get me to smoke but I would not be led down the wrong path with him. That is probably why we broke up was because I was responsible for my actions, and he was not.

- Ok I have had enough, and I am quite satisfied. You only have two more people to be interviewed by and if they agree then I will offer you the position.

I had a smile from ear to ear and I wanted to rush to the dealership right away and tell Dad.

Their names are Kale and Simon. They are 8 and she laughed again and this time with Mom.

The boys live in another province and that is why Mrs. C wants to spend more time with them. She then gave me a list of the rules and all the important phone numbers on this list. The rules were the basic ones and there was nothing surprising. I would arrive on Monday morning and leave by 2 on Thursday. She said my pay would be.

I gasped. I did not even think about money, and I just about said that l would do it for free.

- $700.00

I thought wow about 115.00 for 3 days work a week.

Then she continued for a week. Because of my age and the nature of my position there would be no deductions, and her accountant would be doing a direct deposit every Friday.

She looked at Me and asked if I had a blank check with me.

I was going to say no and then Mom came to my rescue.

- Bec, we will get one for you when all this starts.

Bec said this coming Monday, but Veronica would have to come over on Saturday to meet my daughter and the boys.

- No problem, Veronica can drop it off to you this afternoon.

- That would be wonderful and at that time I can show her around this big dust bowl. She then said that the cleaning lady is here on Mondays, Wed, and Fri. and the Lawn guy is here every Monday, but I think I will change that to a Friday.

We shook hands and left with a bunch of papers and forms to be filled out by my parents. I asked mom if we could go and see dad and she was not going to deny me this excitement. Dam, I was actually getting wet like when I had a boy touch me down there.

The reason I went into all this detail was to show you all how excited I was about getting this job and how professional Mrs. C. was.

Well, we had everything in place and Saturday came and went and the boys loved me as well as their daughter Casey.

I could not imagine getting paid 700 dollars to look after 2 boys and spend time away from home for the first time in my life. This will get me prepared for university. My room was large, and the bed was so comfortable, and I had the run of the house and the pool in the back yard.

There was only one room that was locked, and I was told that this was her private room, and I should not go there but anywhere else in the house was fine.

The first week came and went and I was having the time of my life. These boys were so well behaved, and I loved spending time with them.

By this time, I was calling Mrs. C. Bec, and we always had long talks at night. She always got comfortable in the evening and wore really revealing sexy night gowns that hardly covered her large boobs.

Occasionally her friend would come over and her name was Jackeline. The first time that I met her she had a smile on her face from ear to ear and she was really looking me over. It was kind of eerie and also kind of exciting. Jackeline and Bec were really close friends as they were always hugging and slapping one another. They went for late night swims to gather, and I would go to my room and read or watch some TV.

Some nights I could hear faint moans and cries coming from Bec's room down the hall. I thought she was crying from her loneliness and missing her husband. I never knew that Jackeline was sleeping over and in Bec's room, but I was naive.

Well by week 4 Bec and I got along so good that our conversation's got really personal. I could talk to her about anything including sex. I told her about my 2 times, and we were like sisters.

She asked me if I ever had an orgasm, and I could not answer that because I did not know. I told her that I would get moist down there and I had a little butterfly going through me when I kissed a boy.

She told me about meeting her husband and not being very good at sex and then that all changed once he passed away. Her experience really came later on in life and now she has a private life that she will let me in on in due time.

I did not know what she meant but I was not going to pry or ask her personal questions.

She told me that Jackeline was coming over and she wanted me to join them in the pool later. I agreed. Well, an hour later Jackeline and Bec had two of the skimpiest swimsuits I had ever seen.

I had a one piece. We jumped in and played with the beach ball and l was having a lot of fun. Jackeline was about 25 and not much older than me and she seemed like she was a touchy-feely kind of girl. She would slap my ass and wrestle me in the water and once I even though she touched my breast on purpose.

Bec was getting closer too and she was also being a little closer to my inner space, but the strange thing is it all felt so natural, and I enjoyed their affection. When I went home on the weekend all I talked about, to my friends was Bec and Jackeline. I am sure that they were tired of hearing about them.

6 Weeks just flew by and here I was thinking that I was losing my best friend. I even had a tear in my eye when the boys left the driveway to go home and there was Bec and I standing on the steps, and she was really sad.

I gave her a hug and my head came up to her shoulders. We went inside and sat on the couch and talked some more about how things are going to be different around here now without the boys and then she stroked my hair and said, I will also really miss having you here.

I was getting goose bumps and did not know why. Bec said that I was welcome to come to her place anytime day or night and if I wanted to meet for lunch or dinner that would be excellent.

I smiled and said that I would love that. Then my cell phone rang for the 10th time that day. It was Jack, my ex-boyfriend. I did not answer it.

Bec looked puzzled and I told her he has been bothering me a lot lately and then I got bold and said he was just horny and wanted to fuck me again. He is such a rude and arrogant guy and if my dad knew he would have slaughtered him.

Bec laughed and said here sweetie let me have your phone for a minute.

I gave her the phone with a puzzled look on my face.

She dialed his number from my phone, and he answered on the first ring. She introduced herself as my lawyer and told him he had better quit harassing me or he would be sued. She then asked him to get a piece of paper and a pen. She then gave him the number to her office and told him to phone her right back and ask for Mrs. Connor. He had 2 minutes to make the call and then she hung up.

Bec handed me the phone and said that she did not think that he would be a problem in my life if I did not want him there. Then her office phone rang.

She has a separate phone for her work. She answered it and said yes please put him through Patty and thank you.

- Mrs. Connor speaking, Ok Harry, that was to show you that Veronica has retained my services and you should try and find another girl to seduce with you small dick and you should also get some sex education lesson's and learn how a lady needs to be treated in and out of bed.

- Good day sir and I trust that we will not be having this conversation again.

She hung up and I was smiling from ear to ear and was amazed at how professional and abrupt she was.

Bec had another idea but said that she wanted to speak to my parents first before she told me and no it has nothing to do with him.

I had to leave and get home for supper, so we hugged, and she gave me a kiss on the cheek, and we said goodbye. I drove home with tears running down my face and the silly thing is that I know we will be seeing each other soon.

A few days passed and my final deposit was made to my account with a thousand-dollar bonus. Dad wanted me to return it because this was more like club med than a job.

The next day I phoned Bec up to thank her and also to question her, but I got her voice mail. I left a message and thanked her a million times and told her that I missed her and Jackeline and our conversation.

Bec was at the cottage and when she returned, she went to see dad at work. Then she went out for lunch with Mom.

That night she phoned me and asked me over to her place for some lunch and a swim. I eagerly agreed.

It was so good seeing Bec again and we had lunch by the pool and then we swam and played, and it was like being with a long-lost love. After being there for a few hours, she said let's sit down, I have a proposal for you. I would like to hire you to help me paint and work around my cottage. This would be for about 5 weeks, and you would stay there with Jackeline and me. I have taken the time off work, and we might even travel out to see the boys.

I was wide eyed, and I wanted to jump at the opportunity, but I had to ask my parents first though.

Bec said that she cleared it with them, and they thought it would be a chance for me to be productive and to get some education on life. Your Dad is going to give you a car to use, and he thought it would be great for you to get ready for university. I also invited them out any time that they wanted to come.

I jumped up and gave Bec a big hug and said when.

She held me close and leaned back and said we would be leaving in 2 days, and I could follow her and Jackeline out there.

I went home to pack and Bec said that all I needed was a swimming suit and grubby clothes.

When I got home, I ran into the house and there was mom with a big smile on her face and said that employment was following me around. I had luck of having picked up the newspaper when I did.

The next two days took forever to arrive and then I was up at 6 a.m. to make sure I was at Bec's for 9. Dad had brought home a loaner for me to use and his credit card. What a sweetheart. I packed up the car and said my goodbyes. Mom made sure I had my charger with me for my phone. I had spent the last couple of days doing some shopping and I even got a real skimpy bikini which I did not show my parents for obvious reasons. I wore a T-shirt and shorts, and I was off.

I stopped at a gas station and went into the washroom and changed my T-shirt and shorts to a skimpy and revealing halter top and very short and tight shorts. I don't understand why but I think I wanted to look and feel like Bec and Jackeline do all the time.

When I got to Bec's they were outside loading up Bec's van. She had so much stuff in it and there was also some kind of exercise equipment in the back of it. Bec and Jackeline whistled in Unison when I got out of the car and Jackeline said, it is a good thing that she was not a guy because she would for sure try and hit on me. Bec said, why would gender stop you and we all laughed.

Jackeline said that I hope I don't mind but she will hop in my car because the Van is full, and she knows where we are going in case I got lost. I did not mind at all.

Well, we were on our way, and this is the first trip I have ever taken without music. Jackeline and I talked the whole trip. She knew about Jack and the kind of unselfish lover he was and still is. She also spoke of her first real orgasm and how it sent her to another planet. I asked her question's and was really curious about sex and what the big deal was with it.

She laughed and said Sweetie, I think that going to this cottage for a month with her and Bec will be very educational, and I don't mean just for painting a cottage, then she reached over and softly patted my leg. I had goose bumps and could not understand why.

We finally arrived and Bec was behind us. I was amazed at this cottage on the lake and there was no one or buildings around for miles. It was secluded on a lake behind a forest of trees. There was a swimming pool with gorgeous furniture. Inside the cabin was an open concept. It had a sunken living room and on the second level were two rooms overlooking the whole cottage. We unpacked the vehicles and put this piece of exercise equipment on the patio. They looked after that, and they also kept it covered up.

We were going to bar-b-q, but first we had to change and have showers. Jackeline and I stayed in the living room drinking some beer and Jackeline went first. She went into her bedroom and changed and left the door open. From where I was sitting I could not but help to look up and see her totally naked and with a firm body that men die for. She exited the bedroom and went to the shower and did not cover up.

- OK cheeky, you are embarrassing our guest.

Around here at the cabin you will soon notice that clothes are optional, but if that bothers you just let me know and l will speak to her about being a little more discreet.

I said no it doesn't bother me and if my body was full and firm as that l would want to flaunt it So when do we start painting and fixing.

Jackeline laughed and said, "My little Veronica is trying to change the subject. We will start on Monday but for the next couple of days it is unwinding time and fun fun fun.

We all changed and had our showers and then it was time for dinner in our swimsuits. I came down in my bikini and they both just stood there and were amazed. How can such a beautiful creature like you not know the true meaning of seduction?

- If you would allow me, I would show your body what attention is all about Bec said and Jackeline said that goes for me too. We all laughed again but l was a little shy at first.

We took our drinks out to the pool side and talked and drank for hours. I was not used to this drinking, and they were laughing about some of their sexual exploits. The good ones and the bad ones and I was amazed at their stories.

I got up to go use the bathroom and fell back into my chair. Bec came to my rescue and helped me inside. She took my bikini bottoms off and I sat on the toilet. I think I pee for what seemed like a gallon. Then when I was finished Bec helped me up and that is when it hit me. I was going to be sick. She helped me to vomit in the toilet and I stayed there on the floor for quite a long while hugging the toilet bowl. Bec had left me alone and she returned with Jackeline, and they helped me take off the top of my bikini. I was apologizing in my slurred speech and they both laughed and said that I needed a cold shower and some sleep.

Both got naked and helped me into the shower, but l had no sense. I just knew the water was fucking cold and I was really drunk. The next thing I knew was waking up in bed and I heard someone weeping and moaning. My head really hurt, and I crawled to the bathroom to pee.

The moans were quite loud, and I did not understand but I also had my own dilemma. Unstable leg, a hurting head, and trying to move around in the dark in a cabin that I was not familiar with.

I made it back to bed and the next thing I knew I was waking up to the smell of coffee and bacon cooking. I was naked and I was trying to regain my senses to understand what had just taken place in the last 12 hours. In walked Jackeline totally naked and a coffee and some orange juice with aspirin.

- Here sugar, take some of these and a good cup of coffee and a shower and you will feel like a million dollars. I covered myself up and said, thank you I hope I was not any problem last night.

- Not at all, she said.

- Now have a shower and meet us downstairs. As she turned, she said, but you did say that you wanted another real live penis, but we might have an alternative for you, and she winked and left.

I showered and went to my room to get dressed. I was confused as to what to put on and I glanced downstairs, and they were both walking around naked. What the hell I thought and went downstairs naked too.

Good afternoon precious, said Bec and she came over and hugged me and kissed my forehead.

We had breakfast and talked and laughed and they were telling me stories about my singing to the toilet bowl and wanting a penis in the worst way.

- Girl says Bec. You have got to unwind and let us teach you the joys of life.

I thought I was unwinding I laughed, you mean to say that sex is not puking.

They both split some ribs laughing and then led me to the pool and pushed me in. I jumped out of this shock and chased down Jackeline and wrestled her into the water. We were rolling around and splashing and then we teamed up and got Bec into the water.

After playing around for a while I said that I needed to lay down for a little nap to get rid of this headache. Bec gave me a couple of aspirins and told me to go to her bed because it would be way more comfortable, and the late evening sun does not go in that window.

I awoke and it was dark outside. Night had fallen on us. I was in Bec's arms, and she was stroking my side. Jackeline was on the other side doing the same thing. Bec looked me in the eye and in a very soft and serious voice she sent a shock to my senses.

- Honey, Jackeline and I are going to give you something that you have never had before.

- This is going to be your first orgasm.

I tensed up a little and was kind of scared.

- Precious if you want us to stop, we will but I think you owe it to yourself to at least see what an orgasm is all about.

- Do you trust me honey?

I looked into her beautiful face and nodded.

- Ok I will explain everything to you and Jackeline will be the demonstrator. There are many sexy and vulnerable places on a female that feels really good to the touch.

- Our bodies are like Veronicas. If you crush them, they will not bloom and if you softly stroke them and care for them, they will respond.

As Bec was softly talking to me I felt Jackeline shift and start to stroke my forehead and softly kiss my eyes. Little tingles were starting to run through me. I was starting to shiver like I was cold, but I wasn't.

Bec said, Kissing is a very big part of love making.

Jackeline lowered her lips to mine and slowly I opened to receive her, and this was the most romantic kiss that I have ever received. I wanted to do this over and over again and as she was kissing me, I felt Bec stroking my nipples. I let out a soft moan and I could feel myself getting wet. This was different though because I have never been that wet down there.

She went on to explain how the nipples are really sensitive and now Jackeline was softly kissing and sucking each nipple. Jackeline cradled my head and said that she will just let the nerve endings do all the talking. We both watched Jackeline enjoy my breasts and her hands were stroking my legs now. She spread them apart and crawled between them and continued to suck and lick my nipples.

I closed my eyes and was moaning with pleasure. I then whispered to Bec, my god this feels good, and I think I have to pee, or something, YYyyees I have never felt this before, my god.

- No, you don't have to pee, and I want you to release whatever you are feeling.

I was shaking and Jackeline left my nipples and was working her way down my belly and my breathing was very erratic and I started to tense up.

- Ohhhhh! God! What is happening?

Don't fight it just let it go and then Bec leaned over and kissed me for a long time. I was moaning into her mouth and now Jackeline was licking my inner thighs and l let go a lot of pee I thought, and I shook and moaned into Bec's mouth.

- Oh! My...! Now her lips were licking my pussy and I started to convulse. I shook and screamed, and I did not want this to stop and by God it didn't stop, and Jackeline was licking my pussy lips and then back to my clit and I had another strong orgasm.

- Yyyyeeeesssssss mooooree please mummy! As I broke away from the kiss and now she inserted two fingers into my pussy and rubbed on this hard button and I shot liquid out of me and I shook and shook and shook and wanted more and more and I was screaming and tears were running down the side of my cheeks and then Jackeline started to work her way back and in unison Bec worked her way down my chest and belly and to my pussy. Jackeline leaned over to give my trembling lips a deep kiss and I now started to feel what Bec was doing.

Oh, my Fucking God was all I could say, and my body tensed, and I shook again, and this time seemed stronger than the first. Jackeline straddled my chest, and I had my eyes closed and I was screaming, whining, and crying. I knew what the noises were now, and that Jackeline got eaten by Bec.

Jackeline slowly moved her pussy up and over my mouth and when I opened my eyes, I could smell her sweet pussy. I stuck my tongue out and I sloppily started to eat her to a mini orgasm.

I had a hard time doing this as I was convulsing and shaking too much but I liked the taste of pussy.

Bec came up and cuddled me and Jackeline took her place beside me, and I was trying to calm down and think about what had just happened.

Bec said: that my dear is what an orgasm is, and a woman has many! After all mother nature is a woman.

*"The only queer people are
those who don't love anybody."*
Rita Mae Brown

BLACKMAIL

My name is Zara, I'm going to be 41 years old, I'm married with 2 children, already teenagers and I'm about to achieve a great professional dream. I am about to be appointed president of a major bank, where I have been working for a few years. It's a bank that defends traditional family values and they're looking for someone who embodies them, and I give that profile. A married woman, a working mother who makes time to devote to her family. Of course, they also say that I am quite attractive, brunette, medium hair, green eyes and a very nice body, maybe a little short, but with quite large breasts and a matching butt, a curvy woman. I wear big, round glasses that give me an intellectual look.

Of course, although I am a fervent defender of marriage and its values, from time to time I cannot avoid falling into temptations. My husband has never suspected anything, and I hope it stays that way.

I have to give up those things, if they were known it would be the end of my career at the bank. The last time was at the party of a rich businessman, I met his son, who was not even 25 years old, he was very handsome, he took me to his sister's room and there we did it several times, he was such a good lover... I thought that had been forgotten, but a couple of weeks later it was going to bring me quite a few complications. I was in my office working when the secretary came in.

"Sorry, Zara," she apologized, "A girl has come forward who says she has to see you urgently.

- Now I'm quite busy, tell her I can't and make an appointment for another day - I asked.

- But it's Lucy, Nicholas' daughter still wants to do some big business.

For a few moments I was quite thoughtful, what did this girl want? Whatever it was, I had to see her, her father was an important client, I was doing business with the bank, so I told my secretary to let her in. She was a young girl, perhaps a little older than her brother, tall, thin, red-haired, with curly and rather short hair, her face was a mixture, although it seems contradictory, of innocence and mischief at the same time, highlighting her large green eyes. She was wearing tight flared jeans and a red blouse that left her belly button uncovered. In addition, she sported a necklace and several bracelets that seemed to be quite expensive.

I greeted her by giving her 2 kisses on the cheek and invited her to sit across from me.

- Are you Nicholas' daughter? - I asked.

"That's right," she replied very confidently.

- I am Zara, I help your father in some of his businesses, and I hope that, very soon, I will take over the management of the bank.

- I know, I'm Lucy, delighted.

- Delighted too, Lucy. How can I help you? Is there a problem with your father's affairs?

- No, Zara, this visit has nothing to do with my father. Actually, I'd like to do a little business with you.

- Do you want to invest in any of the Bank's funds? You look like a thrifty girl. You have come to the ideal place; I can advise you several that will go very well for you.

- You didn't understand me, Zara, I'm not interested in anything about the Bank. The business is going to be done by you and me.

I was quite surprised to hear that answer, while she looked at me quite seriously.

- And what business do you want to do with me? "We've never met before," I asked.

She smiled, stood up, took her mobile phone out of her purse and stood next to me.

"I'd like you to see what I'm going to show you very carefully," she asked with a smile.

She plugged it in and what she taught me left me paralyzed and totally pale. She put her phone away and sat down again in front of me.

- Did you like what you saw? You look great, you're very photogenic, Zara. I'm sure that if I post this video on social media, you'll become very famous - she told me very seriously.

I was paralyzed and speechless, I wanted to tell her many things, but I couldn't get a word out. In the video he had shown me, her brother and I were seen in bed having sex.

- Don't you tell me anything, Zara? - She insisted - Maybe your husband or the people of this traditional bank would like to see how well you go and what you do with my brother.

- That's a set-up, I've never been with your brother, I'm a married woman. - I replied trying to discredit her.

- And how do you know it's my brother, Zara? The 2 of you were fucking in my room and it looks like you had a great time. I was inside, in the bathroom, we rich girls have bathrooms in our rooms, and it occurred to me to record you, you were so busy with you that you didn't even notice.

I thought again, it seems that this little girl had me well caught. If the bank found out that I had slept with her brother, I could say goodbye to the promotion I had fought so hard for. Not to mention my marriage, even though I sometimes cheated on him, I loved my husband.

- If you make that video public, you will also harm your brother...

- Do you think he cares? One of his favorite pastimes is bragging about how many mature women he sleeps with. Maybe he even thanked me for it and everything. Besides, I don't have any special regard for my brother. So, I don't care what he wants or doesn't want.
- And your father? The scandal would also spill over into your family.
- I don't care about that, Zara.
She seemed very sure of herself and had an answer to all my arguments. If I didn't play along, I'd take out that damn video.
- How much do you want in exchange for not making the video public? Is that the business you're proposing? - I asked indignantly.
- Zara, Zara... I don't want money; my father gives me more than I need. - she replied with a somewhat malevolent smile.
- So, what do you want?
- For the time being, your phone number - Lucy replied confidently - be very attentive, in a few days you will receive a message from me. And if you don't follow my instructions, you're going to become very popular on social media.
I would have liked to say so many things to this little girl, but I couldn't risk my promotion or my marriage, so I gave her my phone number.
- See how easy this is? - She commented haughtily - I command, and you obey.
- And what are you going to do now? - I asked resignedly.
- Nothing at the moment, Zara, in a few days I'll send you a message with what you have to do.
I didn't say a single word, but my face says it all.
- Don't be like that, Zara - Lucy told me with a smile - You'll see how we'll end up being good friends. Now I have to go, but we'll see each other soon.

She got that smile again of someone who had all the cards in her hand and left my office, shortly after my secretary entered.

-What did she want? - My secretary asked curiously.

"Nothing important," I answered, "You have made an inquiry about where to invest some savings you have.

- She seemed happy, what you recommended must have convinced her.

-I don't know.

- You, on the other hand, look dejected, has something happened to you?

- Don't worry, nothing has happened to me, maybe I'm a little tired, I have a lot of work.

- Well, now you can't rest, remember that you have an important appointment with Counselor Matthews in half an hour.

I had to calm down, Matthews' support was very important to me, put aside, for the moment, Lucy's and wait for her to make her move.

Although I tried not to be noticed, the following days I was quite nervous, I was waiting for Lucy's message, but it did not come. I'm usually very quiet, but this was beyond me. At home, my husband blamed it on nerves about getting that promotion and tried to support me more than ever. I felt pretty guilty, but I couldn't tell him the truth. The days went by without any news, and I began to believe that Lucy was not going to do anything, that she had only played a rather cruel joke on me. Or, perhaps, that her brother had found out what had happened and had stopped her blackmail. But a couple of weeks later, I got a message from an unknown number.

"I'm Lucy, I hope you haven't forgotten me." After that, he would give me the address of a hotel room and ask me to come there on Wednesday night.

What could I want if I didn't need money? All I could do was show up there and play along. I had to lie to my husband, I told him that I had met an old colleague and had invited me to his birthday party, the excuse was not very successful, but he believed me, he even encouraged me to have fun, to leave behind the nerves of these days, he said.

"I don't know if I'll have much fun, darling," I answered.

"You have to try," my husband insisted, "I think you're dressed too formally for a birthday party."

- No, I'm fine like this.

We said goodbye and I headed to the hotel. I was formal, with my suit of black jacket and white blouse, my husband was right, it wasn't an outfit for a party, but I wasn't going to one either. I managed to park the car, went into the hotel and went up to the fifth floor, where the room was, I knocked, and Lucy came out to open it.

- Hello, Zara - she greeted me - I thought you weren't coming.

"Hello, Lucy," I replied, "I've had trouble finding parking, this area is pretty bad for that."

She invited me into the room, she was wearing an orange bathrobe, she looked like she had recently showered.

- Sit down, Zara, do you want to have a drink? - offered me.

- No thanks, I'd rather stand.

- If you don't abandon that hostile tone, I can get angry and that would be very bad for you.

- Please, Lucy, tell me what you want from me! I'll try to give you what you ask for.

- I told you the other day that I don't need money, I don't want that.

-Then what? I didn't do anything to you, I just slept with your brother one night, I don't think it was something that affected you. Besides, she agreed.

- That was noticeable when the 2 of you were in my bed. But you're a married woman, Zara, a mother with a promising career, it's not right for you to sleep with other men and, moreover, much younger than you, don't you think?

-Not me... It's just...

Lucy stood up and stood in front of me.

- You don't have to give me any explanation, Zara, I don't care about your motives.

She came even closer and began to run one of her index fingers over my lips slowly, then down my neck and up to my pants, again distributing the same thing.

-What are you doing? - I asked surprised.

- As I am the eldest sister, I have always been jealous of my brother, when they bought him a toy, I wanted it for myself, and, since they did not give it to me, I was angry - she replied again and again, passing her finger.

- I don't understand where you want to go.

- Don't you have any little brothers, Zara?

- No.

Lucy took off my jacket, now it was the fingers of her 2 hands that were gently running over my blouse over my upper body.

- Then you won't understand that I'm a little envious and want what she has.

The situation was quite embarrassing to me, Lucy kept moving her hands over my body while looking at me lustfully.

"Lucy, I only slept with your brother once," I tried to explain, "I haven't had anything more to do with him.

She didn't answer me, just put her lips on mine. I denied them.

- You're wrong, Lucy, I'm a married woman - A married woman who sleeps with young guys.

She put her lips on mine again.

- This can't go well, Lucy, I don't like women!

- How do you know if you've never tried before? Besides, you don't have a choice, have you forgotten the video with my brother? So don't resist.

She was right, it was in her hands, now literally, so I stood still. She kept trying to kiss me as she completely removed my blouse, her tongue, my neck and my ear, her hands were on my bra and caressed my breasts, her fingers on my nipples, she moved them in little circles while she continued kissing my neck, shortly after, while one of her hands continued with my breast, the other went down and began to caress my thigh. And I was starting to feel a special warmth inside me, I liked that her hands were running like that over my body, although I couldn't believe it, it was turning me on a lot. It wasn't just her hands; I felt her body next to mine and I was starting to melt. Lucy was beginning to see the effect that her caresses and kisses had on me and intensified her efforts, although I still couldn't resist her kiss on my mouth. Lucy's hand went up my thigh and into my sex, still covered by my pants, and she began to caress her gently as she continued to lick my neck, first one side, then the other, I had to restrain myself from hugging her because I was starting to want to caress her body. As if Lucy guessed my desires, she took off my bra and she took off her bathrobe leaving her totally naked, she approached me again and placed her breasts next to mine, so that our nipples touched, while she put her hand inside my pants and caressed my panties over my slit, then she took out her hand and showed me her finger, Wet from my flows despite the panties.

- You're a little, aren't you, Zara?

Lucy smiled and put her hand back in, this time inside my panties caressing my pussy, which made me unable to suppress a moan, which she took advantage of to try to insert her tongue inside my mouth again and I no longer put any obstacle. Our tongues moved together in there as our saliva mixed, Lucy's hand continued to slowly caress my pussy and I hugged her back tightly, our nipples touching again and again. I would never have imagined that a woman would make me feel like this, I needed to feel her body next to mine, I wanted Lucy.

She took me by the hand and led me to the bed, I took off my pants and panties and we lay on top of her, Lucy was on top of me, our legs intertwined, our bodies close to each other, we couldn't stop kissing. I caressed her back and also her ass, while she did the same with me, suddenly, she took her tongue out of my mouth and kissed my neck again, it continued to go down my body and her tongue reached my chest, she took it with her hands and began to kiss it, I sighed and bit my lips when I felt hers there.

- What beautiful and sweet breasts you have, Zara!

She licked my nipple, at the same time, she contemplated my face with pleasure and desire.

- Do you like what I'm doing for you, Zara?

- Very much, Lucy, very much. You're wonderful.

My nipples were quickly hardening under her tongue, then she repeated the operation with the other. I was so excited, the sensation of that tongue running and biting my breasts made me vibrate and desire more and more. Lucy seemed ready to give it to me, her sweet tongue went down my belly button towards my sex, which was waiting for her greedily, she kept looking at me as she licked my body, finally, she opened my legs and started licking my thighs, her tongue was getting closer to my pussy, but when it seemed that she was going to get there, she went back to my thigh again. All this increased my desire even more.

"You have to ask me, Zara," Lucy said to me, as she licked my thigh.

- Please, Lucy!

- Ask me, Zara! What do you want me to do for you?

- I want you to eat my pussy, Lucy!

I couldn't take it anymore and she, hearing my words, started licking it, her tongue went up and down my vaginal lips and I couldn't help but moan when I felt it.

- Aaaahhhhhhhhhhh!, aaaahh!

Yes, yes, yes, yes!

Lucy's tongue did not stop running over those lips and also ended up penetrating inside my soaked sex, there it moved very easily and every time it did it transported me to a paradise of pleasure, I had to hold on to the bed to control the tremors that my body produced but that went even further, Lucy's tongue began to lick my, causing me to moan and scream like I don't think I had before.

- Aaaaaaaaah!

Lucy licked and bit my over and over again, very masterfully and I couldn't stop moaning, shaking and shaking my head non-stop, I was going crazy with all the pleasure she made me feel. Suddenly she stopped, she did it to place herself on top of me, in such a way that her pussy was on my mouth and her mouth on my pussy. She offered me hers and I wanted to give her as much pleasure as she was giving me. So, I started licking her pussy, it was something I had never done before, but perhaps because of the pleasure she was giving me, I loved savoring her wet pussy. My tongue moved over her lips as well, and inside them, in and out, sometimes I had to stop for a few seconds to scream, as Lucy kept taking me to heaven with her tongue.

- Wet 2 of your fingers and put them inside, Zara! - Lucy asked me.

And I obeyed her with alacrity, took my fingers to her mouth, filled them with saliva and inserted them inside her pussy.

- Aaaahhhh!, Aaaaahhh!

And I obeyed her again, my fingers going in and out of her pussy hard, and my tongue kept licking passionately, while my hands held her buttocks. So, the 2 of us continued for a while longer, I don't know how much because I was enjoying it like never before and I lost track of time. Until I started to feel something inside me getting ready to burst. Something that didn't take long to arrive, a moment in which I felt transported to another world, a world of ecstasy and overflowing pleasure, something that increased when I also took Lucy to orgasm, her flows filled my mouth, and I savored them with great enthusiasm. The 2 of us, in those moments of madness, screamed and moaned non-stop and very loudly, during a time that seemed like it was never going to end. Unfortunately, though, it did end, even if I was totally relaxed. I just wanted to hug Lucy and have her by my side, which I couldn't, because Lucy got up, went to wash, and dressed quickly. Then she came up to me and gave me a kiss on the lips.

"You have been very obedient," she said, "I must go, but we shall see each other again soon."

And there, in that hotel room, I sat alone and thoughtful all night. I never thought something like this would happen.

*"Love is the flower;
you've got to let it grow."*
John Lennon

LITTLE DETAILS

A few years ago, I walked these streets, they are almost identical to how I remember them. A two-way street, a grove of almond trees. The sidewalk where I used to sit and wait for your mom to come out of the house to come see you. On that precise sidewalk where I spent winters and summers. When I met you, I have to admit that I didn't like you. Presumably, no 8-year-old girl likes to be kidnapped during school breaks to be the victim of a group of infamous and abusive girls, who hang her until she is pale and unable to breathe... Yes, you were in that group of little ruffians. And it was your hands that pressed against my neck. I'll admit that now I find it funny.

When you finished basic you changed schools, I did it a year later. I was thankful that you left and that your abuse ended. I didn't think I'd see you again, you didn't cross my mind at any time. But then, I met you in college and it turned out that we would take some courses together. Don't give yourself credit... I still didn't like you.

You walked through the corridors with your friend, "Barbie," as I called her. By then, the two of you were the coveted ones of the university. More you for your elegant bearing. Your meter 75 gave you a plus of beauty, your jet-black hair, straight and long. Your shapely figure, without many curves, but they were enough, believe me.

Some of the internships were at the university radio station that had just acquired open frequency. You were the announcer of the midday shift, and I was the producer who issued the identification stamps with your name. I had a good time listening to it, not for my liking, but it had to be that way. I remember one day when my impulsive self-exploded against one of the teachers. Troy was literally burning, I was a few words away from earning a penalty if it weren't for you, who came holding my arm and it was that slight touch that automatically appeased my anger.

From that day on, we started talking more often. The next cycle they changed my turn on radio to 3 pm because my previous schedule conflicted with my 6 am class..., as a friend of mine would say, "that's not from God." Having more time together, you and I struck up a friendship. I became a confidant of some of your adventures. You kept them quiet, even though you knew I didn't agree with them. So, the day came when, with your panicked face, you told me that you were pregnant and that you had been taken from your house. I usually talk a lot, but I was definitely silent that day. I didn't know what to tell you, least of all because of the quality of the father the child would have, but in the end, it was your decision.

You had me with that idea in my head for the next 5 hours, until you deigned to tell me that it was a joke, of course you advanced April Fool's Day about 8 months. You laughed at me a lot that day. I was just smiling at you, but in my mind, I was saying things that were not suitable for minors.

Living together had become pleasant; we shared many things. Minus your penchant for finding out if I was tickled. Then you decided to start your cannibal stage, and you bit my shoulders every chance you got. By then I was 20 and you were 22. I had already been hiding my taste for women very well for some years now. And you forbade me to think of it any other way. Even on that occasion when you changed in front of me and were left with your beautiful and rounded breasts uncovered. I looked away, not resting my eyes on you. I felt that if I saw you, a neon sign would be etched on my forehead saying "lesbian."

- Kelly, which blouse should I wear? "You were standing in front of me, and I was sitting on the edge of your bed, you knew very well how high your breasts were on my face.
- I do not know. Whatever you want. I wanted to stand up, but you gave me a pillow that threw me off my feet. That little game we were playing had become more frequent. None of them said anything else. Study sessions at your home or mine went on for hours. We ended up talking all night, caressing each other's backs until we fell asleep.
- Move over to this side, you woke me up suddenly to move to the left of the bed. I want to hug you.
It's just that the left is my side to be hugged and the right to hug. You knew that very well. You knew it, just as you knew my I don't know how many pet peeves that ranged from separating everything to eat, to scratching my left elbow when I cross a street.
Halfway through the year we went to a nightclub, you got a little drunk on vodka. You went ahead to my house, and I arrived at midnight. I found you sitting on my bed with a "swallow me dirt" face.
- I think your parents noticed that I drank..., I'm sorry, you told me to make a face like a scolded girl and with the utmost sorrow.
- Don't worry, they already told me they did, and I started laughing.
I lay down at the end of the bed, felt exhausted, and couldn't hear the last thing you were talking about. I just remember feeling you gently kiss my cheek as you said goodnight. Without opening my eyes, I thought that wasn't very normal for us to say between friends. At least mine didn't kiss me goodnight even in that sweet way. Sleep overcame me and it wasn't until the next morning that I suddenly woke up to a strange sensation..., Someone was watching me. I opened my

eyes and there you were, smiling with some sorrow. A pity that soon evaporated because you started the game of caresses and bites. In fact, that's where I learned the term "eating." I played along, I don't know where you got so much strength or maybe it was my strategy to look weak. She was on top of me, biting my abdomen very slowly and she was biting my hip bone as well.

- Cinthya, can I touch your breasts? – I asked you with some trepidation –.

- Why do you ask me that? Anyway, you did it a while ago and you didn't ask my permission, when you said this, my body was full of blood boiling with shame. I didn't remember doing it..., Deep down I regretted not having enjoyed it.

You saw my face of sorrow, moved me to the side, and placed yourself on my body. I closed my eyes. You went down slowly, and I expected you to stop at my abdomen, but your march continued and the soft and sensual bite you gave my sex over the shorts of my pajamas, took my eyes out of their sockets. You took a couple more bites and I was petrified on the mattress.

You went up until you placed your face in front of mine and looking for my gaze you asked me in a voice so sensual that it still echoes in my head:

- Tell me, what do you want? – I felt your sweet breath invading my mouth –.

- "Nothing, I don't want anything," I replied, turning my head away.

- Don't want anything? Sure? – You said softly in my ear. Already my body was shivering under yours. I was afraid that if I told you what I wanted you would be scared.

While I was thinking about that, you kissed me. What a delicious kiss. There's nothing like a woman's kiss..., A woman like you. I responded to your lips, and you pressed my hands, which you had clasped with yours over my head.

After a few minutes I stepped aside, took you, and placed you next to me. I was silent for a few minutes and then I said:

- Have you ever wondered if what we do isn't so normal?

- Yes. But whenever I'm around you, I can't hold back.

- Ok. We'd better keep our distance. That we avoid each other for a while it passes us. What's more, let's not even greet each other with kisses on the cheeks or anything like that.

I stood up and leaned against one of the walls of the room. That's when my phone rings. She was one of my friends and I had arranged to accompany her to a rehearsal for the runway where I would model next week. You didn't like her, and she didn't like you either. But hers is another story.

You left without saying goodbye and without contacting me. I left the campus upset and near the exit you caught up with me.

- Kelly, wait, what happened?

- Nothing Cinthya, go back. – I continued my march, and you held my arm –

- Wait..., Let's go to your house and talk there, okay?

- What else to do? Honestly, I missed you a lot. We arrived at the house and went straight to the room. I don't even know why, but when I closed the door by inertia, I put the key in. You sat on the bed, and I sat next to you. Without saying anything to each other, we looked at each other and you kissed me passionately. Your intoxicating kisses again, your love kisses like a good Capricorn. Without asking you, I unbuttoned your pants and put my hand under your panties and over your sex. You were very wet, I caressed you more and more while still kissing you. Feeling like this was like no other feeling I had ever experienced before. We could have done more that night if it wasn't for my brother's interruption who came for me for basketball practice.

We dressed in a hurry and tried to look normal, I think it wasn't enough because when I opened the door, my brother's face said a lot. He looked at me and then at you. Those faces are impossible not to give away.

Over the next few days, we saw each other on campus sporadically, each immersed in her own activities, so we only exchanged knowing glances in the corridors or escaped to give each other a quick kiss in an empty classroom or in the bathrooms of the faculty. We finally got to see each other one day the following week. You came to my house in the morning, there would be no one so we would have good weather for ourselves. I made you breakfast. Yes, even I was amazed by cooking. But that wasn't the only meal I made for you. It was the first of many. As well as many others that you prepared for me and all those that we prepared together.

While I was trying not to ruin breakfast, you were wrapping your arms around me and hugging me from behind, you wouldn't let go of me and I didn't want you to. You had a big advantage, being taller than me, you could kiss my neck without a problem, and I didn't complain.

Alone in the room, we kissed between laughter and smiles. That's how it was that day. We didn't plan to do it, but our bodies did have it on the agenda. We stripped each other of our clothes. In the midst of all this, we laughed at each other's clumsiness. I lost myself in your dark brown eyes and the faint dimples that formed in the corner of your mouth when you smiled.

I sat you on the bed without ceasing to see you, now I could do it without reservation and without fear. I kissed your neck, I remember. You smelled of a perfume that felt extremely delicious in you. Your perfume mixed with my favorite perfume. That's how I thought until I met your woman's scent. I tried not to be clumsy, I had never been with a woman, but it was not in my plans for you to be disappointed. That didn't happen with you. Making love was a different experience every time.

Your torso offered me your breasts, they weren't small or big, they were perfect. I ran my hands over your thin arms very gently, I did it slowly so that my skin would know you and as time passed, I would not forget you. I kissed your delicate, feminine hands. Your pianist's hands. I sucked your fingers one by one, then kissed your wrists. I laid you on the bed looking into your eyes. You smiled at me; I remember. I kissed your mouth and let you bite my lips while caressing my bare back. I kissed your neck very slowly and you took hold of my ear. I allowed you to get to know me, I allowed myself to be yours. I will let you discover every point of pleasure that I thought was asleep. But it was because only you knew how to wake them up.

Kissing your collarbone made your skin crawl or maybe it was the feeling you got from feeling my hand running down your legs. Maybe both. I went down to your abdomen and up it with my tongue to the base of your breasts. You moaned and pulled my hair softly. I outlined them slowly, like this until I reached your erect nipple. The skin of your halo was contracted, you brought my hand to your other breast. They were the perfect size for my hands.

I went back to your abdomen and with my leg I separated yours, you were wet, very wet. Suddenly you were on top of me, resting your sex on my abdomen.

The warmth of my skin was now bathed in your moisture. You started to move extremely sensually. As you did so, my mouth again met your breasts. You hugged me and I could feel your moisture getting more and more abundant. You looked at me and repeated what I had done to you. For a moment you stopped on my chin, I never imagined that this was one of my most intense points of arousal. You figured it out. You went down to my south, you tied your hair up, you stared at me and there it was again…, your smile! You started kissing my pubis, the tip of your tongue sliding along the edges of my labia majora. You kissed them as if you were kissing my mouth, it was a delight to feel yours. Your nails brushed against my sides, making me curl up against your mouth. What an invitation to you. Sometimes I saw you, you enjoyed it, you did it with a magnificent feat. Your tongue tasted me and again your mouth kissed my sex. You worked on me and did with it what you wanted. I didn't have to object. You gave me such an intense orgasm that after a scream I fell silent. I could feel your nails slide lightly from me to my vagina. You'd run your tongue over your lips and then bite down on the bottom. You looked pleased with what you had done to me.

You went up a little bit more and a little bit more. You placed your knees on the bed and left my head in the middle. Your extremely wet sex was right over my mouth. I went to it and kissed it passionately. I grabbed you by the hip, I drank it all from you. My tongue would enter your vagina and then I would pull it out, sliding it with some pressure to your clitoris, which I would then suck on. You moved delightfully. After a few minutes you came into my mouth. It was the tastiest thing I had ever tasted. You scratched at the wall and a silent scream gave way to an intense one. Feeling your spasms and contractions is something I will never forget.

We continued at it for a good part of the day until we gave up. You were lying on top of me caressing my cheeks and kissing me.

- "We should give this a name," you said as you slid your fingertip across my body.

- A name... and what do we call it? What are we?

- Girlfriends..., I Guess.

That's how we became girlfriends. At first it sounded strange, but other than that, we were two women who had fallen in love at who knows what moment.

After a few months, we had to separate for a couple of days. You were on the other side of the country. On a Saturday in October, 2 natural events took us even further away. The first one happened while you were traveling, an eruption prevented us from seeing each other as we wished. That same night, I got a call from you.

- My Love, How's It Going? Are you ok? Your family?

- Yes Cinthya, everything is fine. Nothing serious happened here. When you come, you'll find out. I've already talked to your sisters and they're fine. Talk to them because they haven't been able to reach you.

- Yes, I'll call you right now... Kelly...

- What happened sweetheart?

- I love you..., - those two words took me by surprise and transformed my life.

- "I love you too," I answered.

The second event was the day after the eruption. A tropical storm caused a red alert in the country. Zero classes, zero jobs, zero everything. General activities had been suspended due to the storm. There had not been such a case since 31 October 1998.

In our houses we were not allowed to go out, so we could not see each other. Since we had started the relationship, we had not gone so long without seeing each other and it had been 12 days. We ran away from our homes. We went out still under the alert to see each other in a central place for both of us. When I arrived, you were already there. You stood up and went to meet me. You gave me such a beautiful and heartfelt hug. You didn't even care if people saw us. I hugged you and whispered in your ear the first "I love you," how I had wanted to say it to you that night on the phone.

Over time, your family and mine became suspicious about our relationship. I was completely banned from your house, in mine after a time in which we denied it, they saw you as one more of the family. Your family's veto is what made me be on this same sidewalk at 6 a.m. Waiting for your mom to come out, so I could get to see you.

You once greeted me wrapped in a towel and with your body wet.

- Hello, come in and I'll finish bathing. – you said on the way to the shower –.

I closed the door and didn't let you continue; in that same corridor I made love to you. Seeing you like that had turned me on too much. After that day..., Mysteriously there were many more in which by "divine chance" it arrived just as you were showering. You were a pervert, and you know it. But I loved that you did.

I once remember reading that a couple should "fight like married people, protect each other like siblings and play like friends" and that's how we were. Of course, I couldn't argue with you, you always ended up being right. But just because I wanted to, uh.

- Let's see..., and who do you think is in charge here?

- Don't come to me with that, we know that I'm in charge, she replied confidently.

- Aha... who has the last word? "And it was at this moment that you gave me that sensual look..."
- You, my love...!
- You see, that's how we work perfectly.
These weren't our usual discussions, but we liked to fool around like that. The real fights were over silly things that I don't even remember the reasons for.
When the surveillance in your house got worse, it was harder for me to get to see you. So, we got together with a couple of friends who we knew about our relationship but never told us anything. One night we kicked you out of your house with the excuse that you were supposed to do a college paper with them. The plan was to stay at one of our houses, drink and if there was time left, do the university work.
We came for you. But anticipating that your father would go out with you to check that I wasn't going, we decided with our friends that I would hide in the trunk of the car. In fifteen minutes, you'd be out and on our way. It was a wonderful plan except for one thing..., your mom invited them to dinner and those 15 minutes stretched to almost an hour.
The trunk of the car had semi-free access to the rear seats, so some air came in. After a few minutes, the car's windows were fogged up. I assume that those passing by thought that someone was taking action inside. When the only action there was mine to be able to breathe. I heard your voice and theirs coming closer and I swear I felt like I touched the sky..., because I knew I would see you and also because I would be alive to see you.
- And Kelly? –Cinthya Asked–.
- In the trunk – they replied in unison –.
- How do you mean in the trunk?
You opened the floodgate and rescued me..., You were my princess to the rescue. I saw your face with a tender

and worried look. You moved your lips, and I could read "I love you" on them. What more did I want, that was enough.

That art of lip-reading developed very well for us when we were surrounded by other people. Saying I love you to each other wasn't a habit, in fact we were born to say it, we lived it. It was important to us, so we came up with a key. Two light, slow taps with the index finger on the other's shoulder indicated the two words that gave us life: "I love you." And so, it often happened, with people around it was enough for us to do that to feel.

A few nights later we had a party with them and other friends. There were 4 of us in the same room. Our accomplices and us. They are in an inflatable car, and we are in bed. I fell asleep after you. I've never been a heavy sleeper and that day I was woken up by a caress on my cheek. I woke up thinking one of the guys was getting too smart, but it was you. Caressing me, smiling at me. It was so intense what you made me feel, so much feeling with that detail, that I still feel that touch when I close my eyes.

We learned to share a lot of things. To this day, you have been the only woman I have danced with, whom I have held in my arms to the beat of a ballad. My two left feet and your two right feet complemented each other.

This complement was adapted to those moments when, in the weakness of one, the other protected. Like during one of the many earthquakes that we have to live in our country. My niece would have been about 8 months old at the time and we were both taking care of her. We were playing with it on the floor when a fairly strong earthquake shook us. I remember standing up:

- Ok, don't worry, nothing happens, don't be scared, everything is fine – I moved from one side to the other while saying this –.

- Kelly...
- No, don't worry, nothing is going to happen...
- Kelly..., Calm down. We are calm..., you're the one who's upset – you told me with that smile with which you told me: "You're crazy and that's how I love you, I must be crazier."
The papers reverse with thunder and lightning in the rain. They scared you. Fear that I was grateful for, when we slept together. That way you hugged me and didn't let go.
A few more months passed, and we held a personal ceremony as a commitment between us. You made your vows, and I made mine. You cried that day as you said to them. I stayed strong; you were the one moved... whom I deceived..., I cried more than you did.
We exchanged some rings, a year ago we had bought some at a fair. You saw them and since you were fixated on us having an identical item, we bought them. I think both cost us less than a dollar. And well, it lasted me a couple of days..., You know me and I'm clumsier than clumsiness.
For the ceremony we had had some very different ones recorded from those of the fair. But the meaning was exactly the same. We just wanted to commit to that love.
A couple of months before our 4th anniversary together, we had a conversation that had started as we always did. There was a moment of silence and then you said:
- I think we'd better get it over with –.
I didn't know what to say. It took me by surprise, and I thought you were joking. We went to the supermarket to do some shopping. Then we returned home to get ready for a party we would be attending. We got together with a friend who did know about our relationship, we greeted each other normally and when

he asked how are you? You replied, "Kelly and I are done." He made fun of us about it, he didn't believe it and neither did I.

It's been 8 years since I kissed you for the first time. It's been 20 years since you choked me during my elementary school breaks. I was left with more questions than answers and with only one truth: Now I remember you with a smile as I walk through these streets, along this double lane surrounded by almond trees. I wanted to wish you a Merry Christmas, but I remembered that you are no longer here.

I remember you with a smile that comes from the depths of my soul. The magic of your small details gives me the assurance that you did love me and that is worth more than your goodbye.

> *"Love is about finding another piece of yourself that you never knew was missing."*
> Laura Jane Grace

A CRY OF ABANDON

When I woke up, neither Lewis nor Diane was still in bed. We were at Lewis's house after our second real date. I slipped from under the covers, my body thick with the remains of the sex from the night before. My pubic hair was crusted, my pussy swollen from fucking. Nude, I stole from the bedroom and into the living room. Diane was there, wearing one of Lewis's shirts and nothing else, drinking coffee and reading the paper. She looked as disheveled as I, her hair on one side sticking up over her head.

- "Hi," I said softly as I slipped onto the couch beside her and kissed her cheek. "Pete is at work?"

She nodded. Pete was Lewis's housemate.

- "Where's Lewis?" I asked.

Diane smiled and turned to kiss me more fully. "He is helping Jack move, remember?" she said. Dropping one side of the paper, she put an arm around me and drew me closer. I laid my head on her shoulder and cuddled. Ah, yes, I remembered vaguely. He'd mentioned it on the way to the movie the night before. The movie we had gone to on a date, we three. I felt sexy to think I had been on a date with both a boy and a girl. There was a wonderful, quiet moment then, Diane sharing her coffee with me as we sat together without speaking.

- "You're a mess," she said finally, putting aside the paper and the empty cup. "Come on, let's take a shower."

She led me into the bathroom and shrugged off the shirt as she turned on the water. Turning, she kissed me again, naked this time, arms circling me as our bodies pressed together. She was as big a mess as I was, I thought and smiled. Sex all over her. I thrilled at the touch of her. The sensation of her bare breasts on my skin always has that effect on me. Still kissing me, she drew me into the shower and under the hot stream.

"Yenny," she said as she lathered up the washcloth and began to swab it over my breasts, "I want to make love with you."

I pressed my shoulders against the stall wall to give her more access to my body. "Mmmmm, I love making love with you, Diane."

Her hand moved lower, over my tummy, washing away traces of the night's passion there.

She shook her head. "We haven't made love yet, Yenny, just you and I."

I draped an arm over her shoulder and looked into her eyes and listened to her.

- "We've had sex. We've fucked. Five times now. But there was always someone else there, every time. I want to make love to you, just by ourselves."

She was right. The night we met and first had sex there were a bunch of other girls around. And the second time, we had a foursome with two boys, one of them Lewis, because what is there to do when stuck. And then came our dinner for three at which we decided to try being a threesome, followed by two other nights together, one of them only the night before, of sex. Diane and I had never just made love with one another.

- "You had Lewis to yourself last year, when the two of you dated. And I had him last month. But you and I, Yenny, need to just be together. If this is going to work, we need that."

Her hand was washing me between my legs, but it was a caring, gentle touch, not one meant to arouse just then. She was loving me and washing me. Or was it love? We hadn't quite gotten around to using the word. I understood what she meant though. I loved the physical intimacy I had with her. But I had also loved the physical intimacy I had with Caroline that night when I first made love to another girl. And I felt it with the other girls. And I loved the physical intimacy of two boys in my body at the same time, with Diane there too. I loved the passion and the closeness and the hot, raw, driving sex. I loved sex. But did I love any person?

I thought I loved Lewis. When he stopped calling last year, I felt ever so lonely. But was it just his cock inside me that I was lonesome for? How close had we really become in such a short time? I had let him do me on our first date. I thought I enjoyed spending time with him, being with him, going to movies and out to dinner, but were those only preludes to sex? And what was there between Diane and me? In my fantasies, I saw us going on as a trio, making love, spending time together, loving one another, sharing, growing, and being in love. I thought I loved her. But what had we ever done together except have sex?

I wanted to photograph them both nude, practicing my art on subjects of my love. I'd never photographed a nude, but now I wanted to do so. I wanted to have my friends accept us, and my mom. I wanted us all to graduate and find good jobs so we could get a nice place together and make a home. I had let my mind run all over the place after only three dates. I must be crazy to be thinking such things. Still, I felt those things.

Diane turned me around, ran soap over the cloth once more, and began to scrub my back. It felt so nice. I sighed and just enjoyed her touch. Her fingers moved lower, between the cheeks of my ass, washing me there too. I heard the cloth drop with a heavy wet plop as her fingers continued to touch me. They were slick from soap, and she touched the bar of soap to me, getting me all squeaky clean. No one had ever washed my ass for me before.

Placing my hands on the wall, I braced myself and arched my back, thrusting my bottom to her. I felt her slick, wet hip brush to me as I did. She held herself there, touching my star with one soapy finger. It slipped into me, and I cried out. I hadn't felt that sort of thing before, a warm soapy finger delving into me, but I had enjoyed anal sex.

It felt strange and good too. Diane simply slid her finger in and out of me, slowly, gently. Her body pressed to mine, and I could feel her breasts grazing across my back as she moved her finger inside of me. Her lips found my neck under my wet hair, and the fingers of her other hand cupped one of my boobs. I made little grunting sounds, but I didn't try to pull away from her.

Her lips moved down my back, kissing me, as she dropped to her knees. I spread my legs wider as I felt her going down. Her tongue was firm and insistent as she moved between my cheeks. I felt a shiver as she touched me there. I flexed my fingers and curled my nails into the tile. The water splashed onto my back as she moved out of the way, running down my skin, cascading over my butt. It was too much. I turned, leaned over and brought her up, kissing her to let her know it was all right as I took the soap from her and began to wash her. I picked up the dropped washcloth and moved it across the soap, then her body. She looked at me, her eyes big and questioning. She looked so beautiful. I moved in and kissed her, holding her tight to me as the hot water splashed down over us.

My hands drifted down her body, over the curves of her bottom. Running my fingers down, I opened her cheeks and touched a fingertip to her star as she had done me. She murmured around our kiss and came up onto her toes, pressing her full breasts into mine. I rolled my finger over her, pressing her and wanting her to tell me what to do, but already knowing. As she lifted again onto her toes, I let my soapy finger into her ass. Diane pushed back, taking in my finger and settling back onto her feet as she let me do her butt. We kissed, holding one another as the water began to cool.

- "Come on," Diane said finally, reaching around and pushing my finger out of her and turning off the water.

- "Let's make love now, Yenny." She took my hand and led me out of the shower, dabbed me dry with one of the towels and then let me do the same for her. Hand in hand, we walked slowly back to the bed, bending together to toss off the blanket and spread. I felt shy and nervous, considering how intimate we had been before, how intimate we had just been in the shower. Sliding one knee onto the mattress, I moved onto it, lying face down and reaching out with arms and legs for the corners of the bed. I didn't expect Diane to tie me up, but I felt the need to let her know she could if she wanted to. I wanted to please her so much, and I hoped I was doing what she wanted of me.

The bed moved as she got on it, between my open legs. Tender hands lay on my thighs and damp hair fell to my ass. Her fingers moved up, spreading my cheeks. Dipping lower, she touched her tongue to me again. I knew she wanted this. It was there in almost every time that we had had sex, this hint, the suggestion of her desire for more. I sucked in a deep breath and let her do what she wanted, even knowing that she would be hoping I would do the same for her.

I had liked it when she licked my ass before, and I had put my tongue to her. It was interesting, kind of sexy because it was also kind of dirty. But I knew this was going to be different. Her tongue was probing me, swabbing my ass. I dug my fingers into the sheets, clawing them as she loved my ass. It felt good. Her fingers pulled my cheeks wider, and her tongue curled, flicking over my delicate skin. I remembered what she had done something very like this before, just before putting Lewis's cock into me.

Now, it was her tongue she was pushing in to me. I gasped as I felt her wriggling it, opening me. I lifted my head back, straining against my clawed fingers as I pushed my bottom back at her, trying to tell her to go ahead, to do it. My mouth gaped as I felt her tongue open me.

It was amazing to accept what her tongue was doing to me, where it was. This was entirely different: this was the act, not the prelude. Her tongue was in me, wriggling and writhing, unlike a finger or a penis. I released the sheets and drew my arms down, folding them across my back, crossing them and grasping them in my fingers, holding on against the pleasure.

One of her hands left my cheek and slipped between my legs. As my hips bobbed to welcome Diane's licking, I rose up and came down to feel her crossed fingers touching gently to my pussy. I was wet, I knew. The tips of her fingers grazed between my lips, exciting me further as her tongue moved. Slowly, very gently, she pushed her fingers inside of my cunt. Her other hand raised, and, as she pushed her fingers all the way into me, she brought her hand down sharply on my ass. I cried out, gripping my arms tighter under my fingers, but not moving away from her.

- "Yes," I murmured, knowing what that little smack had done inside of me. I wanted more.

Diane's tongue seemed to speed up, her fingers curled inside of me, dancing across that rough spot up and inside of me. I cried out again, and felt her hand come down on my flesh again.

Suddenly, her tongue was gone from my butt. I turned to look back at her, the desire and frustration hanging heavily on my face.

- "You love this, don't you?" she asked, licking her lips while looking up at me.
- "Yes," I told her. "Please."
- "Please what, Yenny?"
My heart fluttered. I wasn't sure what she expected me to say. "Please, keep spanking me."
Her hand smacked on me again, catching my left cheek this time, the one she hadn't spanked yet.
- "Please what, Yenny," she repeated. Her hand snapped down again, stinging my bare skin.
- "Please keep licking my ass."
Her tongue swept across me again, even as her hand landed on me once more. There was fire under her hand, spreading across the plump flesh of my bottom, searing into me. My pussy gushed.
- "Please what, Yenny?"
- "Please keep fucking me." I bobbed my hips again, moving on her fingers still inside of me. I wanted to cum so.
A rain of spanks fell on me, first one cheek and then the other. They were hard and sharp, but they excited me. I could feel my bottom flushing. I wriggled on her fingers, knowing she could make me cum so easily now.
- "Please, Diane, make love with me..."
Her mouth was back on me once again, her tongue burrowing into my ass, her fingers churning in my pussy. The spanking had heated me, made me even wetter than before, I held fast to my arms behind my back as I cried out again and again.
- "Make love with me, Diane," I gasped again. My orgasm fired up. I bent my knees and raised my legs, my muscles taut and on edge. I held tight to my own arms behind my back, holding on as pleasure rushed through my tense body, until I let go of everything and cried out loudly with the intensity of my cum. It rolled through my body, curling my toes as I writhed and

thrashed my legs. Drawing in a deep breath, I calmed slowly and let my arms fall to my sides as I lay gasping beneath my lover.

Her fingers inside of me brought me up again. I pushed up onto my hands, arching my back and pushing toward her, my hair dangling down onto my back, fingers tearing at the sheets as she licked at me and moved her tongue. I cried out again, coming for her again, the delicious sensation of lust and love mingling the physical with the emotional. I said I loved her. Out loud.

Barely giving me time to breathe, Diane took me over yet again, spanking me more softly now, but continuously. My ass rose up as I half knelt on the bed, legs apart and my sex thrust to her mouth and fingers. Her lips left my star and softly sucked in my clit, pressing to it and gently running her tongue around and around. I was calling her name, telling her I loved her, lost in sensation as I came again.

Oh, it was magical. I eased my body back onto the mattress, lifting the now untucked sheet under my fingers simply for something to hold onto with the pent-up energy that ran out of me. I breathed deeply, slowly, recovering myself after the heights she had taken me to, gentling down again, and being soft. I simply lay there for a moment.

Twisting around, I struggled to get my arms around her. Diane came up to me as we lay together, her warm skin skimming over mine. I felt a sheen coating me, feeling slightly slippery as we moved together. We kissed, long and deeply, our tongues running over one another as I laid one hand over her breast and fondled her. Her breasts are bigger than mine, not huge, but plump and round. Her nipples are different too, and my fingertips curled around each one as I moved from breast to breast as she rolled over onto her back.

Diane got up on her elbows and reached for the water on the night table. She took a long drink, then gave it to me. I sipped, glad of it after coming so. Our eyes met over the brim of the bottle.

Diane took the bottle back and set it down before lying on her back once again, one arm draped over her forehead. I rose above her as she did, dipping my head to use my lips and tongue on her nipples. I smiled to myself. I really liked sucking on her boobs. Six months ago, I would never have imagined how much this simple, endearing thing could make me so happy. Even in my most secret, forbidden bi-curious fantasies, and there weren't many, licking nipples had not played a very big part. I love having my own teased and played with, and, I had recently discovered, hurt, but I hadn't focused on playing with another girls ever. While self-conscious in some ways, being small-breasted does have advantages: I rarely wear a bra; I can get away with wearing lots of styles that more endowed girls would not look good in. (Okay, so I don't fill out a tight top. I wish I did, but I don't.) Lewis told me he really liked my breasts and would fondle me under my clothes in public when we were dating. One of the nicer things about not needing a bra.

I adored Diane's breasts. I eased over her body and between her legs, which she opened for me and let me slide between. I felt the closeness of her thighs around my ribs as I dipped my head to her boobs and ran my tongue around and around each stiff nipple, closing my lips over them to suck, pressing with my lips. I ran the tip of my tongue around the edge of each wide areola. O la la, I was sucking another girl's nipples. I wanted to shout out with glee and let everyone know how much I loved it. Yenny Henderson likes boobs.

Diane's fingers played in my drying hair. She lifted a tress here and there and let it fall, gently massaging my scalp as I just licked and sucked on her breasts. Soft mews filled the air. She is not nearly as noisy as I am when excited. Or she hadn't been. As I loved her breasts, she seemed to let go a little. I wondered if groups intimidated her. So far, they hadn't seemed to inhibit me at all. Funny about that.

Sighing happily, I finally left her breasts and moved down her body. The soft curve of her tummy came up, and I kissed her navel, trailing my lips lower. My hands fluttered over her body, touching here and there. I moved them over the swell of her hips, around her ribs. I just touched her. Pursing my lips, I laid kisses across her mound, her short hair there almost prickling. It reminded me of the suggestion they both had made that I should take away all of my hair down there. I wondered how I would look.

Diane's pussy is also very different from mine. Her labia minora are more pronounced, extending lower and showing even when she is not aroused. She was aroused right then though, and, as I lowered my mouth to her, she sighed even more loudly and laid her hand on my head once more. I knew I was going to use my tongue on her ass. I just had to work up to it, and sweet Diane was not hurrying me. She cooed and whimpered softly as I loved her with my lips and tongue, taking my time.

I had not done a lot of pussy licking up to that point. Okay, so I had gone down on the fabulous Ruby, another girl named Tina, and one named Lauren, as well as Diane, at that party back in the fall. I think that was all. The details are kind of fuzzy. Caroline's pussy was entirely different from Diane's, I remembered as I lapped. Absolutely the most gorgeous in the world, probably. But, for all of having licked four other girls, I was not exactly an expert. I thought I was pleasing Diane when I touched her with my mouth, but I was sure there was more I could do. I wanted to do more. I wanted to be really good at this and for her to like what I did.

Thinking of Caroline reminded me of something she had done to me. I slid my hands under Diane's ass, pulling her closer, and furrowed my way up between her lips, tasting the heavy, musty womanliness of her. I love that taste. My tongue coated with her cream, I loved it over her clit, listening as she cried out more loudly than before and her fingers tightened in my hair. Circling her clit with just the pointed tip of my tongue, I pushed and pulled at her skin there, the folds of her moving under me. I wasn't sure if I would do this right or not, or if she would like it, but I went ahead. I opened my teeth just a little, closed my lips over her clit and inhaled. The suction drew her clit up and into me, past my teeth so that they grazed over her skin. I hoped I was doing it right, because when Caroline had done it to me, I nearly lost it.

I guess Diane loved it. With a cry of abandon, she came, raising her ass up off the bed and pulling my hair as her orgasm rolled through her.

I smiled happily into her sex as she came. I had done this, with my lips and tongue. Yenny, you are getting better.

Diane sat up, leaning on me as I came up onto my hands, and we kissed. This time, it was flavored with the creaminess of her pussy. I quite liked having her all over my face. It made me feel sexy to know she had drenched my face because she was so wet and excited. We kissed deeply, sharing, touching, then she drew away, looking me in the eye, questioningly. Didn't she know I would do anything for her? I wanted to take the questions away.

*"The best thing to hold onto in life
is each other."*
Audrey Hepburn

PHOTO SESSION

Andrea bit her bottom lip nervously as she approached Nikky's house. It was late Friday evening and the sound of her feet striding along the sidewalk seemed to be the only sound in the usually busy town. Even the black sky above seemed to be casting an ominous tone on the events ahead.

Andrea was a stunning twenty-three-year-old with straight raven hair that cascaded down each side of her face and rested gently on her shoulders. Her emerald-colored eyes were offset by a pair of luscious ruby lips shaped perfectly for her face. She was blessed with a pair of 36-B breasts encircled by soft brown areola, and pert nipples that grew hard at the slightest provocation. Her tight abdomen and long, slender legs gave her a stunning sight.

Nikky was twenty-five with fiery red hair that twisted in locks on each side of her feminine face, soft pouting lips, and doe-like eyes. In contrast to Andrea, Nikky's breasts were a size 34-C with soft puffy nipples. Her 5' 4" frame would give the appearance of a rather shy and demure character.

Both had met while attending art and photography classes at a prestigious college. As they shared the same interest in fetish art and erotic photography they often chatted at breaks or lunch. During these chats Nikky had learned a few things about Andrea that had piqued her interest. Andrea, like herself, was bisexual, currently not in a relationship, had many of the same interests as she, and best of all Andrea had all the signs of a submissive female. Nikky was always the dominant when involved with another female. Instead of pursuing anything with Andrea though, Nikky had chosen to devote her time and effort to her classes.

Fate intervened as both Andrea and Nikky soon advanced to being the top two students in the class and found themselves locked in a contest with each other to submit the best overall artwork in the category of digital art. The winner would be given a show at a trendy art gallery known to launch several local artists. In the weeks leading up to the contest they worked fervently at creating what they hoped would be the winning entry.

Andrea submitted a brilliantly colored painting with an oversized, monstrous dragon confronting a nude female warrior brandishing a shining sword that rested on her shapely ass. The details of the painting were incredible and would have easily won if not for Nikky's more erotic themed fantasy of a nude female in a dark and eerie dungeon being guarded by a muscle-bound hunk. After careful appraisal, the art professor declared Nikky the winner. A deep sense of dread overcame Andrea as she recalled the conversation two days earlier.

The professor had presented a way for the students to earn some extra credits by pairing off and one agreeing to model for the other in a photography session. For this event he wanted it to be sexual themes, exploring the worlds of dominance and submission, BDSM and other fetishes. He wanted them to explore lighting, texture, and creativity in their shots.

Both Andrea and Nikky agreed that the winner of the art contest would do the photography, and the loser would be the model. The professor accepted the pairing, and Nikky had instructed Andrea to be at her house at 11 P.M. Friday night, and to be prepared for a long night. For Nikky it presented a golden opportunity. She could work on her photographic skills and also manipulate Andrea. Under the guise of modeling, she could dominate Andrea through the lens of her camera and that is precisely what she intended to do.

Andrea ascended the two-story brick house that Nikky lived in alone. Ringing the doorbell, she was soon greeted by a beaming Nikky, wearing a bright red midriff top and faded jean short. She was holding a glass of wine and motioned Andrea inside. The smell of incense filled the air as Andrea looked around the spacious living room. It was decorated in a casual style, but what caught her eye the most were the erotic paintings and drawings that adorned the walls. They were BDSM themes, and some very explicit.

- "Shy?" Nikky remarked coyly as she caught Andrea's response to the pictures.

- "No, I like them, they are very...intense," Andrea remarked cautiously. Even though Andrea knew Nikky was interested in fetish art, she expected Nikky to be a studious recluse; instead, Andrea was already seeing a different side of Nikky.

Moving quickly, Nikky carefully changed the subject. "I do my best work at night, which is why I asked you to come over at this hour. I am more motivated," she grinned as she looked Andrea in the eyes.

- "Good for you," Andrea remarked, not fully knowing how to answer the remark.

- "I am so excited to have you as my model. Remember you did agree to anything. We will be going down to the basement for what I have in mind, but would you like some wine first?" Nikky remarked with a slight impish grin.

- "Sure, why not," Andrea remarked as she slumped down onto a nearby couch and tried to get more comfortable amid the growing apprehension of what she had gotten herself into. Even though Andrea had lost the class competition, the extra points would still put her in a good position to be recommended to one of the art galleries.

The two began chatting about various things as they drank the wine. "What I have in mind is a series of photos around the theme of you being kidnapped by a cruel Mistress. A helpless captive being forced to submit to her every desire, that sort of thing. I hope you find it exciting. Remember it is like acting. You really have to possess the mindset of a captive and put yourself into the situation for the pictures to look authentic," Nikky mused as she sipped her wine; carefully setting up the seduction she had in mind.

Andrea's heart was racing wildly as she tried to imagine what Nikky had in store for her, and trying to convince herself it was only art, yet there was something lurking beneath the facade that Andrea sensed but could not yet fully determine.

Shortly before midnight Nikky suggested they head downstairs and get things ready. Andrea followed Nikky down the wooden steps that led to the dark basement. The sense of dread Andrea had been feeling was confirmed the moment the basement lights were turned on. To her shock and utter amazement, the entire basement was a well-equipped dungeon; Metal cages, tables with straps, leg irons and wrist irons were fastened to the walls. Whips, feathers, and even candles could be seen strewn on top of a nearby table.

- "Nikky, I know I agreed to this, but..., I am really not into the bondage scene," Andrea remarked as her eyes scanned the array of items with a mixture of curiosity and caution.

Nikky flashed Andrea a cold, icy stare as she picked up an expensive camera and readied it. "It's just art Andrea. We can create some amazing things here, but if you want to back out, I can call the professor and..."

- "No!!" Andrea interrupted as she hung her head sheepishly. "I will do it. I am just nervous is all." she replied. "And by the way, where the hell did you get all this stuff?" Andrea inquired.

A devious smile formed on Nikky's lips as she worked with the camera. "My dear ole uncle left me this place in his will. I found a little antechamber he had covered up. Who knew his little secrets? Over the last year or so I have added some things to kind of fuel the fantasy," Nikky smiled.

- "Have you actually used these things?" Andrea remarked as she paced slowly along a small table of items.

- "Let's get started, shall we? Nikky remarked. "Take off all of your clothes."

Andrea' could feel a wild and strange excitement racing through her at the thought of getting naked in front of Nikky but it was the tone in Nikky's voice that she found even more alluring and provocative. She bit her bottom lip nervously and began removing her clothes until she stood naked and quivering slightly in the strange basement dungeon.

- "Good girl. Let's have a look at you," Nikky remarked as she slowly walked around Andrea. Andrea could feel Nikky's eyes roaming every inch of hers as she blushed slightly. The momentary awkwardness was soon interrupted as Nikky gave the instructions for the first shot.

- "I want you to go halfway up the stairs and lean in against the brick wall with your back facing me." Nikky remarked. Nikky knew the lighting at the top of the stairs would bathe Andrea's body perfectly, creating the illusion of a submissive female in a soft pose.

As she strode towards the basement steps, she tried to imagine what Nikky was seeing and how she appeared to the camera. Nikky took a self-indulgent moment to admire the way Andrea's ass swayed as she began the trek up the steps.

- "Stop! Now lean against the wall. Stretch out your arms wide above your head. Lower your head downward so that you are looking at the floor." Nikky instructed as she readied her camera. The image of Andrea's body casting a shadow against the wall; the soft light illuminating her from the rear, was skillfully captured on film to Nikky's delight.

As Andrea listened to the camera click, the realization that the entire class would soon be seeing these photographs sank in. As Nikky gazed through the lens her keen eyes saw Andrea's fully erect nipples and a crooked smile formed on her lips.

- "Turn around and face me. Rest your hands behind your head and stick out your chest. Your nipples are hard and that will look great!" Nikky remarked as she licked her lips in anticipation of the next shot.

Andrea gasped as she looked down and saw what Nikky meant. Her nipples were indeed rock hard and jutting out from her ample breasts in an erotic show. Under normal circumstances, Andrea would have covered them and ran for cover, but now she found herself willing, even turned on at displaying them for the camera.

Content with the first round of shots, Nikky beckoned Andrea back down the steps as she studied the room for the next shot. Having Andrea naked and ordering her around while she herself was fully clothed allowed Nikky to assert her dominance systematically and she wanted to turn it up a notch.

- "Alright let's do something a little more provocative and intense now, "Nikky remarked as she led Andrea over to center of the basement. "Turn around and put your hands above your head." Nikky directed.

Andrea nervously followed Nikky's directions and watched apprehensively as Nikky bound her wrists and ran the rope through a pulley on the ceiling above. Pulling Andrea's arms upwards until they were amply stretched, Nikky walked behind Andrea studying her next move. Nikky wanted a shot of her own handprint firmly displayed on Andrea's ass and proceeded to slap Andrea firmly, causing Andrea to gasp audibly to the dull stinging sensation on her fleshly mounds.

- "What are you doing?" Andrea asked in a soft but nervous tone.

- "I am spanking your ass like any good Mistress would do," Nikky remarked coyly. "I want everyone to see my handprint visibly displayed on that cute little ass of yours," she continued. The feeling of her hand on Andrea's soft bottom along with the resounding echo of Andrea's ass being spanked sent a decadent thrill of control cascading through Nikky.

When just the right glowing handprint was clearly visible on Andrea's ivory skin, Nikky slipped back to the camera and caught the image perfectly. It would be the perfect lead into the BDSM theme the professor wanted, but even more it played into Nikky's personal intentions for Andrea. Leaving Andrea tied and squirming, Nikky slipped over to the nearby table and picked up a black leather riding crop and returned to her position. Instead of striking Andrea with it, Nikky began running the business end of the crop between Andrea's legs and along the puffy lips of her exposed pussy.

- "Nikky...no!" Andrea gasped in a broken voice. Her reluctance clearly masked the building arousal.

- "Stop? Are you sure? I think you like it," Nikky whispered in a seductive but firm voice as she ran the crop across the hood of Andrea's clit teasingly. There was no response from Andrea aside from heavy breathing.

- "Arousal translates well to the camera, and I want to see you dripping wet," Nikky remarked in a more sinister tone. Andrea blinked her eyes as the heat between her legs began to build. Inside, the battle for self-control and giving in to desire became more desperate as Nikky guided the wand over her sensitive pussy. Taking Andrea to the brink of orgasm, she quickly stopped, returned to the camera and clicked off a few more shots.

Before Andrea could recover and regain her composure, Nikky moved to the next shot. Loosening Andrea's hands from above, she bound them behind her. She bolted upstairs and quickly returned with a pillow. Forcing Andrea onto her hands and knees, she positioned Andrea with her head lying on the pillow and her ass stuck proudly in the air. Andrea was more vulnerable than ever before as Nikky began softly running her fingers along Andrea's puffy lips, teasing her slowly and relentlessly.

- "Try telling me you don't like it now," Nikky snarled.
- "Your pussy is getting very wet."

Andrea couldn't answer. Her body and mind were both prisoners of her own desires. She wanted Nikky to stick her fingers inside her burning pussy and make her cum, but she was still hanging on to the last ebb of control.

As if Nikky had read her mind, she glided two digits slowly into Andrea's pussy and began fingering her, allowing her thumb to torment the bound girl's clit. "Cum for me like a good little slut!" Nikky hissed as she fucked Andrea harder with her fingers. The last ounce of willpower faded from Andrea as her body's growing needs took over. Her body trembled and shook as copious amounts of spray shot from her drenched pussy under the force of the orgasm.

Almost immanently Nikky became inspired for yet another picture. Pulling Andrea's arms under her and backwards she fastened her arms and ankles together. The resulting image showed Andrea's fully stretched ass sticking upwards, her head buried on the pillow, and her pussy clearly in the throes of a recent orgasm. Her puckered hole was aiming right for the camera and Nikky wasted no time getting the shot. The scent of Andrea's aroused pussy filled Nikky's nostrils as she aimed the last shot.

- "That was fucking hot!" she remarked as she ran her hands along Andrea's ass cheeks. "Now let's do a little imprisonment shall we?" Nikky replied.

Andrea was still under the spell of orgasmic bliss as Nikky spoke. Her words seemed muddled and distant. For these shots Nikky wanted blindfolds, cuffs, and ropes. She wanted the scenes dark and edgy as she gathered the needed items. As Andrea came to her senses, she was aware of her bladder filling up inside her.

- "Can we take a break Nikky?" Andrea replied in a weak voice.

- "Oh no babe, don't want to lose the magic and have to start all over," Nikky mused from the distance as she gathered the needed items for the next shots.

- "Nikky, I have to..."

- "Hush," Nikky replied as she poured herself into the next shot. She knew exactly what she wanted and worked quickly to adjust the lighting. Moving Andrea to a padded mattress now bathed in soft light, she hooked two leather collars around her ankles and bound them together with a single chain. She then proceeded to place a studded collar around Andrea's neck and ran a link of chain upwards attaching it to clamp overhead. Placing Andrea on her hands and knees on the mattress, Nikky looked through the lens, ecstatic at the submissive view before her as Andrea's hair fell downward, drawn by the force of gravity.

It was the most erotic picture of the night thus far and Nikky was particularly proud of it as she viewed it through the camera lens.

- "Nikky... I gotta pee!" Andrea whimpered as she felt the desperation building.

Hearing Andrea's pleading voice fueled the dominance inside her as the idea for a mind-blowing picture took place.

- "Great Andrea. Desperation looks great on camera. Hold it for as long as you can."

Andrea's bladder was on the verge of emptying itself with or without Nikky's consent as she tried desperately to remain in control. Nikky led Andrea to several more bondage shots, including some breast bondage, nipple clamps, and pussy play, even making Andrea ride a sybian with her hands bound behind her. The desperation in Andrea's face made the pictures priceless and authentic.

At long last, Nikky quickly grabbed a bucket and sat in the middle of the floor. Losing Andrea's bounds and binding her hands behind her back, she walked Andrea to the bucket.

- "Squat and pee. I will take the pics from behind. Only you and I will know you actually pissed while I took this picture. It will be fucking hot!" Nikky mused.

All defiance and resistance had left Andrea as she squatted over the bucket, totally surrendering herself to Nikky's demands. The hissing sound of the escaping flood soon filled the air as Nikky snapped the view from the rear, taking care to preserve Andrea's dignity while making the picture erotic.

The filming ended for the night, Nikky cleaned everything up and guided Andrea to a hot shower. As Andrea was basking under the warm jets, she felt Nikky slip in beside her. Nikky said nothing as she pulled Andrea to her and the two exchanged a long and passionate kiss. Nikky then bent down and began sucking Andrea's hardening nipples as her hand slipped again between her legs.

In the bedroom, Andrea willingly allowed herself to be tied spread eagle to the bed. Nikky Straddled Andrea's face and lowered herself to Andrea's open mouth. Facing away from Andrea, with her ass and pussy grinding Andrea's face, Nikky leaned over and began working on Andrea's glistening pussy with her own tongue and fingers.

Andrea put her full effort into pleasing Nikky as she worshiped her pussy and licked Nikky's asshole vigorously. Nikky soon erupted in a full-blown orgasm, drenching Andrea's face with her hot sticky juices. Nikky returned the favor by bringing Andrea to a powerful orgasm. Nikky rose from the bed and took a long hot shower before returning to the bound Andrea.

*"Love is not something you find.
Love is something that finds you."*
Loretta Young

SLEEP IN MEGAN'S ARMS

The text arrived a couple of days later. Megan introduced herself and gave a brief description of her and her interests, and I replied kindly. We swapped emails and pictures and arranged to meet a week or so later at a bar near the town center. I put a lot of thought into my dress and general presentation for our meeting, it was going to be a real first for me. I finally settled for a cream-colored dress, buttoned down the front and hemmed about half-way down my thighs. My make-up would be discreet, and there would be just enough cleavage on show to attract attention.

I climbed out of the taxi having touched up my makeup, made sure my dress was not crumpled and walked to the door of the pub. I tried to look sophisticated and confident but inside my belly was churning. I was about to meet, and probably make love with, the only lesbian I had ever known.

As the door swung shut behind me, I spotted her, sitting alone at the bar. She stood up as I approached and kissed my cheek.

- "What's your poison?"

Calm, sophisticated. I wished I was.

- "I'm on Daiquiri. Try it."

The bartender loaded the mixer, shook it and poured my drink.

- "It's delicious."

- "So are you. Kevin warned me, but you are even lovelier than I'd expected."

She was wearing a loose leather jacket, a close-fitting top showing her boobs and cleavage to perfection, and tight shorts which did wonders for the delicious curves of her arse. Both were tailored in white leather, cut to show off her perfectly tanned midriff, and she wore knee length boots Jack Sparrow would have been proud of.

She was fairly tall, maybe five foot eight, her hair closed cut on one side and gathered up on the other, jet black with a flame red streak, and she had a beautiful rather than pretty face. A couple of tattoos were on show as were a couple of body piercings, and as I was to discover later, she had more in some in quite interesting places. I have to say I was impressed.

We chatted for an hour or so, small talk at first then touched on sexual issues.

She told me a bit about her life, how she had given her virginity to her personal trainer on her eighteenth birthday. He had a flat in the same complex as the gym she used and invited her back to celebrate after her morning workout. She already fancied him to bits, so she accepted immediately. She expected cold orange juice, not the chilled white wine he treated her to and especially not the rampant sex they enjoyed together all day and almost every day until term ended a month or so later. He obviously taught her a lot, not least that sex is there to be enjoyed not to get hung up about.

Leaving college, she joined a holiday company as a hostess at a small French seaside resort. After a few weeks, she had the routine of the job sorted, which gave her plenty of time to herself. She found a small, secluded beach where she could get an all-over suntan and of course, she had her own chalet. She could happily use either or both to satisfy her rapidly developing sexual curiosity.

At first, she concentrated on boys, checking through the guest list looking for likely talent. Having eliminating guys obviously with partners and the groups who were there to get pissed, there would normally be at least one or two to choose from, and it was then a simple matter to get them to bed.

However, she soon began to realize that this was far from satisfying. With a few very notable exceptions, sex consisted of a bit of inexpert groping. A tumble into bed, almost always with him on top, a few grunts as he came, maybe a fart or two and he would be happily snoring while she was left to finish herself off as best she could.

About halfway through the season, a rather attractive lady arrived on a solo holiday. Megan helped her settle in and they started chatting. To cut a long story short, a couple of days later Megan showed her to the private beach, and they spent the rest of the afternoon fucking. She had been introduced to girl-girl sex, and thoroughly enjoyed it. They now spent most of their time together, either naked on the beach or in the chalet where they both now chose to sleep.

Megan was shown so much she had never imagined. Different ways to pleasure another woman, the sensitive spots on her own body, that a woman can have multiple, or even a continuous, orgasm, various sex toys and how to use them. By the time Zara left for home, she was quite an expert. It was time to change her tactics.

Now she was scouring the list for likely girls. She was surprised to find that it was quite easy to get a girl to her beach, especially if she offered a picnic and a bottle of wine, with the promise of sunbathing without the attention of leering men. From then it was just a matter of time before they were both getting an all-over suntan, skinny dipping and generally having girly fun. It was inevitable that they would end up fucking, if not on the first day, then very soon after.

Even nubile young daughters with their families were fair game. She would check from her passport details that the girl was pretty (of course) and of legal age, then befriend the family. Fathers were easy. A little flattery from an attractive girl and their minds turned to putty. Mothers were more cautious, but a promise to take personal care of their little darling while Mum and Dad enjoyed their own holiday usually did the trick. And, of course, she did take personal care of their little darling, fucking her senseless while they sunned themselves by the pool.

Once or twice she even took the father. A good-looking guy, late thirties maybe early forties, loads of experience? Mmmm. Tasty. Gave him something to remember from his holiday.

Coming back to the UK at the end of the season, she was promoted to research manager, tasked to check details of potential new holiday locations. This was where she came across Kevin's little project and joined the Troupe, both taking part in the filming but also finding new locations. And in particular developing new talent, in this case, me.

- "I doubt if you know too much about the gay scene?"
- "Nothing at all."
- "No problem. We'll have another drink here then I'll take you to my favorite club. Don't be nervous, you'll enjoy it." She gave me her hand and a reassuring kiss. I felt I could trust her, and relaxed. Just a bit.

The taxi dropped us off outside an unpretentious building with smoked glass doors. The doorman greeted Megan by name and ushered us in. As my eyes adjusted to the dim light, I could see a large room with a central stage surrounded by booths but no bar.

We were greeted by a very pretty girl in uniform who showed us to our table and took our order. I sat down and Megan joined me on the small, intimate, even, sofa. I looked around to find that the audience was made up of couples and small groups, mainly girls with just a few boys. Girls with girls, boys with boys. Arm in arm, shoulder to shoulder.

Our drinks and small eats were delivered to our table, the house lights were dimmed, and the stage floodlit. Two girls danced on, scantily clad and very pretty, and started their routine. The jokes were mainly at the expense of straight men, and they had the whole place howling with laughter. When they thought they had finished they were called back for two encores.

As the spotlights dimmed the stage became a dance floor, mainly girls dancing together but occasionally boys. The dancing became quite intimate, people grinding into each other. Megan stood up and drew me to my feet. I was about to have my first meaningful dance with another woman, and in public. I was very nervous, but at the same time aroused.

I was a little bit distant at first as she let me get used to the situation, then she drew me to her, and we kissed. As she drew me to her, I felt her hands explore my back and shoulders, and I responded by caressing her back and arse. The soft leather of her top and pants responded warmly to my touch and must have felt even more erotic for Megan. She pressed her pelvis into me, and I pressed against her.

After a few dances, she suggested we return to our drinks, and of course, I agreed. She sat down, her leg extended. Instead of inviting me to sit alongside her she maneuvered me so that I was straddling her and lifted her thigh until it was pressing against my fanny. Without a thought, I began to rub myself along her lovely leg.

- "You're enjoying yourself. Look at the state of my leg." Sure enough, even in the dim light, I could see my juices glistening on her thigh. I continued taking my pleasure with her as she ran her finger along her leg then lifted it to her lips.

- "Mmm. Delicious."

- "I can't wait to taste you properly, lick you, kiss your lovely pussy. To give you such a screaming orgasm you won't know what has hit you," She whispered in my ear. I had noticed couples disappearing, normally arm in arm, toward the back of the building. I had assumed they were heading for the toilets, but Megan enlightened me.

- "The club has a couple of rooms upstairs which they rent on an hourly basis. We could have used one, but I have somewhere a little more, how shall I say, classy, for you and me. And we have all weekend. Are you ready to go?" At that precise moment, I was so bloody horny I could have happily fucked just about anything, and Megan promised to be by far the most attractive option.

Walking in the warm evening air, we would have looked like two girls walking home after a pleasant night out. A more discerning observer might have noticed that Megan had lifted up my skirt and was caressing my arse. We paused and kissed. Delicious.

The hotel was only a hundred yards or so from the club, and to describe it as discreet would be an understatement. A small lit sign announcing it as "Exquisite" and a pair of automatic doors just about summed it up, at least from the outside.

The foyer, however, oozed opulence. Deep leather sofas and chairs, subtle decor and lighting, images of men and women in various stages of undress and mutual enjoyment adorning the walls. You get the picture. The receptionist greeted Megan with a wave and a blown kiss as we headed for the lift.

"I've been with her a few times. She's gorgeous and has a body to die for, plus she's randy as hell. Great in bed, but she's not got the smartest brain in the universe so it can be difficult to find anything to talk about after we've fucked."

By now we were in the lift, and kissing. Not the aggressive kiss between a man and a girl but offering just as much promise. Soft, sensuous but with a depth of passion I had never experienced before. Our lips touched; our tongues explored but they didn't try to fight. They loved it.

Once in our room, Megan held my shoulders and just looked at me up and down.

- "You are absolutely gorgeous. Can I undress you? Please?"

And she did. My shirt, carefully unbuttoning it and folding it onto a chair. Then my bra.

- "Those are absolutely wonderful. Perfect. Can I kiss them? Please?"

And so, she did. My left, then my right. Kissing, suckling, teasing. My nipples rapidly stand to attention, waves of pleasure welling through my entire body.

By now she had released the zip of my skirt and eased it over my hips, together with my little thong. A slight wriggling of my legs and I was naked, the last of my clothes pooled around my ankles. Her lips slowly moved from my breasts down my body, paused at my tummy, down again to my thighs. Instinctively I spread my legs, willing her to kiss me just there but she didn't, instead, lowering her head to kiss the sensitive back of my knees. She was kneeling by now, her hands exploring my thighs and arse and her lips placing little butterfly kisses up the inside of my legs.

Carefully, gently, she maneuvered me to the bed and sat me down. Now it was my turn to watch as she undressed. Slowly, sensually, carefully. What a body she revealed to me. Perfectly tanned, not even a hint of bikini lines. The gentle curves of her hips, full breasts, proud nipples, firm thighs, the soft lips of her fanny. And, if only for tonight, she was mine.

She bent over me, and we kissed. The gentle kiss of expectant lovers. Her hands found my breasts, tweaking my nipples. Then a hand moved down and found my fanny. At last, I'd been waiting all evening for this moment. At first, she caressed the outside of my lips, one side then the other. Now slowly, carefully, she separated them. I could feel my juices running freely as she ran her finger up and down my slit. And still, we kissed.

Now her finger found my clit, peeking out of its little hood. Carefully lubricating her finger with my juices, she rubbed it, gently at first then more vigorously. I was in heaven.

- "I want to taste you."

Her lips played with my thighs, licking, kissing. Now they were playing with my lips, licking, kissing. At last, they found my clit, licking, kissing, suckling. I felt a finger at my entrance, then a second. Slipping deep inside me. And a third. "Yes, yes. Just THERE. Please, please don't stop."

I simply exploded. My body shook from my toes to my fanny, from the depths of my fanny to the depths of my brain I completely lost myself in ecstasy, the most fantastic orgasm. Slowly, very slowly Megan let me down from my height, caressing and kissing me. Softly, gently. Lovers' kisses.

We rested in each other's arms, and maybe I fell asleep for a few minutes. I felt her stir, stand up. She lifted me to my feet.

- "We're both dripping with sweat. Let's clean up."

The bathroom was large, very large by hotel standards. Apart from the essentials it consisted of a sunken bath – actually more like a junior swimming pool – filled with warm, slightly fragrant water and with fresh rose petals floating on the surface. A bottle of Champagne sat in an ice bucket on a small table, together with two glasses. Megan popped the cork and poured, and we toasted ourselves and our night(s) together.

Carefully, I made my way to the pool, slowly lowering myself into the water until my breasts were just covered. My glass was still safely in my hand, so I took a generous sip. The cool wine tasted delicious against the background of the warm water and steamy atmosphere. Megan joined me and we clinked glasses again, then kissed. I slipped my leg between hers and rubbed it against her fanny. I wanted to give her the pleasure she had so recently given me.

Suddenly the water began to churn. What had been a calm pool was transformed into a Jacuzzi, small jets of water coming at us from all sides, tickling and tingling our legs and bodies. There was even a pipe, a bit like a small shower head, snaking around the bottom.

We kissed, breasts pressed against breasts, legs between legs, mons against mons, hands groping backs and bottoms as the water caressed and aroused us. Breaking off our kiss I lifted Megan to sit her on a cushion at the edge of the pool, her legs apart and her beautiful pink fanny on full display. She lay back, lifted and spread her legs, offering herself completely to me. I accepted, immediately.

She tasted gorgeous. Slightly musty, salty even, with the fragrance of the pool water adding a subtle touch. As I licked and suckled, she squirmed, clearly enjoying my attention. I reached down and found the shower head, which I could easily play onto her lovely pussy. It helped that the spray was pulsating, and I could direct jets of warm water to the most sensitive parts of her delicious body.

As I worked, I slipped a finger into her, then a second, curling them to touch just there, rubbing gently but firmly. At the same time, I worked on her clit, alternating kisses and suckling with pulses from the spray.

I glanced up. Her eyes were shut, her head rolling from side to side, her breathing erratic, a hand grasping her breasts. Suddenly I felt her fanny clasp around my fingers.

Her orgasm was loud and forceful. Her whole body trembled and shuddered, she was screaming and groaning, she held my head against herself as slowly she unwound. Finally, she let her head fall back, her legs flop into the pool, and smiled.

- "Phew," she said, her breath slowly recovering.

- "That was awesome. Where did you learn to fuck like that? I thought you were an innocent."

- "I just followed my instincts."

- "Those instincts of yours, Lauren, are going to make this girl and I hope many more, very, very happy."

We spent a while longer in the pool. We used the spray jet on each other, discovered that the Jacuzzi nozzles could produce lovely sensations if you knelt or squatted in exactly the right position. And of course, we kissed and caressed each other. Finally realizing that we were tired we climbed out of the pool, dried each other carefully – lovingly, even, with the enormous white towels. We dropped into bed and fell asleep in each other's arms.

I woke first, daylight streaming through the window. I kissed Megan and she stirred, then returned my kiss. We hugged, pressing our bodies together. The morning was full of promise.

There was a discreet knock on the door.

- "Room service."

Megan stumbled out of bed, wrapped a robe around her lovely body and went to the door. The trolley carried our breakfast, which included a bottle of chilled Champagne and a jug of orange juice for our Bucks

Fizz. Breakfast in bed, naked and with a gorgeous girl you are going to spend all day loving. Perfect.
- "There's something I want to show you," she said, pushing the trolley to one side as she climbed out of bed.
- "Wait there."
I was intrigued. She pulled a small case out of the wardrobe, then switched on the TV. Very strange. I was in no mood for old movies or daytime TV. She opened the case, took out a DVD and loaded it.
- "You'll enjoy this. We'll both enjoy it."
We lay back on the soft pillows, my head nestling in her shoulder as she pressed play. After the credits the action started with two lovely young girls kissing, tenderly, undressing each other. As we watched, I rolled toward Megan, and we kissed. Breaking our kiss, I put little butterfly kisses on her neck and her shoulders, making my way toward her breasts as she caressed my head and neck. I glanced at the screen, just to keep up with the action. They were both naked now, kissing.
Lifting her delightful breast with my hand, I kissed her nipple and sucked it between my lips. It was quite firm, like a ripe grape. I turned my attention to its partner, at the same time letting my hand slip down her body and between her legs. She was already very, very moist. Glancing at the screen the darker haired girl was laid back on the bed, legs apart, her partner suckling her breasts as her fingers parted a pair of soft, pink fanny lips.
I looked back up to Megan, who was smiling. She drew me up to her and we kissed.
- "I've brought some toys for us to play with. I call this my weekend away case."
She flipped open the lid to reveal the most impressive collection of molded latex I had ever seen. All sorts of

shapes and sizes, colors from clear to black, some smooth and some ribbed.

- "Are these what I think they are?" Naïve little me.

- "They most certainly are. Which one do you want to try first?"

I glanced at the screen. The blonde girl had a moderately large, pink phallus pressed against her partner's fanny and by the look on her face, it felt good.

- "Have we got one like that?"

- "I'll see what I can find."

She rummaged through the case and brought out an interesting, light brown shaft.

- "It's absolutely genuine. I molded it from an ex-boyfriend, so it's totally realistic."

I was fascinated by the details involved in molding an erect penis, but now was not the time for engineering.

- "His was great when we were together, but this is even better because it doesn't have him attached to the other end. Shall we try it?"

- "Er, ok, if you think so."

I wasn't too sure about being fucked by the disembodied penis of someone else's ex-lover, but what the heck. You only live once.

- "Let's give it a go."

By now the dark-haired girl had the dildo fully inserted and was moving it around, in and out, as her blonde friend suckled and tweaked her breasts and nipples.

Megan passed me the phallus. Although I was not very experienced in these matters – I had been a virgin until just a few weeks previously - it seemed to me to be quite large both in length and girth. The head and veins were very realistic, and it had a nice smooth feel to it. Just like the real thing.

- "Just lay back and relax. I promise you'll enjoy it."

I did exactly that. Megan kissed me, first my neck and breasts then down my body to my thighs. I spread my legs to welcome her, lifting my knees to expose myself completely to her. It felt wonderful as she kissed the inside of my thighs, delicate little kisses. Then to my fanny, slipping her fingers up and down the outside of my lips, then parting them. Her tongue slipping between the lips, finding my clit. Suckling my little bud. Heaven.

I heard a click, then a quiet buzz. The head of the phallus replaced her lips on my clit, vibrating as it pressed against me, slipping between my lips toward my opening.

He slipped into me gently, not the forceful thrust that I had experienced with men. Slowly he moved up inside me, pausing briefly at my most sensitive spot, until he had filled me completely. Megan moved him around, slowly and gently, looking for the most sensitive places and angles for him to please me. Almost instinctively my hand moved to cup my breast, feeling and tweaking my nipple. Megan was kissing me, one hand controlling him while the other played with my clit. The feeling was awesome.

His vibrations were quite vigorous as he moved in and out of me. Megan pressed my clit down, and I could feel him as he rubbed against me. I could feel the tension rising, my whole body ready to explode.

It hit me. Starting deep inside and sweeping out to engulf the whole of my body. Wave after wave, surge after surge. My body reeling uncontrollably, my breath in gasps, my head rolling from side to side.

- "Oh my God. That was amazing!"

I was slowly recovering, nestled in Megan's shoulder.

- "It most certainly was, and there's plenty more where that came from."

I fell asleep in Megan's arms.

*"It takes courage to grow up
and become who you really are."*
E E Cummings

WINTER NIGHT

I was going to meet Gina's family, and I was nervous, if only there was some way to relax...
- Are you ready? Gina shouted.
She was standing down in the hall, with an eye on the clock.
Yep, Ruth said.
Ruth's mind was on other things. She looked again to make sure her new hair color matched the clothes she had picked to wear. Tonight was such a big night that her dark red hair was playing on her mind. She usually slapped any color on her head, safe in the knowledge that it would not be too bad and who was going to care? But did match the red dress she was wearing? Did she look a slapper? -
- I thought you said you were ready.
Gina had appeared in the bedroom doorway. She had a brown shirt on that complimented the dark lustrous hair that framed her face. Her black trousers showed off her fine curves.
- My hair, what do you think about it? asked Ruth.
- Same as a week ago when you started asking me. Perfect. And it goes with the dress. Do not stress. You look drop dead gorgeous.
Gina, the older lesbian by five years, came over and pulled Ruth's face round to Her's so the young one would not keep taking worried glances in the mirror.
We are only visiting my cousin's, right? It is not like I am taking you to meet my parents. Ruth looked panicked again, so Gina added: not that my parents will hate you, but I thought we would take introductions slowly...so you do not panic. Not doing much good, is it?
Ruth calmed looking into Gina's warm brown eyes, but as their relationship was only a few months old

whenever they got this close, they always felt excitement rise and lust speed their hearts. After a few seconds of rising heat, they gave in and kissed. They held on to each other and let their hands roam over the other's body, enjoying the firm curves that made up the other's body.

Why had it taken her so long, Ruth thought, to realize she was lesbian? This was love; Gina was what she had always needed.

She enjoyed the slow, tasty kiss, and the heat of their bodies through their clothing. Then it was over, and they parted.

- Time to go? Ruth whispered, still clinging to Gina's waist.

- Yes, but plenty of time tonight for more. Come on.

Suddenly Gina looked down and smiled. Oh dear.

- What? Ruth followed her gaze.

Around the tight fitting dress a line of underwear was visible. Before Ruth could react, Gina was on her knees with her hands up Ruth's skirt.

I thought you said we did not have time. Ruth asked, a wide smile spreading across her face.

As Gina's hands passed along her thighs Ruth felt an exciting tightening deep inside.

Well, I was trying to avert a fashion crisis, but what the hell! Always time for you, you come so easily. Like you are permanently horny. Must be your age.

Gina's hands came down with the red frilly panties. She pushed the skirt up revealing a shaven pussy with brown lips, the thin inner pushing out of the outer covering. Gina kissed Ruth's pussy, dipping her tongue between them, lapping at Ruth's quickly moistening pussy. Ruth moaned softly at the warm touch of the moist tongue.

Gina parted the lips and looked at the smooth swelling nub that was growing with her touch, she put her tongue to it. Ruth parted her legs further and leaned back on the sink to help Gina get to wherever it was she wanted to go. Gina's tongue went to work on the clit. Ruth felt it harden fully as Gina passed her tongue over it hard and fast. Tingling soon passed up through her stomach.

- I am not horny all the time because of anything I do, oh, Ruth broke off to moan.

After a few short moments ripples of pleasure began passing though her pussy and Ruth's moaning got louder and more passionate.

- Oh, fuck baby, your tongue feels so good. Fuck, fuck, fuuuck.

Ruth rolled her aching breasts and squeezed hard on the nipples that were pushing up two little points on her dress. She pulled her breasts up out of the dress and freed them. She squeezed hard on the long nipples and satisfied her need to touch them.

A great sigh signaled the onslaught of another powerful orgasm. She lowered herself on to Gina's tongue; the message was understood, and Gina licked faster, forcing her tongue hard over Ruth's clit.

Gina's tongue threw wave after wave of pleasure through Ruth as her climax rose to a peak and began to decrease slowly. Eventually, with one last lick of her pussy hole and a sucking noise Gina came out from between her legs.

- Calm now? asked Gina, with a beautiful smile that made Ruth feel dizzy again.

- "But you don't get anything," Ruth said, recovering slowly, but still leaning against the sink.

- I have. I had been drinking your spunk. Gina's licked her lips. Your lips are bright red, she pointed out. And your cheeks, and your tits! You are all red tonight!

Ruth looked in the mirror. Her lips had flushed as had her cheeks, and tits.

Gina carefully squeezed Ruth's perky little tits and then put them back inside the dress. The low-cut top had two points where the nipples were still hard.

Cherry red, Gina said thoughtfully as she looked at Ruth's lips. I think we might be late.

They kissed and Ruth could taste her pussy in Gina's mouth. She wanted more: she wanted Gina. Ruth's hands found Gina's ample breasts, heavy and firm. They were trapped in a shirt that was straining, just the way Gina liked it. At first Ruth thought Gina would give in, but she pulled Ruth's hands away and ended the kiss.

- Now we really must go, Gina said flustered.

She took Ruth's hand and led her to the car. The winter night was already dark and chilly, and the long red skirt did not keep her legs warm. The air on her warm pussy made the tingling grow again. She could feel the cold air trying to freeze the saliva and spunk that had oozed since Gina's cleansing lick.

- I have never been out without underwear on before, Ruth said. Not in a skirt anyway. I like it.

- You are not still horny?

- Horny! I was not horny until you started licking me like!

Gina just laughed, but Ruth thought about the night a week ago when they had played with the ice cream. The shivers of the cold cream on their nipples and pussys had mingled with the tingling orgasms to make them both cum wildly. We will have to do that again.

Once Ruth got horny, she got stuck in horny mode. A good lick and fingering would have sorted her out. Gina had only teased her with that short play. Why would she turn me on? I am desperate now. And the air movements down there are not helping.

Gina let go of Ruth's hand and they got into the shelter of the car.

As they rumbled along Ruth's thoughts turned again and again to her wet pussy lips. She had to mop up the mess of oozing cum or it would get all over her dress. In the dark car she pulled the dress up and took a handkerchief out of Gina's bag.
- Hell, you are hot, aren't you? Gina said.
I am drying the mess - she paused as the handkerchief, sodden with her lubricating spunk, moved over her clit. Tingling passed through her and now she really needed to come again. She leaned back in her seat and rubbed faster. They had to stop at some lights. In the car next to them was a man in his thirties. Gina moved her car forwards a bit so the masturbating 20-year-old would give him a thrill. He looked over as the car moved and his gaze passed from Gina to Ruth.
Ruth had her eyes closed and was moaning softly.
- Oh, I think I am a tiny bit too horny tonight.
- So's the guy in the next car.
Ruth instantly stopped what she was doing and looked at the man. He was cute, wide-eyed and his face was flushed.
- Gina! Ruth said reproachfully, while she tried to hide from view.
Gina laughed as they pulled away. The man had not noticed the lights were at green and it took an impatient blast from the car behind's horn to get him moving.
The thrill of been watched passed through Ruth and her tingling grew again after the initial shock had dampened the urges.
- We are going to have to have sex in a public place, she said, resuming the movements of the damp tissue over her clit. She pushed harder to get in between her now swollen labia lips and started rolling it over just her clit.
- You like the danger of been caught? asked Gina.
- I think so.

- Yes, look how we met.

They thought about the lecture in which they had both masturbated. That was the day they had together. Ruth started moaning again as heat passed into every part of her. She rubbed her aching tits. Squeezing hard on the nipples. Another orgasm passed up her clit, pussy and into her whole body. She sighing as the orgasm rolled through her and leaned back into the seat. Smaller waves of ecstasy made her shudder. She calmed down and opened her eyes to look at Gina.

- Having fun?

- Yes, said Ruth, you wet?

- God yes. Soaking. Glad I am wearing underwear. You owe me, teasing me like this!

- You started it!

- I gave you one orgasm to help you relax, now look at you, preforming for strangers!

- Ha! I will make it up to you tonight.

- Promise?

- Promise.

Gina pulled up outside the house and leaned over. Ruth could feel in Gina's kiss the passion and the need. She had not been joking, she did want Ruth desperately.

Gina took the tissue out of Ruth's hand. While they were still kissing, she pushed it in to Ruth's tight pussy. Both the pussy and the tissue were tightened-up and soon the tissue was deep inside Ruth's body.

- I know you like things in you. This will help remind you own me.

- No, all it will do is make talking to people embarrassing. I cannot be horny when it is your family. They will not notice. It is already 7pm, they will be pissed already. Keep it in. Dare you.

Whenever Gina dared Ruth, she felt unable to refuse, she was competitive, but she liked the thought of keeping a secret like this in a public place.

\- Come on.

The cold night air circulated Ruth's pussy again, giving her a thrill, but the tissue had mopped up the cum. Hopefully it wouldn't drop out during the visit. She felt the pressure of the folded tissue and thought of ways she wanted to it make up to Gina later.

In the house Ruth was introduced to Gina's sister, who was older than Tan but also good-looking, and her three cousins: a man of thirty and two girls between thirty and forty. All had their partners there. In total there were eight people at dinner.

The conversation was soon fast and furious. They were a close family and talking seemed easy, even for horny Ruth. Whenever the conversation took a dive though the sodden tissue in her pussy began to turn her on again. The night was a cycle between turn on and pleasant distraction.

Ruth got up last after the meal when the others were going into the living room. She knew her pussy had continue to water thanks to Gina's glances and the throbbing had probably loosed some juice on to her dress. When the people were ahead of her, she turned round to look at her arse to see if any wet patch was visible.

Shit, there was.

\- Is the seat wet? asked a voice.

Shit! Isabel, Gina's sister, was behind her.

\- Er, I think I split my drink.

As if she believes that now I have gone bright red!

Ruth quickly looked around for a cloth and her heart stopped when Isabel came over and wiped the sticky liquid from the seat. Isabel went red when she saw the fluid was obviously not wine but made no comment. Going to the loo would probably look suspicious right now.

- Ruth? Isabel called her as a burst of laughter came from the other room.

They were both red-faced and avoiding too much eye contact.

- Yes? Ruth panicked.

She did not know why, we all have pussies, right, and they get wet, right?

My sister has only ever had one other girlfriend, when she was a teenager, she always picks beautiful women to go out with. Isabel smiled warmly.

- "Thank you," said Ruth shocked, but flattered.

- I have been worrying about meeting you all.

- You relaxed now?

Yes. No, she thought. I did not know Gina had a girlfriend when she was younger.

- Yes. Our mum and dad did not know of course, Gina keeps herself to herself, but she was so desperate to show her off she told me, she was called Leanne, very pretty. Moved to America though. Gina was heartbroken, but they were young. It was the same with you, she wanted us all to meet you. To show you off.

Isabel took Ruth's hand as Gina had done and led her gently into the other room. Ruth was overcome with happiness, and thoughts of her pussy were, for the moment, forgotten.

The night went on quickly and eventually she did get to the bathroom. As she went up the stairs the movement caused a big sticky drop of her slick spunk to slide out of her pussy and hit the carpet. She looked down at the door that led into the room, it was open, but no one saw. She rubbed it into the carpet with her shoe and rushed to the bathroom.

She pulled her skirt up and mopped up the fluid trapped between the lips. She tried not to rub too hard otherwise she might cum, and she wanted to wait now.

Let it build up. The next time I cum I want it to be with Gina.

Gina was the quiet member of the family, just as Isabel had said. She sat to the side laughing and watching. Gina, after months of being with her, could still drive her wild with passion even from across the room with those big brown eyes. Her hoarse voice was getting worse. Can they tell she is horny?

As Ruth sat waiting for the conversation to move round to her again, she fantasized about Gina, imagined her naked on their bed. She lingered on her cherry lips, her large firm breasts that she liked to feel squashing her own, and the wet, thick-lipped pussy shaking in climax around her fingers. Her stomach knotted in almost overwhelming excitement.

- Ruth? asked Gina.

Someone must have asked her something while she had been dreaming.

- Sorry. Miles away. Ruth gave Gina a wink.

Finally, the party ended. She had had fun. The people were interesting, they never stopped laughing. The promise of what was to come was in the air, and in Gina's glances. Ruth knew that the slow increase in excitement would mean a more powerful orgasm later. They said good night and left at about midnight.

- You had fun? Gina asked as they walked hand-in-hand to the car.

- Yes, but we still have more fun to come, right?

- Oh, yes.

The air circulated Ruth's pussy and made her realize how wet she had become again; she wondered how she had not de-hydrated.

The car ride was long. They hit all the red lights. They passed the time by saying what they would do to each other.

- Sixty-nine? asked Ruth.

And that. And... tribbing, I want our pussies together.
Ruth leaned over and put her hand on Gina's thigh. She stroked back and forth for a while before running her hand up further. She found the fly and unzipped it. As soon as her hand was in Ruth was surprised at how wet Gina's panties had become.
- You have got a leak, said Ruth, kissing Gina's cheek.
Gina stayed quiet, not wanting to talk and ruin anything.
Ruth could feel Gina's thick lips through her panties. She pulled them to one side, moistened her fingers in the feminine nectar and found Tan's hard, hooded clit hiding under her labia. At the touch of her smooth throbbing clit a fast breath was forced from Gina, Ruth – who was leaning over – breathed it in deep, sharing in Gina's pleasure.
- Oh, baby, you are making me cum. We will crash. Gina's voice was thick with desire.
Gina pulled the car over. They kissed deeply. Between mouthfuls of each other Gina moaned loudly. Ruth felt Tan's body moving in time to her fingers. Now Ruth needed to cum, but she ignored her own pussy. Gina's long clit had been weak under her rubbing at first, now it was fully erect.
Gina gasped and came while their tongues moved back and forth in each other's mouths. The kiss slowed, as did Gina's body rocking.
Get us home quick, Ruth said, barely able to keep her fingers away from her aching pussy. I need you.
She licked the spunk off her fingers while Gina watched.
- Mmm.
Ruth did not dare go near her pussy, but as Gina drove, she pushed her breasts together. They ached again and wanted to be set free.

They no longer noticed the chilly night air when they got out of the car. Gina practically kicked the front door down when they got back. They found moving to the bedroom difficult as they kept kissing and tearing each other's clothing off.

Both women's nipples could be seen through their clothes, briefly – as Ruth's dress was off as soon as they got through the door and Gina's bra was thrown off somewhere along the stairs.

Breasts rolled free as they ran into the bedroom, the bouncing was a pleasant feeling for their tender breasts. Both women were used to walking round naked, so cloths sometimes felt constrictive.

Tan turned the lights went on, the curtains were open, but there was no time to close them; if there was anyone out there, they were welcome to watch tonight. Ruth closed her eyes as Gina's skilled hands worked her breasts. Ruth stroked Gina's hard nipples in return. They were both drawing things out.

A slow kiss brought shivers to them both. Their tongues moved into each other's mouths. The kiss's speed became faster, more urgent. Gina had one hand on Ruth's right arse cheek, rolling and kneading slowing, the other was in her hair, keeping her head – not that she needed the encouragement – to Gina's lips. Ruth's hands were all over Gina's toned body. When their mouths were free of each other they moaned softly.

They were thinking about each other's pleasure so much that they were not taking what they wanted, but Ruth knew that Gina could take no more, she needed to come, she was getting rougher now she was desperate. Ruth longed to make her love come furiously.

- I love you, Gina said.

- I love you.

Ruth pushed Gina down and pushed her pussy into Gina's. Control slipped away from Gina; she could only lay shaking under the vigorous grinding of Ruth's pussy. Their pussy lips moved in and around the other, their slick clits gliding over each other built up the waves of ecstasy. Heat flooded their limbs, their tummy's knotted and suddenly their pussies twitched.

- I am coming, Ruth cried, she came first and tried to stay in control so she could give Gina the orgasm she had promised.

Fighting against her own orgasmic shudder Gina reached down into Ruth's pussy and yanked out the handkerchief. With a damp noise a load of spunk came out with it. The movement dropped Ruth to the bed in pleasure. Paralyzed by her orgasm she could no longer rub their pussies. Gina jumped up and ground her swollen pussy against Ruth's as Ruth squirted all the trapped spunk from her pussy and into Gina's groove. That made Gina reaches the height of her orgasm. She shouted out in pleasure, competing with the sounds Ruth made while she trembled under Gina's forceful thrusts at her young pussy.

Panting and shaking they gazed into each other's eyes as the powerful surge of their orgasms held them in their grip. The smell of the long trapped pussy juices surrounded them as they struggle for breath.

As the orgasms strength passed the grinding slowed down. Ruth had nearly fallen off the bed, so Gina gave her legs a quick pull, so she was safe from falling before collapsing completely onto her lover.

- Hell, babe, you squirted again. Wish I could. Gina said.

I could feel all that cum in me and, well, Ruth struggled to talk; she was still panting, it came out. Wow.

Their bodies were in full contact: mouth to mouth; Gina's large breasts squashing Ruth's pleasantly into her. Their nipples were still hard, but Ruth's slowly softened as they lay together. The dizziness passed. Gina's nipples were still hard.

Ruth moved under Gina to kiss her cheek, her jaw, then she reached the soft smooth flesh of her neck. As she kissed, she breathed in the sweet smell of her hair. Then rolled so she was on top and continued kissing all the way down Gina's body, collar bone, breasts.

The nipples were stood erect in the middle of large brown areolas. She played with them, squeezing, and rolling the breasts while she licked and sucked. She pulled the long brown flesh and watched as it stretched. Gina moaned louder as the pain got more intense a sure sign that she was as horny as fuck. Ruth felt the weight of each breast, squeezing tenderly.

- Are you going to make me come already? Said Gina smiling.

- Mmm, answered Ruth.

Ruth's played with Gina's aching heavy breasts driving her close to another orgasm, but she waited. Let it build again. Tan took a deep, slow breath. Then Ruth moved down, over Tan's toned tummy, kissing all the way down until she was between Gina's long smooth legs.

"I owe you a lick," Ruth said when she was comfortable between Gina's thighs. She looked up to see Gina's longing gaze. You want to cum? she said teasingly.

- Yes. I want you to make me wake the neighbors. Make me cum baby.

Gina's reached down to stroke Ruth's hair, then she lay back and played with her own breasts. Ruth felt a tremor run through Gina. She loved to feel her love's body rive in pleasure under her.

Slowly she kissed up Gina's thighs. Making her painfully slow way to the thick red lips of Gina's cunt. It was wet from the mixed pussy juice, red and swollen from the night's teasing and Ruth was surprised by the amount of spunk that came out when she parted the lips. When freed it ran over Gina's beautiful curving arse. Ruth quickly bent in to lick it up. Her tongue and lips on Gina's arse made her giggle in pleasure.

- Now, fuck, now! Gina begged.

Ruth had no intention of putting a decent orgasm through Gina just yet. She kissed the sensitive thighs right at the top. And ran her tongue up them, getting painfully close to her throbbing leaking pussy. Gina whimpered in frustration.

Ruth watched Gina's heavy breathing lift her heavy aching breasts while she kissed between Tan's hips.

Gina reached down to her own pussy.

- No, said Ruth, pulling the hand away. Wait.

- Let us trib, Gina's husky voice was begging again.

Ruth moved the wet lips apart to look at Gina sex. Gina's pussy was oozing cum, her clit was long, red, and throbbing. Finally, Ruth's tongue found Gina's smooth hooded clit. She kissed it, then licked soft and slow.

The shock of the contact brought tingling waves of pleasure up Gina's body.

- Oh, Gina sighed, Ruth. Harder, babe, faster, please. I am...'

She could not finish; Ruth had pushed two fingers in Gina's pussy at the same time as pushing her tongue hard and fast over her clit. Gina's toned body had a tighter pussy that Ruth's, but she forced two fingers in easily because she was so wet. Ruth found Gina's mound inside that she liked rubbed hard: her G-spot.

Gina's body tightened. Her stomach fluttered. Gina shouted in pleasure as her pussy clenched Ruth's rapidly moving fingers.

- Oh, Fuck, Ruth!

The spasms made Gina's breaths short and jarred. Her back arched slightly as the highest point of Gina's orgasm hit. Her quivering was shaking the bed.

Gina bucked and squirted spunk from her pussy on to Ruth's chin. Gina's cries descended to soft moans as Ruth finished seeing her through her shuddering orgasm.

- You squirted!

- Whuhos.

Ruth laughed at how drained Gina was. She lapped up the cum. Savoring the taste. Then crawled up to lay beside Gina. Gina licked her cum off Ruth's chin. Ruth pulled the sheet over them and hugged Gina as they both lay satisfied.

They talked about the night, before Gina rolled onto her side. Ruth, the tallest of the two, put her arm round her and squeezed momentarily, before putting her hand on Gina breast, and they spooned.

- I love you.

- I love you too.

And they drifted into a deep sleep.

"Love is a rebellion. As an act of resistance against everything that tries to keep us apart."
Alok Vaid-Menon

GIRLS ACADEMY

On Thursday, Marie eagerly awaited the arrival of her friend Tifanny. Marie knew they were going to participate in an unofficial tradition: the wearing of "naughty girl" panties under their Catholic school uniforms. Tifanny had gone and purchased new underwear for both of them.

No one could remember when this practice had started, but it seemed to be a way for many of the girls, a way to express their repressed sexuality. They were supposed to all be dressed uniformly. At this time of the year, they had their summer outfits of short-sleeved white blouses, light-blue skirts, white knee socks, and brown shoes. Underneath these, the requirement was that they all had to have ample white underpants. Of course, some of them did something different in the way of underthings.

Since their school, the Mount St. Evangelina Academy, was run by strict nuns, there was some risk in violating the underwear sartorial protocol. This was also unofficial, but the nuns would run random "panty-checks" to see what the girls were wearing. Anyone caught with anything, but ample white ones would be taken to the "paddle room" and be spanked, first on the seats of the offending drawers, then on the bare buttocks.

Sometimes girls got paddled for some other infractions like poor grades or a sassy attitude, but the panty issue was the number one reason for a spanking punishment.

The girls who did this panty stunt often enjoyed the whole business. They liked walking around knowing that they looked chaste in their uniforms, yet they had slutty underthings hidden underneath. The cat and mouse games with the nuns were entertaining too.

Finally, some girls actually liked getting a wooden paddle applied to their behinds; they got a sexual charge out of it.

Afterwards, the young females would be sent home, if they lived close enough, to change into proper drawers. They would often have an aching need to masturbate, which they indulged in at home while imagining the discipline they had just received. If family members were around, they would come back to school and try to do it in one of the girls' rooms, or if they were really bold, behind one of the trees on the school grounds. Of course, others had to wait until they were in bed at night before they pleasured themselves with their own hands.

On this September morning, Marie arrived early and waited outside the gate for her friend. She did not have to be there long. When Tifanny arrived, she could not contain her enthusiasm. "Tifanny, I can't wait to see what you bought for me."

- "Actually, there were two candidates, but I could not decide on which one. Thus, I got you both of them."

- "That's great, I really appreciate that."

- "You should see what I got for myself."

- "When can we look at them?"

Busy Bronx streets did not offer many places to examine women's underwear, but Tifanny was clever. "We still have a half-hour. If we go into one of the booths in the back of that pizzeria in the next block down, we could get away with it." She cautioned Marie, "Just be quiet about it. Do not be squealing with delight when you see them."

Once in the booth, with their slices and sodas, Tifanny could see that they could examine the underwear if they were subtle about it. "I am just going to take them out briefly. Remember, keep your voice down. Here is the first thing I got for you." She got it out and put it on the table.

It was a pair of lacey black briefs, and Marie was impressed. "Oh, they're so wonderfully sexy."

Tifanny said, "I thought you would be impressed. Here is the next thing." She put the first one back in her bag. The next one was white and amply cut, but it was so sheer that it was virtually transparent. "Believe me, when you wear these, your pubic hair and ass crack are going to be very visible."

When she put that away, Tifanny said, "Some women used to wear these over a garter and stocking straps, which of course would show through panties like these."

- "I've heard of garters, but I've never seen them."

- "That is because they have mostly been replaced by pantyhose. Or by thigh-high stockings that hold themselves up."

- "But I have heard that you can still buy them." Maybe we should try that sometime."

Tifanny giggled at that. "You certainly have a creative mind; I don't think that's ever been tried at our school."

- "Maybe we should be trailblazers then."

- "Keep in mind that we'd still get spanked if caught with them on too." She leaned forward. "You know what some ladies used to do? They used to wear garters without any panties. And the garters are open at the bottom, so basically their crotches would be exposed underneath."

- "That sounds positively wicked."

- "See, garters come in all different widths. Some are so narrow that they are little more than belts. Others are bigger and come down to the tops of your thighs. But they are all open below if not covered with underpants."

Marie said, "I'd still like to get some, even if I don't wear them at school."

- "Marie, you are such a dirty girl, I never would have guessed it. Anyway, let me show you what I got for myself." She took out a skimpy garment. "It's a thong." It was held regather with black strings, and the front panel was a small pink-and-black piece of cloth. The section in the back was even smaller. Tifanny pointed to it and said, "This part just about covers your butthole."

- "It is totally scandalous. I never knew anyone who had a thong before."

- "I think I am covering new ground here. Now I propose wearing these on random days in the next couple of weeks. Be prepared for a spanking, of course; it could come at any time."

- "I think I'm ready."

- "Are you? I mean, I am totally perverse, and I like to be spanked, even though it hurts. Afterwards I need a good whack-off session sooner or later. But then again, I would whack-off over just about anything."

- "How are we going to put these on?"

- "Do it in one of the girls' rooms when you have to go in there."

- "I would really like to go to our lover's rock again this afternoon like we did a few days ago. You know, play with our new underpants."

- "Marie, I already have that on our afterschool agenda. You are really turning into a very bad girl now."

- "I was wondering why we do not use the Botanical Gardens. It is so much closer."

Tifanny replied, "I would have to scout it out some more. Maybe there is something beyond greenhouses. Anyway, it is almost time for us to get going."

After the third period, Marie exchanged her regulation white panties for the lacey black ones. When she emerged from the restroom, she felt very different from before. The smooth little black panel in the crotch of the garment was snug and tight against her cunt.

As she walked down the hallway, there was a spring to her step as she walked along; the lacey portions felt good against her hips and ass. Almost unconsciously, she gave an extra sway to her hips.

I do not feel like a schoolgirl now; I feel like a mature woman who appreciates her sexuality. In her classes, she noticed a dampness seeping into her underwear. I hope this does not become too noticeable, like I hope nobody can sniff the aroma of it. Fortunately, the moisture from her body did not increase into full wetness.

In the second lunch period – there were two every day – she met Tifanny, who smiled and winked at her. Marie could not contain her excitement. "I've put mine on; how about you?"

- "You bet I did, and they feel so nice." She slid her hindquarters back and forth on the surface of her plastic chair. "It's almost like being nude under my skirt."

Marie said, "I've been getting turned on today; I can feel the dampness going into them during class."

- "That often happens to girls when they try this for the first few times." She leaned forward and said quietly, "You're getting lubricated so a man's penis can easily enter you."

Tifanny's bluntness often shocked her friend. Marie stumbled over her words at first, and then she said, "Well, of course, I knew about that."

- "I bet you did." Her smile was saucy, but her voice remained a matter of fact. "It also helps another woman get her fingers or even her tongue into your sweet little snatch."

Marie tried to keep her wits about her but could not quite do it. "Please, Tifanny, it's such a nice day today; we must make that trip to Lover's Rock."

- "Relax baby, I have that all scheduled. I hope you can wait that long."

When they arrived in Bronx Park, they could not keep their hands off of each other. After doing some smooching, Tifanny said, "Let us get behind this rock thing. It will give us some privacy from prying eyes. When we get there, kneel for a moment and raise your skirt. We can admire each other's panties."

Both were impressed by what they saw. "Marie, those panties look great on you. Turn around and let me see. Yep, just as I thought, I can see your backside right through that thing."

- "And you look practically naked in that thong."

- "Look at the back; there is this little panel that covers my butthole. Pink and black; an awesome combination. Marie, we are such dirty girls now."

- "That's the point; we're not girls anymore – we're women."

Tifanny was on the tall side with fairly short dark hair. Her friend thought that, with the right clothes, she had fit right in down in Greenwich Village or maybe even the East Village. Marie was shorter, with longer blonde hair. At this point in her life, she could only imagine herself in The Bronx or one of the other outer boroughs.

They sat on the rock. Soon their legs were entwined, and their fingers were in each other's pants. Tifanny, as the more experienced one, soon had a finger on Marie's clitoris while her other hand stroked her vulva. A couple of times they mixed things up by grabbing each other's buttocks.

Marie was moaning, and she said, "Tifanny, you are so good at this."

- "Well, let me arrange your hands, and I'll show you the proper way to do this to me." She guided Marie's hands into the front of her thong. Soon Tifanny was saying, "Marie, you really have a knack for finger-fucking."

She giggled, "Well, really, it is not that complicated, is it? I have had plenty of experience on myself."

Tifanny said, "Bad girls are always masturbating; they can't keep their hands off of themselves."

- "Are you a bad girl?"

- "One of the worst!"

After a little more of fondling each other, Tifanny said, "This is very nice, but we don't have all day for this. There is a simple way to speed this up." Marie had an expectant look on her face. Tifanny continued, "It's quite simple; we have to use our mouths and go down on each other."

Marie appeared shocked, "How are we going to get away with that? And I have never actually done it before."

- "Nor has anyone ever done it to you, I assume. Come on, do not blush, I have a plan. We do not even have to take our panties all the way off."

She patiently explained it to her friend. "We will just sit on the back of the rock. That will give us a bit of privacy. Then I will do you first. Believe me, I know what I am doing. I will kneel in front of you, and I will just pull the crotch of your underpants aside. I will be your teacher; then you can do to me what I did to you."

Marie was visibly nervous, and Tifanny said, "Try to relax; just sit back and let your good buddy do her thing on you. I think you are one of those girls who can come pretty quickly with the right stimulation. I know I am."

- "Actually, I've been feeling horny all day, ever since I put this on this morning."

- "You see; you're already halfway there."

Even though she was at the back of the rock, she did look around nervously. "I still feel kind of exposed here."

- "You will be facing away from anybody passing, probably. Besides, my attitude is, 'fuck them!'"

- "Okay, let's give it a try."

Tifanny knelt between Marie's legs and pulled the panties aside. Then she used her lips and tongue to work on the outer part of her friend's genitals. Marie had never experienced this before, and she was impressed by the intense pleasure she was getting from it. She began to moan, and her hips moved on the rock's surface.

Rather than describe what she was going to do, Tifanny just escalated her muff-licking when she felt it was the time to do it. She used her hands to spread Marie's pussy lips, and her tongue went in deeper, and she began flicking the clitoris. Marie raised her legs and ran her hands through her friend's hair. "This is so delightful; I love what you are doing to my clit."

Tifanny noted that she was not whispering but using her normal voice. She seems to be losing more of her inhibitions. Tifanny had never been penetrated by a man, but sometimes she wondered if being with another woman could be equally pleasing, maybe more so.

She was competent enough to know when Marie's climax was approaching. The other girl pushed her pelvis against Tifanny's face, and she began to rhythmically grunt with each thrust. When she came, she gripped Tifanny's head with her thighs, and she cried out with something loud but unintelligible. Then she leaned back and panted.

Tifanny gave her a few moments to compose herself, and then she said, in an off-handed kind of way, "So, how was your first pussy licking?"

- "I almost don't know what to say about it."
- "I noticed that you seem to have lost some of your – diffidence, let us call it. I mean, you were pretty loud this time."
As in the previous session, Marie felt the rest of the world coming back into her consciousness. She did feel a bit embarrassed again, and she quickly pulled her blue skirt back down over her hips. "I hope nobody could hear me."
Tifanny made a scoffing motion with her hand. "And if they did, so what? They would know that some chick was getting her rocks off but good." She got up on the rock and put her arm around her friend's waist. "Relax a bit. A girl's first cunt-licking is as big a deal as her first fuck."
Tifanny's bluntness surprised her as usual. "You're exaggerating that a bit, aren't you?"
She laughed at that, "Probably, but when I've done it with my first guy, I'll report back to you with my findings."
- "Isn't it's my turn to do you?"
- "There is no rush; get your bearings first. Do it when you are ready." Then they sat together and smooched for a while. "I bet you can taste your own cunt on my mouth."
- "I can, but . . ." She did not know what to say about it next.
- "That's okay, that's one of my favorite things about all this."
In short while, Marie said, "I think I'm ready now."
- "Okay, let us do it then. Kneel between my legs like I did with you." She raised her schoolgirl skirt, then she moved the pink and black thong panel away from her crotch.
Marie had a moment of doubt, "I've never done this before; I'm not sure about what I'm doing."

- "It's easy, I just showed you." She leaned forward and said in a confidential tone. "I have a theory about women; I think they're actually born knowing how to pleasure each other."

Marie suspected that this was supposed to be tongue-in-cheek, but she did not challenge Tifanny on it. Tifanny had some additional advice. "Do not be afraid to use your fingers as well as your mouth on me. And the clit; you must know this from touching yourself. Be subtle about it; put most of the pressure more around it rather directly on top of it."

When she went down on her, the first thing Marie noted was her friend's taste. She had often tasted herself on her own fingers. This does not seem that different from my own flavor. Maybe all ladies are the same in that way.

Tifanny spoke quite a bit during the act, instructing and encouraging her friend. At one point she said, "Baby, you do have the knack for this. Please, give me more on my clit; I can take it. I am just the sexiest, hottest chick in the whole Academy."

Marie thought, well, I am going to give you some competition on that.

Her climax went a bit differently from Marie's, although she did stroke the other girl's hair as had been done to her. Then Tifanny put her hands on the rock and moved her crotch up and down on the other girl's face. As she came, she got her legs up on Marie's shoulders for the final pushes. "Marie, you're so sweet; you're making me come!" She leaned back as the spasms went through her body. Then she slowed down and tried to catch her breath.

She looked down at her friend and said, "Marie, I am proud of you. You are becoming a bona fide bad girl."

- "That's fine, I always wanted to be one and now I'm finally making it happen."

Later they were in a coffee shop on Bainbridge Avenue. "So, are you going to mention this in Confession?"
Marie replied, "Absolutely not. I refuse to say anything about my personal life in there."
- "So, what do you say in that case?"
- "I just make up stuff, like I was mean to my mom or something. The priests seem totally bored."
- "Of course; they are looking for some hot girl gossip. So why go at all?"
- "I don't know, every month I tell my family I'm going there."
- "So go out for a walk and come back. They'll never know where you were."
Marie had never thought of that before. "That's actually a very good idea."
- "You're at St. Brendan's, right?"
- "That's it."
- "It is a very interesting building. Why does it look like that?"
- "It is supposed to be the prow of a ship. St. Brendan the Navigator, remember?"
- "I get it; that's very clever."
Marie said, "I still have to go to Mass, because my family goes."
- "Yeah, me too. So do you get dressed up to go?"
- "Sure, but I do not wear knee socks. In the summer I have white pantyhose; in the winter, it is dark nylon."
- "The next time you go, you're going with a busted cherry." Marie looked confused, so Tifanny explained it to her. "What we did today; I licked you into an orgasm and you did the same for me."
- "Does that really count?"
- "It depends on how you look at it. In girl-loving terms, it certainly counts."

Marie looked away and pondered what she had just heard. Tifanny smiled at her. "Marie, it was all my pleasure to initiate you into womanhood."

"Love is a rebellion. As an act of resistance against everything that tries to keep us apart."
Alok Vaid-Menon

THE PINK NIPPLE

The music was loud. I could feel the beat of the bass notes shake my belly as I sat at a table close to the dance floor with my partner, Orianne. We had difficulty hearing each other talk, what with the music, and everyone close to us trying to shout over it. I started to look around me, people were dancing, mostly in pairs and some were just chatting, probably getting to know each other. I watched the pair of red and blue disco lights illuminate the ceiling, and periodically, the people on the dance floor. Every now and then white lighting would pulse and periodically freeze their motion as they danced.

I love watching people in places like this and I could see intention in some of their eyes. One couple, quite close to me, were openly caressing each other's breasts as they stared into each other's eyes. I guessed, by the way they were looking at each other, that it was early on in their relationship. I instinctively knew they were going to get off with each other as soon as they left the Pink Nipple. If it were a man and woman misbehaving openly like that, in any other place, they would be asked to leave, but it seemed to be acceptable for two women to act that way, in this bar at least.

The Pink Nipple is a gay bar in Brussels. It is where all the sassy girls go for a good night out and it is the best place to meet new and exciting people, of the same sex that is. That is where I met Orianne, my partner. Four weeks later and here we are, chatting and drinking our Gin and Tonics as we survey the room. Between us, we have made a few friends in this wonderful pub and would probably make a few more.

Orianne rose from her seat and motioned to me that she was heading for the loo. I sat back in the chair, cradled my drink in my hand, sighed, and watched the people as I slowly sipped it. For a while at least, I watched Orianne's tight arse sway across the room, but it was not long before my eye caught a stunning redhead across the dance floor from me. She was sitting close to the edge of a table, facing me, and I took it from her body language that the blonde woman she was talking with was her partner or girlfriend. I watched them smile at each other, caress the others' hands, and occasionally laugh. The redhead's smile was intoxicating. She had a broad smile and bright red lips, a bit like the smile of the actress, Julia Roberts. She had an inviting, welcoming face. I could see myself talking to her for ages and slowly making her acquaintance.

As I watched her, I saw her glance at me. A little later, she took a longer look at me, but at both times she returned her attention to her girlfriend. In time, I became aware that I was staring at her and that she was staring back at me. In days gone by me would have averted my eyes, but not now. I was more confident now, and as I saw her look at me, I lifted my glass as if toasting her and took a sip.

She smiled back but her actions surprised me. She opened her legs as wide as she could while staring at me, leaning back into her chair as she did so. I could make out that something was not right with her jeans, but I could not see what that was immediately; the light in the room was far too variable for me to concentrate. I glanced between her face and her jeans a few times, but I had to let my eyes rest on her crotch for some time to try and figure out what was different. I saw her draw her finger across the zipped area, then I saw it disappear inside. I eventually caught on as to what was missing from her jeans.

At that point, I did avert my eyes while I smiled into my glass. I slowly raised it and took another sip. My mind was racing, and I was giggling away to myself at her brazenness. I raised my head but deliberately looked at the people dancing, avoiding making eye contact with her. My curiosity eventually got the better of me as my gaze returned, once more, to her direction. She was still watching me. I did not know where to look. I watched her smile at me, and I watched her finger stroke and then slide into her pussy. I was mesmerized by her overtly wanton display. My own finger entered my mouth as I bit on the nail before sucking on it.

My stare was disturbed when Orianne brushed her hand over my shoulder as she sat down next to me. We started to chat once more. We talked about the holiday we were planning in Asia in the coming year; more about how we were going to finance it on our meagre pay packets, than what we hoped to see or experience.

For some reason, my mind was not on this important conversation that Orianne was having with me. My head kept drifting to one side while I chatted with Orianne, and my eyes kept glancing across the room. The redheads' presence was highly distractive and my mind needed constant updates as to what she was doing.

It soon became my turn to visit the bar, and I topped Orianne and myself up with another Gin and Tonic. I was hoping the redhead would join me so that I could talk to her, but she did not. When I returned to our seats, our conversation continued, but I had become more and more disinterested, and I think Orianne sensed that. I wondered if I could move the conversation to the redhead but thought better of it. At one point I became agitated, when two women stood between myself and the redhead, blocking my view of her actions. I willed them out of the way, but my Jedi Knight training was not paying off. When the couple eventually moved onto the dance floor, my view of her was once more reinstated. She was still fingering herself and still looking at me. The smile on her face was blatantly directed towards me. Her blonde girlfriend was stood by the bar talking to someone else; obviously leaving her to taunt and torture me with her actions.

Orianne nudged me and pointed to my drink. She had finished hers quickly, or so it seemed, and I was obviously lagging behind. I downed the drink and let her wander off to the bar to get another. At last, I could spend a little more time looking at my redhead on the opposite side of the room. Trying to be coy was no longer a necessity. I stared openly at her crotch, completely missing the smile she had on her face. As I stared, I replayed all the information I had gathered on her.

She was very slim, with little or no breasts to speak of. She was wearing a black top, which had intricately cut out flowers arranged over one shoulder and down and across one of her breasts. Her jeans were open at the crotch, and I would be confident betting that she was not wearing any knickers. Her red hair was cropped on top, much shorter down one side but longer at the other, leaving a typical asymmetry in her hairstyle. If I had to judge her, I would have classified her as the strap-on wearing part of the couple. Her blonde girlfriend on the other hand was every bit a girly woman; a bit like me.

I wanted to know her name. I wanted to talk to her. I sighed knowing that that was never going to happen, not tonight, not with Orianne here.

Orianne arrived back at the table with another round of Gin and Tonics, and I took a big sip. Our conversation had eventually moved on from holidays. At some point, though I was unsure when it happened, the music had changed tempo and was now far more mellow and lighthearted. It was not as loud, and we could hear ourselves think. The night was obviously drawing in.

I leant over to Orianne and whispered to her that I was going to the loo. I could see there was a queue snaking its way through the corridor to the ladies at the other end. As I walked across the edge of the dance floor, I could not see my redhead at her table. I did not know whether she was in the loo, or elsewhere, and I wondered where she could be. Her blonde friend was at the bar; still talking. I waited until the cubicle became free. I entered, closed the door, and pulled my knickers down, taking them completely off in the process. I pulled my short skirt up, sat down and started to pee. I was unsure as to what to do with the knickers and reckoned I would palm them and calmly hand them to Orianne when I got back to the table. That sort of behavior always brought a smile to her face.

After doing the honors with the toilet paper and flushing the loo, I stood to leave. I flipped the lock and opened the door. I was startled as I pulled the door back towards me. A body was standing directly in front of me and moving in my direction. I had nowhere to go. I pulled myself backwards to avoid a collision with her and nearly stumbled.

A shocked gasp left my mouth, and my eyes widened at the impending impact.

It was the redhead. She was inches away from me. I felt her hand on my chest, directly over my left breast as she pushed me backwards into the loo, turning me at the same time so that my back was against the cold stone wall. Her left hand raised and pushed my hips backwards as she crunched herself into me, pinning me against the wall. Our mouths collided and she forced her tongue inside me. I was taken aback by her directness, my hands, although free, were helpless and refused to respond by pushing her away. I suddenly started to kiss her kindly and met her advances one for one.

I pushed my tongue back at her. Our mouths and tongues battled for quite some time until we settled into a frenzied rhythm of passionate kissing. At one point, I became almost breathless and lost in the most amazing kiss of my life. My hands came around on her backside and I let my knickers drop to the floor as I groped the cheeks of her arse. In no time at all, her hand had cupped my sex, and she was caressing it, probing it. Her middle finger snaked along my slit as she fingered me, moistening my pussy so that she could gain immediate access.

I heard the loo flush in the cubicle next to us and was aware that our door was still wide open. I heard the cubicle door unlock, and someone step out of it.

My redhead stepped back from me and while still holding onto my top, she pulled me towards her. She reclined herself on the loo and pulled my legs either side of the toilet seat until my pussy was over her face. I held up my skirt and watched as her tongue made contact with my sex. I let out a loud and audible gasp as she flicked her tongue across my lips. I quickly parted them with my fingers to give her access.

Behind me, a woman had appeared outside the cubicle. - "We have a situation here, girls. Someone is going for it," she announced to all that were present.

I could sense the woman behind me make a fucking motion with her hips in an attempt to let others know what was going down. All I knew, was that my redhead was already down, and she had a fucking wonderful tongue that she was putting to good use. Her tongue darted into my pussy and licked all over my clit. She was as horny as hell and attacked my pussy with the same gusto that had me pinned against the wall earlier.

A voice behind me brought me to my senses, "Fuck me Vivian, you look so hungry down there!"

I looked over my shoulder and saw that it was the redhead's girlfriend. I froze as she walked into the cubicle and I thought that that was it, I had transgressed a boundary, but the blonde kept smiling at me.

She leant into me and licked my earlobe. "My name's Lauren, fancy a double?" she asked.

I was a little perplexed, I had not heard of a double before, but I knew that if I said nothing back to her then I was going to find out what it was, pretty soon. I felt her slide down my torso until she rested on her haunches behind me. I felt her hands on the cheeks of my arse, pulling them apart and lifting my dress up further around my waist. Then I felt her tongue on my arse as she licked all over my anus.

The combined sensations of having my pussy, clit and anus licked all at the same time, was excruciatingly pleasurable. I found it difficult to concentrate on one feeling at a time, and both sensations seemed to attack my senses with different intensities. My orgasm was building rapidly with the attentions of both women. I found my hands grasp the nape of Vivian's neck as I pulled her into my pussy. I held her firmly with one hand while my other attempted to come around behind Lauren's head as I tried to push her into my anus from behind. I sighed and shook my head from side to side as I worked my anus and pussy between these women. It was bliss, especially when I started to come.

By now, an audience had gathered outside the cubicle. I could hear words of encouragement from different people, mostly aimed at Lauren and Vivian, telling them how they should tongue me! How they should give me a good time! Others shouted out that the slut was asking for it, in a non-derogatory sort of way. I gathered that everyone outside was having a great time watching the three of us.

I lost it big time when both women had their tongues pushed up inside me at the same time; both tongues wiggling in unison. Vivian eventually rested her tongue over my clit and flicked at it. That was when my orgasm came crashing down. I reached for Vivian's head and pulled her upwards in the hope of stabilizing myself as my legs started to buckle, I found that I had to push my hand forward onto the wall to stop myself from falling forward. I was gasping for air and screaming at the same time. My stomach was clenching involuntarily, and I felt my anus contract against Lauren's tongue while it was right up inside me, my anus pinched it almost stopping it from retracting. All the swear words and expletives I knew left my mouth, to the rapturous applause of the audience behind me.

- "Fuck me, I am cumming... I am cumming..." I shouted, between gulping in lungsful of air.

One onlooker was instrumental in telling me how I had been 'tongued by the best' as I panted and gasped for air. I wondered if she had experienced the same thing with the same two women. I eventually had to push Vivian away from me. Lauren, realizing that I was spent, leant backwards at the same time leaving me to desperately try and prop myself up against the wall, panting heavily. Every part of me was on fire and I loved every minute.

I looked behind me, at Lauren. She was smiling like a Cheshire cat and licking her lips. Vivian was still reclined on the loo and giggling away like a little girl, on the verge of hysterical laughter. I turned to look at the crowd of onlookers and found that they were all smiling away at themselves; probably feeling horny from watching our show. I spotted a familiar face at the back of the applauding crowd.

- "Fuck no...." I cried.
- "Em..." I shouted, "Em..."
I watched as Orianne turned and ran from the loo.
I quickly stepped over Lauren as I rushed out, in close pursuit.
As I approached our table, I could see that Orianne had gathered her handbag and coat and was heading for the door, pushing past anyone that got in her way and leaving a wake of people behind her. I followed her out to the street. The busy traffic stopped her escape, and I eventually caught up with her next to the traffic lights.
I placed my hand on Orianne's shoulder, but she shrugged it off, "You bastard!" She spat at me before turning back to the road ahead. The lights turned green, and Orianne ran across the road.
I started to run after her, "Em...please listen to me, please."
On the other side of the road Orianne turned and looked at me, anger was written all over her face, "Just fuck off Amy, your body language in there said it all, now fuck off!"
I stopped and watched as Orianne walked away from me. I watched her leave me, forever. This was it, the end of our relationship had come, and all I had to do was resist the temptation set before me.
I slowly turned to walk back inside the Pink Nipple, I made my way through the crowded bar and saw that Vivian and Erika were sitting side-by-side, they looked pensive as they hugged one another. I looked in their direction and Vivian caught my eye. She smiled, almost apologetically, and patted the seat next to her. I contemplated picking up my jacket and leaving the pub altogether. My life was in ruins, and over what?
I did pick up my jacket but found myself inextricably drawn towards the seat that Vivian was patting with her hand. I was mesmerized by the movement of her

hand as I sat down next to Vivian. She placed her hand on my thigh as I rested my head on her shoulders. I closed my eyes. I felt her hand snake upwards, and I found myself grinning. I opened my eyes and looked at Erika.

Erika leant in towards the both of us. "We want you to come back with us tonight. Would you like that?"

I smiled and nodded.

I had lost Orianne, and if truth be told, I did not really know what I was getting myself into with these two, but I felt an adrenaline rush flow through me. My nipples felt like icicles; hard and erect, on the verge of melting and I felt my pussy leak fluid onto the seat.

I was ready to find out.

*"I'm in love with you.
And I know that love is true."*
Whitney Houston

ART CRUSH

Julia was two years old when she met her babysitter, Brooklyn Turner. She lived two houses down from Julia's family. She was such a loving lady and treated the little girl as though she were her own. Kelly could not conceive due to a rare disease of the uterus she contracted at a young age (21), thus having it removed. It was a very difficult time for Kelly because she wanted children. Having Julia around along with the other neighborhood kids made things easier.

Ms. Turner was the one who taught Julia her ABCs and 123s since her parents worked all day. She even taught her how to bake cookies at the age of six. Julia grew quite fond of Ms. Turner as her personality was so warm and cheery. Not only was her demeanor captivating, but she was also spellbound by the artwork Ms. Turner had hanging around her house. Ms. Turner had impeccable taste. The art was rare, finely detailed, and looked rather expensive. It did not seem like artwork from regular stores.

Ms. Turner's cultivated paintings and sculptures made Julia very interested in art. At the age of eight, she began drawing. She even attempted to copy some of the paintings on the walls. Though she had not mastered three-dimensional drawing at the time, her pictures looked very similar to the paintings. Julia's art was so superb she passed all her art classes throughout grade school with flying colors. In seventh grade, she already set the goal of majoring in art in college.

Over time, Julia developed a serious crush on Ms. Turner. She found herself drawing pictures of her. She threw most of the drawings away to keep her attraction secret but kept one which was a 3D pastel of Ms. Turner holding a gemstone rose. Behind her, in the drawing, the sun shined like a halo.

The thing Julia loved most about Ms. Turner was her touch. Ms. Turner hugged her when she came over. She always gave Julia a pat on the back whenever she did a good job on something such as gardening or baking. Sometimes, she held Julia's hand when they had conversations, especially deep ones. At times, she would come up behind Julia and surprise her by playfully wrapping her arms around her waist, lightly squeezing her. Julia loved it because of the feeling of Ms. Turner's warm body against hers. Also, she loved cuddling. When Julia was little, she would sit on Ms. Turner's lap while watching television and fall asleep on her chest. Her heartbeat had the most soothing rhythm. Plus, her breasts seemed to be the softest place on earth...softer than her own pillow. When Julia was four, out of pure curiosity, she squeezed Ms. Turner's breasts, not knowing what they were, and asked, "Ms. Doddy, what are these?"

Gently, Ms. Turner took the little girl's hands off and laughed while replying, "Honey, you're a little young for that now."

- "Will I get those too?" Julia quizzed.

- "When you're older, sweetie. Now let us concentrate on washing these dishes, shall we?"

That was the last Julia heard of breasts until she was twelve years old. Then Ms. Turner and Julia's mother sat her down and gave her a lesson on having her period, sex, boys, dating, and STDs. Julia was a bit of a late bloomer. She did not start her period until she was fourteen and did not develop breasts until she was seventeen. From age 17 to 18, her breasts sprouted from AA to C. Plus, she went from having no curves at all to having shapely hips, round buttocks, and slim, toned thighs and legs. Standing at 5'6", many friends and family suggested she try modeling, but Julia was more interested in art and Ms. Turner than showing off her body to complete strangers.

Now, Julia was 21 years old. Instead of majoring in art, she decided on communications in college. She felt she would do art as leisure, not pursue it as a full-time career. She scanned her works and put them on Instagram and Snapchat for fun, but people were interested in purchasing them. Depending on the size of the canvas, Julia sold her watercolor and oil pastel works for as much as $400. Though she worked in a coffee shop, she made better money with her artwork.

Julia was very scared to tell Ms. Turner of her attraction to her. She felt Ms. Turner would not be interested, especially due to her age. Ms. Turner was near fifty...forty-seven to be exact, but Julia thought she looked good for her age. She admired her shoulder length curly blonde hair, blue eyes, and creamy skin. Her hair did not have a single strand of grey. She always kept her skin soft and moist. Julia considered herself a plain Jane compared to Ms. Turner although many thought otherwise. She had honey brown skin, long dark brown hair that came down to her butt, and hypnotic dark brown eyes. Her racial background was a wonderful mix of Arabian, Black, Italian, and Asian.

Though Ms. Turner relocated to another house outside of Julia's old neighborhood, Julia still visited her every now and then to help her with gardening, house cleaning, or they would just have fun together. They visited art galleries that came to the community and had funny debates on which work was better even though Julia, though the best work ever made was Ms. Turner herself. She was the ultimate masterpiece no matter where she went.

On this particular day, Ms. Turner wanted to look at Julia's art portfolio and possibly add a piece to the many she had hanging on her walls. Julia became very excited despite having a long day at work and spending a few hours organizing her new apartment. She put on a pair of jeans, a black blouse, and a pair of old sneakers. Then she tied her hair in a ponytail and made her way to Ms. Turner's place.

It did not take her long to get there as she only lived 30 minutes away. When she arrived, she drove on an unpaved driveway through a set of trees. When she entered the clearing, she saw the big, blue house. Julia drove up to the garage and parked in front of it. The second she stepped out; the potent scent of roses entered her nostrils. With every step she made toward the door, her heart raced faster. To calm down, she closed her eyes and breathed in the rosy scent surrounding her. It encased and warmed her heart causing its hyperactive beating to slow down. Then she opened her eyes and rang the doorbell.

Seconds later, there was a hard click and a turn of the knob. When the door opened, Julia swore her heart stopped at the alluring sight she saw. There stood Ms. Turner. Though she wore a plain pink shirt and black slacks, Julia felt an overwhelming amount of calming, positive energy radiating within Ms. Turner's aura. Gently, she took Julia by the hand.

- "Come in, sweetie."

As she entered Ms. Turner's home, Julia was greeted by the warming scent of lavender and vanilla candles. Leading her to the living room, Ms. Turner hugged her and asked, "How are you, honey?"

- "I am fine, thank you," Julia replied trying not to let the quiver in her stomach transfer to her vocal cords.

Cheerfully, Ms. Turner said, "That's good. Why don't you have a seat here and I will get you something to drink? What would you like?"

As Julia sat down, she wanted to say "wine", but she did not want to give Ms. Turner any clue of her crush. She

deterred her answer to "a glass of juice or iced tea with lemon if you have any."
- "You are just in time, sweetie." I just made a fresh batch of sweet tea. I added some raspberry flavoring if you don't mind."
- "I like raspberries. That's perfect."
- "Ok. You get comfortable while I get the tea."
As Julia waited, she sank into the couch and took in her surroundings. The atmosphere was very welcoming, not just with the scent in the air, but the couch had absorbed the scent. Plus, it was very comfortable. The window across from her had beautiful, custom-made, sky-blue drapes with bluebell flower designs at the bottoms. The wall behind her had a painting of a sunny meadow a couple of feet above the couch. The grass looked almost real, the birds and flowers nearly lifelike, especially since the painting was almost four feet across. Julia's mind wandered into the image of her and Ms. Turner in the meadow, the breeze blowing...
- "I've got your iced tea. I also sliced a few apples if you'd like."
Julia's imagination shattered like glass revealing Ms. Turner holding two trays. One contained two glasses of iced tea. The other had sliced apples.
- "Oh, the apples are fine, "Julia said. "And you have the red delicious kind too. My favorite!"
Ms. Turner sat down next to Julia and sipped her tea. - "Let's get down to business, shall we?":
Julia picked up her big, black binder and asked, "Which theme would you like to see?"
- "Mmmm...the gemstone themed pastels."
Julia opened her binder and first showed Ms. Turner a 3D pastel drawing of a leaf shaped emerald with 3 diamonds shaped like raindrops seeming to run down the leaf. Then she turned to the next drawing which was

a sapphire shaped like a bluebell flower. It had leaf shaped emeralds as well as the stem.

- "I love that one," Ms. Turner commented. "It is so beautiful, so lifelike. I almost want to pick that flower. How does $500 sound for the drawing?"

Surprisingly, Julia did not want money. She wanted Ms. Turner herself. The $500 sounded great, but money just did not match the attraction she felt.

- "I'll lower the price to $250," she said in protest.

Ms. Turner countered mildly, "I know you're doing your best to be reasonable with your pricing, but you put a lot of effort and timing into this drawing. I can see passion in every speck of color. Actually, a superior work of art like this would be worth about $1200 if you were to auction it."

Flattered but still disinterested in the offer, Julia insisted, "Ms. Turner, I've known you for a long time. I cannot be greedy. $500 sounds good, but don't you think it is a bit much? I couldn't take that from you."

But Ms. Turner was already writing a check. "Sweetie, you already know money was never an issue with me. You are a great artist, and you sacrificed a lot of time to create such a masterpiece. How long did you take to draw this?"

- "About four and a half hours."

- "Commitment, concentration, precision, and passion deserve to be well compensated."

I would rather be compensated with you, Julia thought, but she said, "I guess. Thank you, Ms. Turny."

- "Call me Kelly, sweetie. I know you are used to calling me Ms. Turny. You have known me since you were a tiny little thing, but you are all grown up now. I'd like to have more than a friend connection rather than just being your former babysitter."

The first step in getting closer," Julia thought. Calling her by her first name.

Suddenly, Julia heard a clicking sound. It came from the front door. Who was coming to Kelly's home? Her confusion only increased when she saw a man in a suit come in the living room carrying a suitcase. He was taller than Kelly and had a head full of silver-grey hair. Julia finally pieced the puzzle together when she saw Kelly's eyes brighten.

- "Hi, honey! You are home!"

Kelly stood up and pecked the man on the lips. She turned to Julia and said, "This is my husband, Nicholas. I've known you for so long and never got to introduce you to him because he travels so much."

Husband! Julia thought. Husband? Ok how did I miss this from age two to fourteen? I know Kelly mentioned something about Nicholas when I was little, but I never knew who she was talking about.

Julia's stomach burned as she stiffly stood and shook Nicholas's hand. She smiled weakly as she greeted, "Hi. I am Julia. Kelly used to babysit me."

Nicholas smiled. "It's nice to finally meet you for the first time! Kelly told me so much about you and she was right. You have blossomed into a very sweet, young woman."

- "Not only that," Kelly added. "She has the most talented hands ever. I bought a new addition to our art gallery. Look at this beautiful pastel she drew! Doesn't it look almost like you want to pick it from the paper?"

Nicholas nodded, looking at Julia's drawing. "Wow! That is impressive. How much did you pay her, Kelly?"

Before Kelly could say anything, Julia cut in. "Well, I offered her $250, but she paid me $500."

Kelly added, "And I told her commitment, concentration, precision, and passion deserve to be well compensated. She spent nearly five hours drawing this magnificent piece."

- "That's a long time!" Nicholas gasped. Then he changed the subject. "Kelly, honey, would you like for us to head out to dinner? Then we can come back here and spend some quality time together. I have missed you."
- Kelly obliged, "Certainly, Nicholas. Would it be a bother if Julia came with us?"
- "Not at all. Julia, would you like to join us for dinner? It will be our treat."
- "Umm..." Julia hesitated. "I think I should go. Thank you for the check, Kelly."
- "Oh, I am sure you are hungry dear," Kelly persisted.
Julia lied, "It's ok. I am fine. I am sure you two would like to be alone. Besides, I am not that hungry."
But her growling stomach proved otherwise.
Kelly laughed. "Sweetie, you are eating! There is no way I am letting you go hungry. I never let you go home hungry when I babysat you."
Julia had no choice but to accept, but she tried to get out of it once more by protesting, "I'm not dressed."
- "Honey, you are beautiful," Kelly countered. "It doesn't matter what you wear. Now quit trying to get out of eating with us. I will put on some slightly better attire and then we will go."
As Kelly went to get dressed, Nicholas said to Julia, "Kelly is right, you know. You are beautiful. You have lovely skin. How do you keep it looking so nice?"
- "I just wash with soap every day. Nothing special except I exfoliate once a week with a sea salt scrub. I paid $60 for it. Expensive, but it works."
Nicholas took Julia gently by the hand and felt the back of it. "I see it does work. Your skin also seems to have a natural glow to it too. You are blessed!"
Julia shuddered at his touch. Briefly, she sighed as her eyes wandered to the stairs where they locked Kelly coming down. She looked like an angel gliding down.

She wore black dress pants with a sparkling blue floral print blouse with ruffled sleeves.

- "Are we ready to go?" she asked.

Nicholas took her by the hand. "Of course."

- "Am I going to be following you guys?" Julia asked. Deep in her mind, she contemplated pretending to follow Nicholas and Kelly, then purposely getting lost, but her plan failed as Nicholas replied, "You may ride with us. Save yourself the gas, hun."

Reluctantly, Julia slithered into the back seat of Nicholas's car. She put on the seatbelt and slouched letting her body sink into the black leather. As she stared out of the window, watching the sunset beyond the winding road, her stomach plummeted at the sounds of Nicholas and Kelly's cheery conversation and giggles.

The arrived at a relatively small Italian restaurant. Nicholas opened the door where Julia sat, softly took her by the hand, and helped her out of the car. Then he playfully interlocked her arm with his. He had Kelly on his other arm.

- "Let's go, ladies," he chuckled.

Kelly shook her head in amusement. "Are you a ladies' man for tonight, sweetheart?"

Nicholas snickered. "I guess so! I must be one lucky man with two beautiful women on my arms!"

They walked into the restaurant, Julia feeling like a third wheel. When they were seated, the second Julia opened the menu, she blurted, "I guess the checks will be separate?"

- "No, sweetie," Nicholas answered. "I'm treating everyone."

Julia ordered fried calamari along with angel hair pasta in a red sauce with mussels, scallops, and baby shrimp. She started eating quickly until Nicholas giggled. - "Hungry enough or is the food really good?"

Embarrassed, Julia's cheeks reddened. The fact that her redness was visible did not help the situation. Only when blushing did Julia wish her honey brown skin was darker. Kelly and Nicholas were tickled by her blushing. She did not find it funny. In fact, she became irritated. Briefly shutting her eyes, Julia suppressed her embarrassment, and her cheeks returned to normal. She ate the rest of her food mostly in silence unless Nicholas or Kelly spoke to her.

When the three returned home, Julia announced, "Well, I guess I should be going now. I must work in the morning. It was nice meeting you, Nicholas, and thank you for dinner."

- "I haven't been to the coffee shop in a while," said Kelly. "Nicholas, how would you like to have a little coffee date in the morning? It will be a plus with Julia there. She knows exactly what I like!"

- "Definitely!" said Nicholas. "We'll see you in the morning, Julia."

Julia politely waved goodbye to Nicholas and Kelly, got into her car, and quickly drove off. As she sped through the dimly lit roads, her chest hurt as though it had been hit by a bowling ball. Her heart felt crushed. She also felt dumb because she did not put together the pieces. There was no way Kelly could afford the exquisite artwork hanging in her house. Plus, how could Kelly afford to throw away $500 and say that money is no issue? Unless Kelly's family was wealthy, which Julia knew they were not, those words would have never crossed Kelly's lips.

At work the next day, Julia felt sluggish and out of focus. Her concentration went into even more distortion when Nicholas and Kelly floated through the door. They sat at Kelly's same spot by the window in the middle of the cafe. Julia prepared Kelly's hazelnut coffee with a slice of marble cake and a blueberry muffin for Nicholas. She walked quickly towards their table, but she was so out of focus she did not pay attention to her footing. Julia's foot seemingly wrapped around the leg of a table before Kelly's, throwing her completely off balance. Instantly, she reached for the empty chair at the end of the table, but she missed. The coffee flew out of her hand as well as the marble cake and blueberry muffin. The two pastries landed on the floor right before Julia fell over like a tree. Her face went into the marble cake slice while the cup of coffee cartwheeled twice causing the lid to come off and the hot liquid to spill out. It all landed on Julia as she slid across the floor and crashed into the leg of the table where Nicholas and Kelly sat.

- "Oh aw," she groaned in pain.

Immediately, Nicholas got out of his chair and helped Julia sit up. The coffee shop manager came running to her side.

- "What happened, Julia?" the manager asked.

Kelly said, "She was bringing us our orders, but it seemed like she either slipped or tripped. I am surprised the coffee did not burn her, but oh, sweetie, there is a bruise on your arm and... oh my goodness! Your lip is swollen and bleeding!"

Not only that, Julia's entire body ached. Although the coffee did not burn her skin, she felt as through her had been stung by needles. Her head hurt more than anything else.

The manager said, "You don't look like you're in shape to work any further. Your shift is almost over anyway. Go ahead and clock out early. Besides, your hair and face are a sticky mess now."

Both the manager and Nicholas helped Julia to her feet.

- "Go put some ice on that lip, hun," said Nicholas. "Drive home safely. I hope you feel better."

- "I'll come over to check on you," Kelly said.

After wiping the marble cake from her face, Julia got in her car and drove away. On her way home, her emotions went haywire. First came embarrassment from her slip and fall at work, her swollen lip, coffee-stained work uniform, face covered in marble cake, and now, sticky, hazelnut smelling hair. Then came anger. How on earth did she let yesterday's events get to her like that? It was dumb to even think that Kelly would ever have any kind of feeling toward her, especially due to the age gap and the fact that she had a rich husband! Julia's feelings were so intense she did not notice the speedometer had gone up to seventy and she was in a 45-mile zone. Snapping out of her trance, she slammed the brakes causing the tires to squeal.

"Oh fuck!" she yelled. "Dammit, Julia! Get it together! Get over that woman already!"

After regaining some form of composure, she drove the rest of the way home, this time, staying within the speed limit.

As soon as she arrived home, she dropped her purse and shoes by the door, stripped off her work uniform, left it in the living room, and jumped into the shower. Each drop of the steaming hot water stung her body, melting her aches and pains away. She washed her hair and body with extra soap to get rid of the embedded smell of hazelnut coffee. When she made sure she was thoroughly clean, she turned off the water and flew open the curtain.

"Dammit," she thought out loud. "I forgot my towel."

Dripping wet and naked, Julia opened the bathroom door and started to make her way to the bedroom, but she nearly screamed seeing a figure sitting in the living room.

"WHAT THE FUCK!"

It took her a second to realize it was Kelly.

- "Take it easy!" Kelly shouted, trying to calm Julia down. "It's me!"

Julia shook her head in bewilderment. "Damn, Kelly! You could not knock or call? Are you trying to have me go through another slip and fall?"

- "The door was unlocked," said Kelly. "I knocked several times, and you didn't answer. Then I turned the knob, and the door opened. That is when I heard water running, so I knew you were in the shower. I did not want to scare you by walking in there, so I waited for you out here.

- Besides, I said I was going to come over to check on you."

Julia's mind was in such a twist she nearly forgot she was naked. "Oh great! I cannot get any privacy either?"

Kelly just laughed. "It's nothing I haven't seen before. Don't forget I bathed you and changed your little Pull-ups when you were younger."

- "Um...yeah but these aren't baby parts anymore. And I am dripping water all over the carpet! Ugh!" Julia went to her room to get a towel and dry it off.

"Remember to lock the door next time," she said to herself.

There was a knock on the bedroom door. Then it opened.

- "I'm not dressed, Kelly," Julia called out. She only wore her pink bra and lace thong set, but Kelly came in anyway.

- "Just wondered if you were ok, sweetie. How is that arm?"

- "Please don't touch it." Julia backed away from Kelly and sat on the bed. "My entire body still hurts a little, but I think the shower helped. Now all I need to do is lotion up and I think I'll take a nap afterward." She grabbed a bottle of lotion from the floor, but gently, Kelly took it from her.

- "Let me take care of that," she said. "You're hurting. You should relax."

Julia retracted. "It's ok, Kelly. I will be fine. Thank you for coming by though."

But Kelly took her by the shoulder, turned her around, and pushed against her. "I insist. Just lie on your stomach and unwind."

Julia did what Kelly said, but she still protested, "Kelly, don't worry. I said I"

The second Kelly's hands began massaging the lotion into her honey brown legs, Julia fell silent. As Kelly's hands slid up the young woman's thighs, she bit her lip and bit the pillow fighting to relieve the throbbing in her clit. Then she buried her face in the pillow, not believing what was happening.

- "Are you ok?" Kelly asked.

Instantly, Julia jerked her head up. "Huh?"

- "You made a noise there. Am I hurting you?"

- "No, you're fine."

Oh no, not my butt, Julia thought as Kelly's hands glided along her bare bottom. She really wanted to moan out loud then. Kelly's touch was relaxing yet very arousing. Was awakening her libido really Kelly's intention? She did not know, nor did she care at this point. The moment became more intense when Kelly had her flip over and went from her feet to her flat torso. Julia's body shifted and slightly shuddered beneath Kelly's delicate touch. She took in very little air as she did not want to show Kelly any signs of her arousal, but she knew her racing heart would give her away. Good thing her bra had some padding to it, or else Kelly would have definitely noticed her hard nipples. Julia flinched when Kelly rubbed lotion on her sore, bruised arm.

- "Ouch!"

But even with the pain, the young woman's arousal did not leave. Before she had the chance to moan out loud, Kelly stopped.

- "Ok. All done, sugar."

- "Thank you." Julia's voice slightly trembled. "I think I should put on some more clothes." She only threw a big t-shirt over her underwear."

- "Feeling any better?" Kelly asked.

- "Yeah, that relieved some of the soreness. Thank you. I guess I needed that."

- "I'm glad you're ok. That was some fall! It looked like something out of a cartoon. Hey, I see the swelling on your lip came down. That's good."

- "I'm surprised it came down so quickly."

The sound of Kelly's cell phone interrupted the moment. She dug it out from her purse.

- "Oh gee. It is Nicholas. We are supposed to be doing an at-home dinner tonight. Looks like I need to get going. I will call you soon, ok? Take care of that arm for me."

- "Oh, I don't want to keep you from Nicholas," said Julia. "Go on ahead. Thank you again." She led Kelly to the door.

After Kelly left, Julia was still aroused. Her clit still tingled. Her thighs felt like Jello and her nipples were still erect. She took off her t-shirt and bra, laid back on the bed, and let her body sink into the mattress. As the warmth of her body heat reflecting from her bed cocooned her, Julia closed her eyes and let her libido be her guide. Her hands explored her smooth thighs, soft belly, and delicate breasts. She squeezed them while giving her nipples a light pinch. Shuddering from the sensation, she guided her left hand down between her thighs. While running her right hand across her breasts, her left hand pressed against the fabric of her pink thong and rubbed gently. Then she pushed her thong aside and fumbled for her clit while playing with her nipples. She slid her hand down further and felt her damp, moist folds. As soon as she found her swollen, sensitive button, she pressed harder and lightly quickened her strokes. Minutes later, her vaginal walls contracted as she bit her lip and moaned loudly, feeling the orgasm jolt through her body. She took a minute to let it subside and catch her breath. All the while she thought, Oh my goodness! What did Kelly do to me? How did she do it? This is crazy. I cannot think about this! She is married!

- "Oh, this is dumb!" Julia snapped out loud, rolling her eyes. Rapidly, she rolled out of bed and changed into her underwear. Then she dug out her pastel drawing of Kelly from under the bed. Taking a lighter from her desk that she used for candles, she held it under the drawing and laid her thumb against the igniter ready to press it, but she could not do it. The drawing was very beautiful, and Kelly meant so much to her. She dropped the lighter, slid the drawing in its plastic cover, and put it back under the bed in her portfolio. Then she bit her lip in frustration, fighting to rationalize and suppress her feelings.

I must be crazy, she thought. Is this a crush or an obsession? I live only fourteen miles from her. I work at the coffee shop she has been going to for years before I even got hired there. I have been drawing pictures of her for who knows how long. You are crazy, Julia. She is married.

She is married.

That is what Julia kept telling herself, but her emotions did not seem to care.

As night settled in, Julia was just putting the finishing touches on a sketch of a cardinal sitting in a tree behind her apartment. She laid in her hammock on the deck watching the bird chirp while looking off in the distance. Afterward, she closed her sketch book, covered herself with a blanket, closed her eyes, and let the steady summer breeze rock her to sleep.

A warm, tender hand slid up Julia's thigh beneath the blanket. Not long after, a pair of lips explored her belly up to between her breasts. Julia's hands felt for the stranger and came upon silky, curly blonde hair. She pushed her hands against the back of the stranger's neck wanting to look into the mystery lover's face. She found herself looking into blue eyes. As she smiled, at the angelic face looking upon hers, she lifted her head to kiss the soft lips begging to be devoured....

Her cell phone rang.

Rubbing the sleep from her eyes, Julia looked into the distance.

Sunrise. It had to be 7:00am.

Damn, she thought. I slept out here all night.

The cell phone rang again.

- "Who the hell is calling me at this hour?" she groaned. She reached for her phone at the foot of the hammock and answered. It was Kelly.

I dream about this woman, and she calls me. Please tell me I am still asleep.

- "Good morning, sleepyhead," Kelly greeted her cheerfully. "Did I wake you?"

- "Kelly, you know I'm not a morning person."

- "Well, rise and shine, girl. I thought we would have an early breakfast at 8:30, gardening at 10:00, then a nice outing at the park by 2:00. What do you say?"

- "Where's Nicholas? Is he coming?"

- "Nicholas left early this morning at about 5:45. His flight left a good fifteen minutes ago, I believe. I would like some company if you're not too busy."

Julia wanted to reject the offer, but it would not have made sense to do so. Besides, what excuse did she have? She could not make up one as it was early in the morning and her mind was not clear just yet.

- "It's no bother. I just need to shower and get dressed, ok?"

When she arrived at Kelly's house, Julia already smelled breakfast cooking. Her stomach gurgled when she went into the kitchen and saw Kelly putting the finishing touches on the food. When she was sitting herself, Kelly turned around and walked toward her. Jokingly, she said, "Now you don't sit down without giving me a hug."

Julia stood up and hugged her.

- "I made home fries, eggs, and biscuits with gravy," said Kelly. "I also cooked some sausage. I remember you loved my biscuits and gravy when you were little. You always asked for more, then made the cutest sad face when I said you had to save some for the other kids."

Julia giggled. "Yeah, your biscuits and gravy were my favorite food. You have always made such a slamming breakfast! I'd take your home cooking any day over McDonald's or Burger King."

After the two ate, they went outside to the garden. The 10:00am sun caused beads of sweat to pour down Julia's chest between her breasts. Luckily, she wore a sports bra and shorts, but that did not stop her abdomen from sweating too. Thoughts raced through her mind as she pulled weeds with a hoe.

I wonder why Kelly asked me to come over. Was she lonely? Why am I so attracted to her? Nicholas is one blessed man. I guess some fantasies will have to remain.

For a minute or two, she stood and watched Kelly use her mini shovel to dig small holes to plant her cucumber seeds. The mere presence of her made Julia feel happy inside.

Well, if we just remain good friends, I guess that is good enough. As long as I get to be around her, that is all I need.

- "Are you ok, Julia?" Kelly asked, looking up at her.

- "Oh yeah," the young woman answered. "It just seems to get hotter by the minute."

- "Well, we are just about done now. I just must plant this last seed. Then we'll head back inside and clean up for our outing at the park."

As soon as they were finished, Julia hurried back inside the house to shower. She made the water lukewarm due to the summer heat radiating from her skin. She washed away the dirt and sweat on her body. Suddenly, she realized she had left her salt scrub and lotion in her car.

She called out, "Kelly! Will you get my salt scrub and lotion out of my car please? The keys are in the kitchen on the table!"

- "Will do, sweetie!" Kelly called back.

After Julia scrubbed down, she stepped out of the shower and wrapped a towel around her wet body. She made her way to Kelly's bedroom to dry off and relax, but Kelly was already sitting on the bed looking through Julia's portfolio. Julia froze in horror when Kelly pulled out the portrait, she had drawn...the angelic portrait she had kept hidden from Kelly for a good number of years.

- "When did you draw this, Julia?" Kelly asked.

- "When I was sixteen," Julia replied, her voice trembling.

- "This is the most beautiful drawing I have ever seen! I took your portfolio out of the car so your pastels would not get ruined by the heat. Wow! This picture is so amazing! You have every single detail of my facial features here! Eyes, hair, lips, everything! It is almost like I am looking into a mirror. Five years and you never told me or showed me? Why not? Why did you keep this picture such a secret? I would have loved to have this."

Julia still stood frozen. That drawing was a special, yet hidden part of her...the love and appreciation she had for Kelly. The crush that never went away. Now it was revealed plain as day. Julia had no idea whether to be scared or upset. Finally, she said, "You're special to me, Kelly. I have always loved your aura, and you are such a positive person. You have a good heart. I wish there were more people like you in the world."

Kelly took Julia by the hand and sat her down next to her on the bed. "I can see it in your drawing. You mean a lot to me, too. From the very first day I saw you, I had to take you under my wing. You went from a sweet, little girl to a beautiful, wise young woman. I truly believe more people like you need to be in the world. You have the whole package looks, brains, and personality. I cannot imagine why no man has whisked you away. You deserve a good man in your life."

Kelly then planted several small kisses upon Julia's cheek. She paused for a moment, then kissed Julia's other cheek several times again, but a lot slower this time.

Julia jittered even more. So much so, her hands were visibly shaking. She was frozen stiff.

- "Oh, honey, you're shaking," Kelly pointed out. "What's wrong? Are you ok?"

- "Oh, Kelly, I've been attracted to you for so long, ever since I was a teenager. I kept that from you all these years because I did not think you would be interested. Plus, you are married to a rich man. What would you want with a working-class girl like me?"

- "Julia, Nicholas knows that I like women too and he is ok with it. I have not been with a woman for a while now. I had this friend with benefits when you were younger, but she moved. Nicholas is gone for quite a few months out of the year. Sometimes, dildos and masturbating to porn does not help. Now I will never have sex with another man ever. Nicholas is my one and only. I would like to have a lady friend too. You seem like the perfect fit. We have known each other forever. I trust you and I hope that you trust me. We are adults now, so let us take this friendship to the next level. Are you comfortable with that? I do not want you just for sex whenever I get horny. I want you around for company. I want us to continue all the things we always do together. Nicholas already knows how I feel about you."

Julia was very surprised. "You told him?"

- Yes, and Nicholas said it was a wonderful thing since we have known each other for so long. Ever since you turned eighteen, I could not get over your stunning beauty inside and out.

Julia was floored. "I was so afraid you wouldn't feel the same way."

Kelly kissed her on the cheek again. "Hmmm...why don't you lay back and take that towel off? I'll lotion you up."

Still nervous, Julia laid back, but she did not take the towel off. Kelly opened it, exposing the young woman's honey brown body.

- "Well, your body definitely doesn't look the way it was when you were two," Kelly joked. "Your body looks delicious now. Tell me something, honey. Has someone ever touched and caressed your body to the point of orgasms?"

- "Um...no," Julia gulped.

- "Well, I am glad to be your first. You do not have to do anything. You will love the way I touch you. I promise."

Kelly squeezed a little bit of lotion into the palm of her hand. Instantly, Julia melted the second the older woman's hands were placed on her body. Kelly began at her feet and worked up to her neck. She also ran her hands through Julia's long silky hair. Kelly knew Julia was getting wet by her heavy pants and shivering, but never did she touch between her legs, nor did she touch the woman's rock-hard nipples. She continued rubbing her legs, thighs, torso, chest, and next. Meanwhile, she seduced Julia with her voice.

- "You are aroused by my touch. I can see your body quaking. Do not be afraid to let yourself go, sweetie. Mmmm....your skin is so soft. I can't stop touching it."

Julia became wetter by the minute while Kelly's creamy white hands slid all over her honey brown skin. The sound of Kelly's voice and her touch had Julia shaking so hard. Soon, all she could let out were moans and sighs.

- "Mmmmm....oh my God, Kelly, yes!"

No matter how much she fought, Julia's body was under a deep spell. She had no other choice but to give herself totally to Kelly. At that very moment, one of the most powerful orgasms came through her like a strong storm. She screamed loudly, her body stiffening from such unique pleasure.

- "Mmmm...turnover, honey," Kelly whispered softly.

Julia grabbed the pillow and bit into it as Kelly's sweet caress went from the back of her legs to her shoulders. Her pussy began dripping when Kelly deeply massaged her round bottom. Just the feel of her loosening muscles made Julia have yet another roaring orgasm. But Kelly did not stop there. She kissed the back of Julia's neck, down her spine to her luscious ass. She focused there for a moment, then kissed down to Julia's calves. Kelly kissed more deeply, going back up to the woman's bottom. She bit each of her butt cheeks then spread her thighs to see her glistening pussy soaked in juices. As Kelly's hand crept to her drenched area, Julia's entire body convulsed.

- "Oh, sweetie, you're so wet," whispered Kelly. "It is so slippery down there. Baby, your clit is so swollen. I feel it poking out of its little hood."

As her sensitive button received small amounts of stimulation, Julia moaned and clenched the sheets tightly. She had never experienced this type of pleasure before. Every touch upon her clit made her toes curl and caused her teeth to clench harder. As she had another orgasm, she bit into the pillow and screamed into it. She then turned over to see Kelly's angelic smile above her. Kelly stripped off her shirt and bra, lowered herself onto the young woman's body, and slowly kissed her while holding her in a loving embrace.

Breaking the long kiss, Julia whispered, "Kelly, are you sure this is right? How do you know this will not ruin our friendship?"

- "It's so much more than a friendship, honey. I do not just like you. I love you and I know you love me too."

As Kelly's lips totally encased hers once again, Julia smiled inside. Here she had been doing beyond what she dreamed of ever since she was a teen. The tiny hairs on her body stood on end from the feel of Kelly's tongue slithering into her mouth. With her body almost hypersensitive, the second Kelly's lips and tongue touched her neck, Julia moaned loudly, "Oh, God that feels so good!"

She had to take a deep breath when Kelly's warm mouth wrapped around her sensitive, hard nipple. She murmured softly, reacting to Kelly's slow and gentle sucking. With Kelly lovingly holding the young woman's body in place, Julia quivered at the feel of her lips on her bare torso. Each deep kiss and wet lick made her surrender her body even more.

- "I love the way you give yourself to me," said Kelly. "I love how every inch of your body responds to my touches and kisses. I can tell you are ready for me to taste you."

Kelly kissed and nibbled each of Julia's inner thighs before breathing on her pussy which was still soaked. Her tongue slid up and down the young woman's wet slit causing her to arch her back and bite her lower lip.

"You taste as good as I anticipated," Kelly said. "I don't see how anyone could have passed you up. Whoever your future husband is, he does not know what he is missing."

Julia did not care. She focused on the moment at hand, which was Kelly's lips and tongue between her thighs. With every lap on her clit, every thrust inside, every tickle of her outer lips, large amounts of tingling and warm sensations channeled through Julia's body. She could barely watch Kelly as the sight of her led to a sensory overload, but it was beautiful. The sensations through her body became stronger. Minutes later Julia found herself screaming as she had an orgasm that caused her body to go into a brief shock. Everything in her body seemed to stop. Heart, lungs, brain, everything. Then Julia came back to life, sucking in huge amounts of air, trying to get her body back to a normal state.

- "What was that?" she panted heavily. "Did I just die?"

Kelly came beside Julia and pecked her on the cheek. "For a second there, it seemed like you did. You just had an intense orgasm. You came so beautifully. I wanted to cum myself from watching you."

Julia laid there recovering from her orgasm with Kelly planting kisses on her face and touching her. Soon, she became tired, but she did not want to sleep just yet. Without warning, she gently pulled Kelly's face to hers and kissed her lips. She then rolled on top of Kelly and kissed her way to the older woman's soft neck. Rapidly, she made her way to Kelly's breasts. Her nipples were already erect, waiting for a mouth to embrace them. Gladly, Julia obliged and slowly savored each one. Meanwhile, Kelly ran her fingers through the young woman's hair and tenderly murmured, "Your mouth feels so good on my nipples, baby. You can suck a little harder."

Julia wasted no time guiding her head to between Kelly's thighs. She could see her pussy shimmering, begging to be tasted. Her lips and tongue circled her labia, causing Kelly to moan in response. The circling became smaller and faster when Julia found Kelly's sensitive pearl which had already poked out of the hood. The second Kelly felt her little mouth closing in on her clit, she shouted, "Oh yes, honey! Right there!"

It was not long before Julia felt Kelly coming close to a climax. Just when Kelly's orgasm kicked in, Julia slid a finger inside, making her cum harder.

- "Oh my God, you're good!" Kelly said through heavy breathing. "Come here, sweetie."

She pulled Julia up from between her legs and gave her another passionate kiss. They cuddled together for a moment. Then Julia asked, "So now what?"

Kelly just laughed. "Nothing yet. Let us just hold each other for now. I hope the future holds many good times like this for us."

With that, Julia rested her head on Kelly's bare chest, the older woman's heartbeat comforting her.

"True love is finding your soulmate in your best friend."
Faye Hall

THE HYPNOTIST

I was twenty-four, just out of culinary school and out of the closet. I fell in love with a woman, and we were together for six glorious months until I found out she was cheating on me. This heartbreak motivated my move back to Charlotte where to my surprise things had changed quite a bit in the five years or so I had been gone. The nightlife was great, the local music scene inspiring, new art galleries were opening all over the place. Not much for lesbians it is true, but I was doing the online dating thing and met some cool girls as well as the requisite kooks. I was free and independent and could feel myself becoming the woman I wanted to be. It felt good.

I soon got a job as a sous chef at a high-end place on the Banks development right next to the Baseball stadium. I was passionate about food then. The business had not taken its toll on me yet. My boss, the executive chef, really took me under his wing. If our owner decided to expand into new markets and I did my job well, I might hope to be in charge of my own place in a year or two. The dream was to eventually own and run my own spot. But one foot in front of the other, first things first.

I started making friends and soon had a busy social life going. A chefs' schedule is always hectic and crazy. Maybe that is why so many of us get into drugs and alcohol. You tend to need a lot of stress relief. I tend to stick to booze and weed but if someone offered me mushrooms, I would not say no.

Probably my closest friend there was a bartender named Annie. She was a beautiful shapely strawberry blonde, my age and newly married. Her husband Kyle was one of our floor managers, a really friendly, down-to-earth sort of guy. They were outgoing and I started hanging out with them and their friends quite a bit. Like me they were really into indie-rock, so we were always going to seeing cool new bands and of course getting fucked up. We were heavy partiers. I would come to work early, do my invoices, make out the prep list, call in orders and maybe work on the daily special or the soup du jour, feeling like I had been cleaned out on the inside with bleach and a scouring pad. Dying to sleep but pushing through. As a female chef with mostly male staff, I could not let those boys see any weakness. I had to be a warrior.

Our food was good. Reviews were positive in the local press. People were coming in the door. My owner and my chef were pleased. We were making money.

As I said, our place sits right next to the Baseball Park, so game days were always busy for us. We had glass partition walls separating the inner dining room from our seating outside. We would lift those walls, opening us up to the outside on nice days. All the servers would get to wear their casual baseball gear. We would take large coolers filled with ice and beer and sell them to the passersby, enticing them to stop in for sushi or a burger. This was when the straight boys and I really got to see some girl candy. We had several hotties among our serving staff, and they all knew that looking good for drunken sports fans meant big tips. Annie always wore her little Baseball T-shirt with her push-up bra, her breasts bulging from it. It was hard not to stare. She would wear jeans that seemed painted on, like three sizes too small. It was the same with her skirts when she worked at the host desk. Her ass was delicious, round, and full, perfect in fact. She was so sweet too.

I could hardly even allow myself to fantasize about Annie though, that is how straight she was. Like straight, straight, ex-cheerleader, boy crazy, super femme. Even if she was not attached, I could never imagine her being interested in me. Maybe if Kyle wanted a threesome, she might kiss me a little but fuck no, not my scene.

I have been told I am beautiful, not to make too big a deal of it, but I am raven-haired, dark-eyed, and pale-skinned. I stay in shape. I have a nice body. I was getting asked out a lot by men, both guests and staff and since I do not lie about who I am, directly or by omission, word got out soon enough.

Now dating co-workers is always dangerous. It can bring a lot of drama and awkwardness into your life, especially with young girls who want to experiment. All gay women know the awful feeling of losing your heart to someone who is not serious or who is not comfortable with her sexuality. So, with these hotties at work who loved to party I was resolved to be very circumspect.

We made plans, Annie, Kyle, and I, to see a friend of his from out of town, a famous hypnotist. An entertainer, not a hypno-therapist. He had worked at carnivals and freak shows but did gigs at comedy clubs, bars or wherever he could get people interested. He was going to be in town Saturday night to play the Music Room, one of our preferred hangouts. None of their other friends could go or wanted to. They twisted my arm, and I agreed to tag along.

We got pizza and beer at a little gourmet bistro then walked the two blocks to the club. One night only. People were out. Nice looking girls everywhere and I was getting some second looks. I recently had my hair cut Miley/pixie style partly because it is just a cute cut but also because being single and femme, I was tired of girls mistaking me for straight. I was even mixing in rainbow jewelry just to make sure I got the point across.

We paid at the door and entered the dark, noisy, and crowded club. We took a table. A gorgeous Asian girl took our drink orders. I decided on gin and tonic as my poison for the night. The happy couple took shots of whiskey chased with beer. I looked around the room. A mixed crowd, college kids, yuppies, older academic types, and a few rockers.

The lights dimmed. Some shouts and applause. A great disc of light illuminated the stage. The Hypnotist, plumber of the depths of the human heart, seeker of the mind's darkest, most hidden desires, came on stage. He was blonde, well-groomed, meticulously shaven. A born performer, he moved his arms in great theatrical gestures like a mime. He could throw his voice like a ventriloquist, aiming it like a missile across the crowded room. I did not believe for an instant he could really hypnotize people. I assumed there were a few plants in the audience who would act out for us, all in good fun.

He used one of those spinners and spoke to his victims in a soothing voice, even massaging the temples of a particular gentleman, to put them into trance. It was impressive.

The first man to go up was made to do animal noises. He barked, meowed, cock-a-doodle-dooed and oinked while his friends clapped and laughed. His wife sat their beet-red almost doubled over. The second was a middle-aged woman whom The Hypnotist first convinced was a very elderly man. She limped across the stage, holding her hip, speaking in an imitation of the gruff quaver of a male senior citizen. Next, he told her she was Robert Plant, and she began to belt out Stairway to Heaven in an off-key falsetto. It was hilarious. The drinks were flowing fast and the whole audience was having a great time.

Afterwards The Hypnotist came to our table. He was popular and even signed a few autographs. He and Kyle embraced, and Annie and I were introduced. He was charismatic and strange. His steely blue eyes kept a fixed and penetrating expression. It made me shy. One almost wished to draw a curtain over one's face lest he peer too deep.

The four of us took a cab back to Kyle and Annie's place, stopping for beer on the way. Annie put her Pandora station on while Kyle broke up weed on the sleeve of a Ramones LP, preparatory to rolling a fatty. The Hypnotist was the sober raconteur, telling us about his travels and adventures. He took himself very seriously, considering his hypnotism to be a form of high art. We passed the blunt.

Kyle had overdone it. His eyes were red and swollen and he started to nod off. Annie left The Hypnotist and I alone for a few minutes while she helped him prepare for bed. I was going to sleep in the guest room and The Hypnotist on the living room couch.

I was feeling mischievous and decided to deflate The Hypnotist somewhat.

- I see through you, you know? I asked, dragging deep, coughing, and passing.

His eyes grew wide, and he smiled slightly. What does that mean? He took the blunt but ignored it and it burned in his hand.

Those people were plants. You put them there. There is no way that silly spinner thing could put people that deep in trance. I do not believe it.

- Ah I see...a challenge.... How can I prove it to you? Shall I hypnotize you? Right now? We would best wait for Annie to get back before I make you oink like a pig.

- She can record it on her phone, and you will have your proof.

- No. Do her. Annie is no actress. If you manage to hypnotize her, I will believe it. If she agrees of course.

Very well. What shall we make her do? What thoughts shall we place in her head? Or rather what secret desire of hers shall we bring into the light of day?

Looking back, I am inclined to think that The Hypnotist knew what I wanted and led me there with that phrase. Please remember I was not only skeptical but very drunk. It was as a joke that I leaned across and whispered in his ear: I want you to turn her into a lesbian. I chortled, delighted at having given him a challenge as naughty as it was impossible. He leaned back, his face beaming self-satisfaction. Done.

Soon Annie sat in a chair directly opposite The Hypnotist. I sat a little farther apart out of sight so as not to disturb their concentration. He had an old-fashioned pocket watch on a chain. He moved it like a pendulum in front of her face, telling her in soft words that her body was relaxing, that her mind was becoming open, that all of her inhibitions were dissolving, and she was becoming sleepy. Her eyes closed.

He asked basic things about her, her name, the name of her husband, where she worked, where she lived, where she had gone to school. He made her speak of her childhood memories, her dreams, her first loves.

And then he slowly began to introduce the subject of women.

Hadn't she noticed how much prettier women were than men, how much softer, how much nicer, how they smelled? He asked Annie if she did not agree. She did agree. He mentioned me. Hadn't she noticed how pretty her friend Ritta is? How nicely shaped, how pretty her eyes and smile and hair are? She said yes, she had noticed these things. My heart was pounding, and I began to be vaguely ashamed as well as terribly excited. I could not tell whether these thoughts were being sown into her consciousness from without or rather excavated from the deepest layers of her mind. I wanted to interrupt, to tell him to stop because clearly Annie was hypnotized, and he had proven his point, but I stayed silent and listened while Annie's warm voice talked gently of how she admired my beauty and had dreamed of belonging to me.

Before snapping her out of it at the count of ten he placed a trigger word in her mind. He stole a glance at me as he pronounced it to her and made her repeat it: Ironic. The next time she heard that name she would be reminded of her feelings for women. They would dominate her. They would come over her so strongly she would be unable to control her own passions. Had I gone too far? I thought it was a joke. I did not want to break up the marriage of my two friends. Annie came too. She seemed not to remember that she had agreed to be hypnotized, and we all went to sleep, neither of us reminding her.

The next day I was very troubled. Could I possibly trust myself alone with Annie now? When all I had to do was say that silly word?

I met a girl online, really cute and smart. We were into each other pretty deep for a few weeks, so it was easy for me to avoid Annie and her husband. Eventually we drifted apart though, and I found myself feeling lonely again. Annie had been texting me furiously over the last few weeks, trying to get me to hang out with her. I could tell she was hurt and wondering what she could have done wrong.

A mutual friend at the restaurant was having a go away get together at the Nitrogen Club before she moved away to go to college out of state. I had nothing to do and no excuse to make so I went. Most of my work friends were there, as Annie and Kyle. At the time this was probably the wildest nightclub in Charlotte. If you could not hook up there you would be truly hopeless. Not exactly a gay club but close to it. All the kinky and fetishy types went there.

The music pulsed as hollow-eyed pleasure seekers wandered about. The smell of clove cigarettes hung in the air as I watched the dancers swaying to the heavy rhythms. Many men and a few women let their eyes linger over me, but I kept to myself. I did not want to lose control and end up in some strangers' bed. I set myself a three-drink limit after which I should still be sober enough to drive home. I was just observing, people watching as I love to do sometimes, when Annie tugged at my elbow, smiling. We had to shout our greetings in one another's ears.

She had dyed her hair a deep red. Her pouty lips were of the same fire-engine hue. She wore a slinky pale pink body dress. Every curve richly accentuated. I told her she looked gorgeous.

- Thanks, so do you.

I was rocking boy clothes: jeans, t-shirt, leather jacket and a newsboy cap. But I also wore my smoky eyeshadow, and my lashes were painted, long, delicate, and flirty.

We moved out to the patio so we could hear each other talk. I could see Kyle at the other end, oblivious to us, talking with his friends.

- Where have you been? Are you mad at me?

No, it's just work and was taking up a lot of my time. But that is over. She went back to her boyfriend.

I am so sorry; I know you really liked her. She hugged me again. This time we held each other for a few moments. Her hair smelled like strawberries.

Anyway, you are not the only one having relationship trouble.

- Something wrong with you two?

- Yes. No. I do not know. It is something I cannot put my finger on. I do not know if he has changed, or I have but something is just off now. I do not feel the same, I feel...

She trailed off, looking at the dancers inside. The song changed.

- Oh, this is my jam! Let us dance! She took my hand, leading me to the dance floor.

A few guys made their little attempts to engage us, gyrating or shuffling pathetically near but I got close to Annie and danced with her. She giggled playfully but stayed there with me. I let my hands roam over her sides lightly, wondering if she would pull away. She did not. I turned my back to her, doing a little twerk, rolling my hips, letting my butt grind against her. I felt her hands on me, her hips pushing and reciprocating. I saw a group of our friends looking at us, pointing and talking. I did not see Kyle. I did not care. I turned to her, put my arms around her neck, smiled as I gazed into her eyes and then said softly in her ear, Ironic.

- What? she shouted over the music.

- Nothing! I yelled back.

- She took my hand. Let us get out of here!

We dove into the first cab we saw. I barely spoke my address before Annie's hot mouth closed over mine. She was on top of me, her limbs folded around me. I opened an eye and saw the cabbies' startled but very interested gaze in the rear-view. I hoped he would be able to pay attention to the road. I have never been kissed like that. Our tongues mingling, hardly able to breathe, and the grit of her lipstick crunching like sand in my teeth.

Somehow, I paid the driver, and we got inside. I pushed her to the wall, throwing my jacket to the ground. She dropped her purse as I flipped her around and smacked her ass. I hiked up her skirt revealing a sheer pink thong. I dropped to my knees, spreading her, pushing my face into her crotch, sucking her pussy lips through the thin lace barrier.

Lust shot through us, determining our movements with the instinctive assurance of animals.

I peeled her panties down, relishing the way they slid down her soft ivory thighs, loving the sight of her ripe melon of an ass. I could not help myself. I stiffened my tongue and dove between her butt cheeks. She squirmed and shouted. I stood up, pulling off my shirt. She kissed me hard on the mouth again. I helped her off with her dress. Unwilling to pause, I kept our momentum going towards my bedroom. We made our way there in a rolling movement along the walls, each of us regaining then losing the upper hand in delicious power-play.

I unfastened my bra, revealing to her my full, heavy tits as I pulled her into my bedroom.

I could hear both of our cell phones going off in the hallway where our purses and clothes lay strewn. Annie removed her bra, her lovely b cups dotted with a few tiny moles. Her body writhed in anticipation over my silk sheets. My eyes locked on to her beautiful swollen pussy with its triangle of blondish hair. I did not stand at the ceremony. I was eager to be her first, to show her how women love and to drive this experience myself. I made her hold her legs all the way back, her elbows holding her by the pits of her knees. Her treasure was open to me. I kissed it, savoring the fragrance of her desire. My tongue parted her wet lips, licking long and deep, her savory juices oozing onto my face, lingering under her hood, circling her clitty before sucking it into my mouth. Her body shook. She cried out, oohing and cooing and begging me not to stop. I moved my face around in her, then wiped her hot dampness with one breast then another, taking my hard nipple and moving it around the rim of her pussy. My face and breasts glistening wet now.

I raised her butt in the air, her weight resting on her neck and shoulders, my arm circling her thigh. She was completely open for me. I gave in fully to my desire, letting my tongue play over her rim, two fingers pushing into her cunt. At the mercy of pleasure, she looked up at me, eyes aflame in total submission. My tongue explored her anus, licking it deep, my eyes rolling in their sockets as I lost control, fingers twisting and turning in her, coaxing her G. My own sex was on fire. I lowered her, keeping her spread, and straddled. She gasped as she watched our centers unite, our lips lightly kissing at first. I shuddered with pleasure as she gripped me close, our hips finding a rhythm together, bucking and rolling. I glid in a long trail from inner thigh over hot lips to inner thigh. She pushed herself into me. I was sweating, my clit grinding over hers. Her body quaked and she squealed as I felt my body tense and then release.

I collapsed next to her, arms folded around each other, spooning and kissing, softly and gently. I stroked her hair while she caressed my thigh, my wetness pressed to her ass. It was so intimate. I felt I could fall for this girl, but I had to be honest with her first. I told her about the night when The Hypnotist and I stayed over and about Ironic. She looked thoughtfully at me but only smiled and kissed me more.

- I do not care. I love you, Ritta. I belong to you. I never want to leave your arms. This is what my heart has always ached for, ever since we met.

I watched a smile spread over her face as I removed a special item from my bedside drawer: my black strappy. I fastened it on and re-positioned myself at the same intimate place just behind her. I reached around stroking her clit while my hard girlcock teased her perineum and massaged her lips. Still so wet, the head pressed to her opening, she spread for me and guided me in. I felt the resistance give sweetly away as her walls stretched to admit me, the little nubby worrying my clit as I worked my hips, entering her slowly. As she took me deeper and deeper, she swooned in my arms, my hips slapping her soft round butt as I fucked her. One hand playing with her anus, the other rubbing her clitty as she held the pillow, crying into it. She came in my arms, again and again and again.... I kissed her neck, my erect nipples pressing to her back.

We spent the entire day in my bed, ceasing our lovemaking only for the sake of food, restroom breaks and the discussion of future plans, of our life together. The next morning, I drove her to their place so she could pick up some clothes and other essentials. Kyle was upset but what could he say?

"She's my role model, my traveling companion, my most reliable source of light, my fortitude."
Elizabeth Gilbert

COOKIE

The next morning, I felt different, as doubts started to plague me, while I admit to having enjoyed what had happened to me, yet it also scared me. I had butterflies in my stomach as it occupied my mind as I sat there trying to eat some breakfast. Mother told me she had some errands she wanted me to do for her, and in a way I felt relieved.

It gave me a chance to get out of the house, as I went about the errands all I could think about was how I felt, alone, scared, and was I a queer? I knew what had happened was not right, was not natural as we were supposed to fall in love with a man. In the last 4 months or so I had left home, lost my virginity, and not only that had sex with my friend. Now I was back home and the one woman who I had always looked up to wanted me to make love to her.

My letters to her had apparently triggered what had happened, she had read between the lines and correctly guessed what had happened between Jennifer and me. I had been too stupid and scared to deny it. I took my time shopping for mother as these thoughts were going through my head, but after I got back home mother reminded me, I should get going to help Elaine.

By the time I got there it was mid-morning, and once inside she gave me a big hug and kiss asking what kept me. Since I had left the evening before she had finished stripping the old wallpaper off and was now starting to apply the new wallpaper to one wall. All she had on was a chemise, bloomers, and slippers, and it was clear she was not wearing a bra or her girdle.

It was a relief in a way to me that she wanted to continue papering to finish one wall. I helped her lay it out and cut it to length, then after she brushed some paste on the wall climbed up on a stool to start hanging it from the top. I kneel at the bottom and line it with the edge of the previous one. She then brushed it to squeeze any air bubbles out and smooth it down, and then we repeated with the next piece.

Once we got the first wall done, she stopped and said, "Let's take a break and have some fun," and taking me by my hand led me into her bedroom.

Before I was too timid to say anything and just meekly followed her, she again started to undo my blouse and take it off me followed by my bra. Next, she unzipped my skirt and had me step out of it, and looking at me smiled as she ran her hands over my body.

She told me how beautiful I looked and how I was all she could think of, and that she loved me very much and did I love her too?

- Of course I said, "Yes" to which she smiled at me and said, "Show me dear, I want you to love me very much." During this I saw her excitement rise and noticed her breathing change as she lay back on the bed pulling me too her and placing my hand on her tit, she kissed me on my mouth.

I was aware of her nipple under the light material of her chemise and began to caress it, reminding me about what she liked me to do to her. My own arousal was starting to grow in me, so I did not need much urging as my fingers began caressing her tits, first one then the other. I loved their feeling, so big and soft; her breathing was changing as she whispered instructions to me.

- "Grip it dearie, don't be shy I love it when you do, rub it harder it feels so good" and so on.

She had me on top of her and managed to get her legs around mine holding me in a scissor like way as I squeezed, licked, and sucked her tits. Her moans excited me till with a cry she had her climax, and I relaxed but she still held onto me. I felt her body quieten from her pleasure, and now kissing me again took my hand and pushed it down between her legs.

- "Give Cookie a rub dear," she said as she rubbed my hand over her crotch.

I was fully aroused myself by now and was happy to oblige her, feeling her pussy or her Cookie as she called it through her bloomers. Pushing the material into the crevice and feeling her clitoris, soon she was gasping and moving her arse in time to my hand rubbing her. Then with a cry and gripping me tight, held onto me as the waves of pleasure washed over her.

Unlocking her legs she moved me onto my back, and she leaned over French kissing me, her tongue deep into my mouth, telling me how beautiful it was. She took a moment to remove her chemise to let her tits swing free, then began licking and kissing my tits. I felt her hand at my hips pushing my knickers down, down below my knees. I was on the verge, close to an orgasm as she started kissing her way down to my belly, tonguing my belly button for a minute before moving down to kiss me in my pubic hair.

I was gasping by this time; more like whimpers really it felt so good, incredible feelings flooding through my body. She got up off the bed and pushed my legs apart and next thing I knew she was kissing my pussy.

This had never happened to me before, and it only took a few moments before I spread my legs wide for her and pulled my knees up close to my tits, raising my hips to accommodate her. I had the most powerful orgasm explode inside me, making me scream with delight. I was bucking with the magnitude of it, but Elaine had a good hold on me round my hips, hands on my belly pressing her face into my cunt.

She was not finished, covering my pussy with her mouth she kept probing and licking me with her tongue, soon I was on the crest or another orgasm as beautiful as before, and then on to give me yet another 'till exhausted. All I could do was lie there and let her have her way with me. She slipped her bloomers off and climbed up beside me, and we held each other tight for a few minutes.

It took me a long time to come down, and I was not really aware of anything for a few minutes. I lay there panting as she slid her body up to mine and we kissed long and slowly, as she is expressing her feelings for me.

I tasted my own juices round her mouth as she kissed me, I did not find it offensive at all if anything a little bitter but that was all and enjoyed the experience very much.

Soon she began petting me again, her hands exploring my body, then lying on her back pulled me on top and I brought my pubic arch to hump her. Slowly at first, then increasing the pace one bit at a time, she opened her legs wide to feel me and she raised her hips up to meet my thrusts.

Her tits were swinging up and down like jelly to my strokes, the look on her face was awesome, eyes partially closed, her lips in an 'o' the sounds she was emitting was more than just a groan.

- "Grip them dearie, harder, harder" she commanded, I squeezed them as hard as I could, my thrusts getting more vigorous, then we cried out in unison as we both climaxed, and I collapsed on top of her.

I felt no shame at this time if anything the opposite as I was pleased with my ability to give her much pleasure too. To hear her moans and other sounds as her arousal grew was awesome. She asked me how I liked her kissing my Cookie, as I learned she called a pussy.

I said I loved it, which was true, although I always agreed with anything she said anyway. I knew where she was leading with her questioning as I realized anything she had done to me she encouraged me to reciprocate by doing it to her.

Lying there so close and talking about it, almost whispering saying she had wanted to do that to me for a long time, how wonderful it felt and did I enjoy it too. She kept on about it and like I said above, I always agreed with whatever she said anyway, so it was not really a surprise when she invited me to kiss her Cookie too. So, it is not like she made me go down on her, more like she persuaded me to try it, and if I do not like doing that then that is OK but at least I had tried it.

She sat on the edge of the bed and had me kneel on the floor between her legs, I admit to being scared, my heart was thumping with my anxiety yet in a way I felt excited too. She opened herself up with both hands, so I saw close up how wet and intimidating her pussy was. Surrounded by her jet-black hair, the innards so wet and pink and her clit like a little tit sticking out.

I could smell her sex, frightening as she kept talking to me encouraging me to kiss it, and leaning forward touched her nether lips with my tongue. Now with a hand on my head and her other holding herself open let me take my time, I repeated giving a small kiss in her lips. Now with the flat of my tongue I ran it up her slit to her clit, I heard her moan, but I know that was just for my benefit as I was encouraged to do it again.

I did not find the taste unpleasant, just a lot stronger than I expected so I started licking her again. Now she let herself go and held my head in her hands as I probed a little deeper with my tongue to lick her innards, then flicking the tip over her clit. I looked up at her over her hairy bush to see her concentrating on what I was doing, smiling at me then she leaned back to leave me on my own.

Her cries now more reflective of the pleasure I was inducing in her cunt. She was extremely wet, her juices mixing with my saliva as I was now enjoying what I was doing to her. Suddenly she stiffened for a moment, then twitched a few times calling out as she had an orgasm, I stopped to watch amazed by what I'd done to her but she mumbled, "no no don't stop" and again I repeated what I had done till she twitched again telling me how beautiful it felt.

Finally, I sat back on my heels and looked at her as she sat up; holding out her hand invited me up onto the bed where she could now kiss me, tasting her own juices of mine.

Getting up she made us some sandwiches and tea for lunch, then we got started with the wallpaper. As we worked, she began telling me about how she got started having sex with a lady friend in university too. They lived together for quite a few years and socialized with other lesbians.

I began to realize there were lots of other women like us who preferred other women for their sexual gratification, and that a lot of them were married too. I never heard the term bisexual used, it seemed that a woman who ever had sex with another would be considered a queer and that was it.

That night when I was home, I lay in bed thinking about what she had told me and had me do to her. In those days it would be considered dirty, if not kinky or perverted, what some people might call taboo. I did not care as she had given me so much pleasure, and thrilled I could please her too, as she had pleased me, and by this time I was accepting what she was, and what I had become.

Over the next few days, I went to help her we would spend at least a couples of hours having sex, and that included lots of kissing and sucking on each other's Cookie.

She obviously saw I was enjoying the sex more and more as I was now quite happy to participate and encouraged me to enjoy her more. There was one more surprise for me before we finished the wall papering.

One afternoon we had retired to make love, and I was resting in her arms, she whispered to me, "I want you to meet Robin."

This puzzled me, and she got up and went into her closet and removed something. It was a black rubber thing with leather straps hanging from it, and I watched as she sorted the straps out then strapped the thing round her waist, so the base of it was snug against her pussy. I realized what it was supposed to be as she approached me holding it up like a cock.

She had me lie back on the bed and hold my legs up and apart, and she approached me holding the thing like it was a real cock and brought it to my nether lips. She rubbed it up and down the crevice between the lips and against my clitoris letting me feel the length of it. The rubbing excited me as I watched and soon felt her place the tip into my pussy. Just a little bit, maybe just half an inch or so at first, then take it all the way out, and back in again very slowly. She was looking at me as she did this to gaze at my reaction and each time went a little deeper. I was beginning to respond to the feeling, although it was not as nice as Newman's cock still it felt good.

Once she had it all the way home, I could feel it against my cervix, then she slowly started to fuck me with it. She was leaning over me smiling and moving her arse around to let me feel it against the roof of my vagina, sometimes plunging it into me then with drawing it all the way out and repeating. I watched her do this, her tits swinging in front of my face from her effort.

After we finished the wall papering, we painted the trim round the windows and doors that really brightened up the room. Elaine invited us, mother and my aunt and me to join her and some other friends for a New Years dinner at her house. There were lots of nice comments on the job we did to freshen it up with the new wallpaper and paint job.

I was to leave the next day to go back to University and Elaine offered to drive me to the Station to catch my Train. We left a little early so we could have some time together, have a cup of Tea and last-minute chat.

She held my wrist and told me how much she had enjoyed my company over the holidays, and hoped we could do 'it' again sometime, smiling at me as she said this.

I agreed with her and meant it, and she asked me to stay connected about my love life. I knew what she was hinting at, she wanted me to give her the details of my relationships.

Finally leaving to board the train she slipped some money into my hand, reminding me she knew how little pocket money I could afford.

Then after a hurried kiss, I boarded the train just as it was ready to leave, and from the window watched her standing on the platform waving goodbye as the Train left the station.

"I'd never fallen in love with a woman. But when I did, it didn't seem so strange."
Cynthia Nixon

CONVENT SCHOOL

My mother's decision to send me away to the school to complete my education was made, she claimed, for entirely altruistic reasons; to save my soul and to instill the 'necessary discipline' to enable a young woman to survive and flourish in a harsh and increasingly immoral world. However, as she began to enthusiastically strip bare my wardrobe and feed items of my clothing and other essentials into a wide-mouthed and hungry silver-stucco Mossman, it seemed to me that it was also a decision which, coincidentally, dovetailed comfortably with her own interests. I was not wrong, as I found out later. Within hours of peremptorily depositing my belongings and I on the steps of my new alma mater, my mother had moved her new boyfriend and his irrepressible libido into her now perfect love-nest, and began learning, in my absence, to flourish in an increasingly immoral world.

The Convent School main school building, which dated from the late medieval period, was a rambling, slate-grey edifice with imposing, obese, castellated turrets flanking the main entrance. It was, in any view, aesthetically stunning, although it still comfortably managed to convey a cold austerity that was in keeping with the ascetic regimen that the sisters rigorously enforced. To the front, a phalanx of pyramid yews trimmed obsessively to almost geometrical perfection guarded the approach; to the rear, an idyllic Italianesque cloister garden, complete with ornate stone water fountains, created a mystical, almost magical, ambience. After classes, many of the sisters would spend their time there in quiet contemplation, although this particular piece of manufactured heaven was strictly out-of-bounds to the students. Of course, girls will be girls.

From the outset it was clear that the virtually irrebuttable presumption of the sisters was that every girl who walked through the weighty moral doors of the school was a morally bankrupt whore-in-training and needed treating as such. The gravest punishments were reserved for the slightest infraction of the golden rule that all mention of boys, relationships with boys, communication or attempts at communication with boys or even thinking about boys was strictly forbidden. Despite my Catholic upbringing, or perhaps because of it, paradoxically I had nonconformist blood pulsing through my veins and occasionally decided to push these boundaries. However, as a result I soon found myself pushing table tennis balls with my nose around an ice-cold gymnasium floor at five o'clock in the morning, on all fours, whilst being continuously and ferociously barked at by Sister Martha, a cold-faced forty-something who for a long time I suspected of having been the victim of an unfortunate heart-removal operation at birth. I needed fun, but I soon realized that such pre-crepuscular torment was far from it.

It became apparent to me early on that the regime was designed to starve overheating, hormonal young women of male influence, and in so doing to attempt to deny them of what the sisters saw as their 'corrupt sexual urges.' During each long term, the only contact we ever had with anything resembling a male was during confessions. These took place once a week with Father Nicholas, a priest who parachuted into the school for the purpose, and who none of us ever actually saw but only heard through the cocoa-colored latticework of the confessional grille.

I realized early that father Nicholas had a particular proclivity for wanting full and frank disclosure of 'sexual sins' above all others. Having discovered that the only consequence of breaching the 'golden rule' during confession was the repetition of a few words that I did not really believe in, this weekly event soon became a chocolate box of playful mischief for me and spared many cold mornings in a freezing gymnasium. Looking back, I can now see that my confessional experiences at Convent School fell into three distinct phases.

At first, and exhibiting more than a little naïveté, even at sixteen, I would recount in detail what was essentially my fabricated desire for boys of my own age, and how my body responded to thoughts of them. I would go into ever more graphic detail about, for example, how I wanted to unfasten their trousers, take out their cocks and suck them. I would embroider increasingly elaborate 'desires' from the depths of my febrile imagination, which sometimes took the entire week between confessions to hone to perfection. I gradually became aware that as the fantasies I was relating become more graphic and lurid, noises were coming from the other side of the thin grille that were clearly those of a man in the throes of surreptitious sexual excitement. It was obvious to me what Father Nicholas was actually doing and, if I am perfectly honest, I found the power I could exercise over him in those few minutes each week more than a little intoxicating.

After a while I decided to broaden my imagination. For example, on occasion I would tell Father Nicholas about how I would lie in the warm confines of my bed at night and pleasure myself. What I discovered, however, was that his furtive fumbling and obvious self-gratification in the confessional were almost absent unless I was 'confessing' about young men, and slowly the truth opened its wide jaws; Father Nicholas was fantasizing about cocks, rather than the nubile, playful sixteen year old who was lying her heart out about them. I was not in any way disappointed, although the discovery of this kernel of reality precipitated phase two.

This phase demanded the exercise of skill, timing, and the careful utilization of everything I had discovered in phase one, and if executed perfectly always made me feel delighted. I recall with crystal clarity one instance of this.

- "Tell me, Paola, have you had any sinful sexual thoughts since your last confession?"

- "Yes, Father, I have."

- "About a young man?"

- "Yes, Father, about a young man."

- "Tell me about it, Paola."

- "Well, I imagined I was lying asleep in my bed at night, and when I woke up, he was kneeling astride me. He was totally naked, Father."

- "Oh, and what was he doing?"

- "He was holding his hard length in his fingers and working it up and down, Father. It was covered in this smooth, shiny cream that was oozing from the top of it."

At this point, I heard a rustle of heavy cloth and knew that Father Nicholas was lifting his cassock and starting to touch himself.

- "I see. Describe his long, hard thing for me, Paola."

- "Well, Father, it was thick and long, with veins like small purple rivers running up and down it. It was twitching and jerking in his fingers as he stroked it. And at the base he had these two round things, like soft, slightly hairy eggs, that seemed heavy and full."

Behind the screen I could hear Father Nicholas's breathing building, and a rhythmic, moist slapping sound.

- "And what happened then, Paola?" he panted. "Tell me about this long, hard thing."

- "He was rubbing it, harder and harder, and becoming more and more excited, Father. Then, suddenly…" I stopped deliberately.

- "Go on, Paola," he implored, clearly impatient and more than a little agitated. I paused a short while longer, for effect.

- "Well, then…his hard thing just came off in his hand, Father, like it had broken off." I could almost hear the blood drain from Father Nicholas's body at this turn of events. "And underneath he had these folds of flesh, rather like mine down there. I looked up at his torso and two swollen breasts with engorged nipples had grown. And then this delicious wine started pouring from his vagina, which I began to drink."

- "I see," said Father Nicholas, his arousal by now becoming a rapidly fading memory.

- "And then, Father, the long, hard thing in his hand turned into a shiny, metal vibrating thing, which he brought down between my legs and…"

- "I think our time is nearly up, Paola," he growled.

Just after I turned seventeen, I became consciously aware of my first real sexual attraction to other women. I had noticed that one of the sisters who took us for physical instruction, Sister Monique, who I estimated was probably around twenty-five, seemed to take great interest in me when it came to changing and showering after hockey or softball. Although she was as cold and remote as most of the other sisters, something in her hungry hazel eyes seemed to burrow inside me and create the most delicious tingling sensation between my legs. She would watch intensely as I soaped and lathered my breasts and between my legs. On more than one occasion I allowed my fingers to dwell provocatively on the puffy lips of my vagina and drag them up my slit and onto the sensitive bud, the pleasures of which I was just beginning to discover.

The third phase in my confessional experience with Father Nicholas began at around the same time as these feelings rose within me. My confessions actually became far more open and honest. I would tell Father Nicholas about my rapidly intensifying desire for other women. The lion's share of the pleasure in this was in knowing that he was deriving no pleasure himself from it. He would tell me that I was in danger of falling into the fires of hell if I continued along that path. My heart told me that the very furnaces of hell could not be as hot as the fire that burned between my legs every time, I became aroused thinking of another woman's fingers and tongue pleasuring me to climax. I continued to give up every one of my lesbian fantasies in the most colorful and vivid detail every single week, regardless of the 'tuts' and judgement of, quite literally, a hypocritical old self-pleasurer.

It was also at around that time that I suddenly, and rather surprisingly, found many of the sisters becoming significantly less abrasive with me. In fact, in my final year, Sister Martha gave me the news that they had decided to make me 'Head Girl;' an honor which I received with some confusion and deeply mixed emotions. I knew nothing about the Bible, my prayer life was non-existent, and with my sex drive and feelings towards other women beginning to radiate from between my legs almost continually I knew that the multiplicity of my sins made me the least qualified young woman in the upper sixth form for that particular role.

About four weeks before my final exams, I was in the sixth-form dormitory when one of the sisters approached me and said that Sister Martha wanted to see me that evening after vespers. Most of the girls knew that being summoned by Sister Martha was not normally a positive sign. She was responsible for every disciplinary matter that arose in the school, and usually dealt with it in the harshest possible manner. More than that, I had never really forgotten the cold mornings in the gym, scraping all the skin off my knees and being called a "disgusting little harlot," among other things. It was, then, with some trepidation that I approached her study and knocked lightly on the door later that evening.

When I entered, Sister Martha was not alone. She was sitting on one of three imposing vintage brown leather armchairs, with Sister Monique sitting on another. The study itself was lit in a low, flickering, pulsing gaslight, lending it an almost ghostly, golden-yellow tint. A large, ornate Persian rug was spread on the floor in front of their feet.

- "Ah, Paola. Come in and sit down, please," Sister Martha said with a slight snap in her voice. I walked over nervously to where she and Sister Monique were sitting and lowered myself into the third, sumptuous armchair, taking care to smooth the back of my navy-blue skirt against the back of my legs with the palms of my hands as I did so.

- "Tell me, Paola," she continued, "Have you decided what you are going to do when you have completed your education at Convent School?"

The truth was I had not given anywhere near enough thought to it. I had meandered through most of the previous few months with some vague notion of spending some time travelling, possibly in South America, but with no concrete plans.

- "No, Sister Martha, not really" I replied. "I have really just been concentrating on trying to do as well as I can in my final exams here before making any firm decision about the future."
- "I see," she continued. "Well, I was wondering whether you had given any thought to becoming a novice here."
Sister Martha's suggestion was so unexpected and, frankly, absurd that it was all I could do to stop myself from bursting into spontaneous laughter, but I managed to mask it; or at least I thought I had.
- "Are you smiling, Paola? What do you find so amusing?"
- "Oh no, Sister Martha," I replied. "I am just a little shocked that you might consider me a young woman of such pious virtue to merit such a possibility."
- "I don't, Paola."
- "Pardon me?" I said, more than a little confused.
- "If I did not make myself clear first time, Paola, I do not consider you a young woman of 'pious virtue,' as you so quaintly put it. In fact, I consider you quite the opposite." She looked across at Sister Monique, who was sitting in the chair next to her, exchanging half-smiles.
- "What do you mean, Sister Martha?" I had already asked the question before I could reel in my tongue sufficiently to give my mind some thinking room.
- "What I mean is that sister Monique and I know perfectly well what kind of young woman you are. You are the kind of young woman who has an insatiable, burning desire to have sex with other women, are not you Paola."
- "Oh no, Sister Martha, honestly" I lied feverishly.
- "And the thing is, Paola," she continued, totally ignoring my futile protestations, "I know that you don't have the slightest ounce of shame about those desires

that keep your fingers buried inside your panties in your bed at night, under cover of darkness, do you?" She was absolutely right.

I had not the slightest feeling of shame about it, but to be confronted with the accusation in this way was still more than a shock to my system. I lowered my head and tried to focus on my hands, which were clasped together in my lap.

- "Sister Monique has told me all about how you perform for her in the showers after games, Paola. She has told me all about how your eyes meet hers, and how you try to corrupt her mind by soaping and fondling your needy sex and firm breasts in front of her like some sex-hungry slut in a lesbian porn film."

- "I don't know what to say, Sister Martha," I said, my voice so low it was barely audible, even to myself.

- "I have known your 'secret' for a long time now, Paola. Father Nicholas could not wait to get out of confession with you every week so that he could come to my study and tell me about what he called your 'dirty sins.' He told me that he thought you were beyond redemption, Paola."

- "I don't understand, Sister," I said, my mind genuinely unable to comprehend any of what she was saying. "If you have known all this, why on earth do you suggest I should consider becoming a novice?"

Sister Martha reached over and placed her hand on Sister Monique's knee. With one movement she gathered the rough black cambric of Sister Monique's habit and began to draw it up her legs. The first thing I noticed were the surprisingly sexy black pumps with four-inch heels that Sister Monique was wearing on her feet, and as the skirt of her habit was pulled higher still, the sheer, barely black nylon stockings that were encasing her firm, shapely legs.

- "Sister Monique has exquisite legs, doesn't she Paola?" said Sister Martha. For all my bravado of the past two years, at that precise moment I barely knew what to think or where to look. "You can say it, Paola. We all know what you are actually thinking."
- "Yes, she does," I murmured. "They are lovely." And they were. The higher Sister Martha drew the material, the more my eyes were drawn to the legs underneath. I could feel the familiar tingling sensation beginning to take hold between my legs once more.
- "Here at Convent School, we demand total honesty, Paola," Sister Martha said. "And you are going to start giving it. Are we clear?"
- "Yes, Sister Martha," I said, nodding.
- "You have been having wild sexual fantasies about other women for some times now, haven't you Paola."
- "Yes, I have, Sister."
- "And some of those fantasies have involved Sister Monique, haven't they." I watched as Sister Monique crossed her legs. The skirt of her habit slid further up her thighs, revealing the delicate lace tops of her stockings. Sister Martha's fingers began to glide lightly up and down the firm contour of Sister Monique's thigh. A wicked tingling was taking hold between my legs and my mind was filling with sex once more.
- "Many of them have, Sister Martha," I replied. Sister Monique smiled; her eyes intently fixed on mine.
- "You're wanton, aren't you Paola." I nodded. "Say it!" ordered Sister Martha, harshly.
- "I'm wanton, Sister Martha."
- "You are a wanton slut who cannot stop thinking about sex with other women. Say it."
- "I'm a wanton slut who can't stop thinking about sex with other women, Sister."
Between my legs I was beginning to flood. Sister Martha's words and the provocative sight of Sister

Monique's exquisite legs wrapped lightly in sensuous dark nylon were taking hold of my mind and driving my most basic need to that place it always loved, and longed for, to go. The room, which was bathed in a low, flickering lamplight, seemed to reflect the carnal thoughts that were darkening my mind deliciously and possessing it.

- "Your mind is a hot, insatiable chamber of sin and desire, isn't it Paola," Sister Martha continued, her voice now low, husky and teasingly provocative. "Even now, the need you feel between your legs is consuming you. It is a raging fire of relentless hunger, craving to be satisfied."

My heart was now racing, pumping an enthusiastic heat through every vein. Sister Martha's fingers were tracing their light, tantalizing way over the exquisite and delicate lace tops of Sister Monique's stockings and down between her thighs. Every sense in my body felt as though it was being overloaded.

- "Get on the rug, on your hands and knees, Paola. The tone of Sister Martha's voice left me in no doubt that her intention was not to tell me twice. I pushed myself out of the sunken leather of the armchair and sank to my knees on the extravagant and sumptuously embroidered rug. I was now kneeling directly in front of Sister Monique, just inches from her feet. With a tilt of her foot, Sister Monique eased her heel out of her shoe and dangled it in front of me on her toes for a few moments, before letting it fall to the floor.

Uncrossing her legs, Sister Monique moved the underside of her nylon-clad foot to my face and began sliding her foot around it and exploring it slowly. I looked up at her. In the near half-light, her cheek bones were high, proud, and beautiful. Her eyes were full of both power and wanton mischief. Her toes, with their delicately painted red nails provocatively visible under the sheer material, moved up and down against my bottom lip, flicking it down, before tracing them over my top lip. Sister Monique said nothing, but her lips formed three words that I clearly made out from the movement of her soft, full lips. "Open your mouth."

I parted my lips. Sister Monique pressed her toes between them and began to fill my mouth. I took her foot into my mouth deeper and felt her toes move and slide over my tongue and I began to suck and lick them almost instinctively. My mouth was almost full, and I could feel a reservoir of saliva beginning to cover her toes and then run like little rivers between the tiny gaps at the corners of my mouth. I was greedy for her feet, her toes, and her control.

- "She's a greedy little bitch, isn't she Sister Monique?" Sister Martha purred before leaning down, rubbing her fingers into the torrent of warm saliva that was now covering my chin and sliding it around my cheeks and nose. "Your mouth is flooding, Paola. And I doubt that it is the only part of you that is flooding. Why don't you find out, Sister Monique?"

Sister Monique removed her foot from my mouth. I gasped for breath as my lungs were suddenly overwhelmed with an inrush of air once more. Easing herself out of her chair, Sister Monique moved around behind me. I felt her hands take a firm hold of my ankles, which she pulled apart with a strength that made me understand why she had been made head of physical instruction. As she pulled my legs wider apart, I felt my skirt, which had the tiniest two-inch vent in the rear, tighten against my thighs and bottom. Slowly, she began to run her slender, lithe fingers up and down my calves, all the way to the back of my knees, caressing them with a provocative, delicate lightness of touch.

I then felt those same fingers beginning to snake under the hem of my skirt and higher up my inner thigh. I bit my lower lip and swallowed hard. Sister Martha was sitting in her armchair, her face adorned by a look of deepening voyeuristic satisfaction. The only words I could hear within the glazed confines of my mind at that moment were "You disgusting little harlot." The effects this time, however, were vastly different and very much more pleasurable.

I gasped as Sister Monique's fingers found the flimsy covering of my white cotton panties and slid effortlessly under my crotch. My hips instinctively moved back as her hand completed its journey between my legs and cupped my vulva. The heel of her palm started to press and circle tantalizingly against the now very damp material before she allowed one finger to trail deliciously over my pussy lips, dwelling for an all-too-brief moment on my swollen, sensitive pearl. My knees buckled under the almost unbearable pleasure.

"I think the hungry little slut is in need of more, Sister Monique," I heard Sister Martha say, her voice faint through the intoxicating haze of delight that was enveloping me. "And we want to make sure she thoroughly enjoys the last weeks of her education at Convent School, don't we."

The next thing I knew, Sister Monique had slid her hand from under my skirt. I was now resting on my knees and elbows. I was aware that her fingers had moved onto the hem of my skirt, either side of the small vent. In one swift, powerful movement I heard the ripping of the thin summer material as Sister Monique tore it apart, from the vent almost to my bottom. She hooked her fingers into the legs of my panties and pulled them forcefully down my legs. My breathing was running out of control, and I was letting out small, involuntary gasps with every unfolding moment.

In front of me, Sister Martha, still sitting in her leather armchair, had begun to pull up the skirt of her habit, parting her legs a little as she did so. My eyes barely had time to focus before I felt Sister Monique grab hold of my hair from behind, bunching it in her clenched fist, pulling it tight and lifting my head. Her other hand then moved back under my crotch, this time finding its way onto the slick lips of my now drenched sex.

"Fuck her with your fingers, Sister Monique," Sister Martha urged. "Drive them inside her tight pussy and fuck her." In full obedience, Sister Monique deftly parted the easily yielding lips of my sex and pushed two fingers deep inside me. I moaned loudly as I felt them probe deep within the soft confines of my hungry pussy, before starting to build up a powerful rhythm. At the same time, I felt myself being pushed forward until my head was resting on the soft leather edge of Sister Martha's armchair, between her open legs. I watched as she draped one of them over the arm, before sliding her fingers onto her glistening pussy lips, parting them, and gently vibrating her clit.

- "Can you smell the scent of my lust, Paola?" Sister Martha purred. "Breathe it in, you hot little slut." Although every one of my senses was overwhelmed, the scent of her arousal was beyond powerful. Behind me, Sister Monique continued to plough her stiffened fingers frantically between my legs, fucking me with them deeper and ever deeper, and building my arousal by the moment.

- "What do you need, Paola," growled Sister Martha. "What does a wanton slut like you really need? Confess your sins, you little bitch."

- "Oh god, I need fucking," I cried, my voice vibrating with the power of the thrusts that were driving between my legs. "I need fucking, good and hard."

Almost immediately, and with astonishing swiftness and ease, Sister Monique flipped me over onto my back. My skirt was now ripped almost all the way from the hem to the waistband, and the material was hanging loose around my torso. Above me I saw Sister Monique, her face alive with the kind of ravenous sexual hunger that I had never seen in anyone, begin to lift the skirt of her habit once more, again revealing her strong and shapely legs. As she lifted the habit still further, I became aware that there was something else she was hiding underneath; a ridged, slightly curved purple strap-on cock, fastened tight with black leather straps.

- "Fuck her, Sister Monique," insisted Sister Martha. "Give the wanton slut just what she needs."

Sister Monique brought the head of the thick rubber cock to my now drenched slit and looked deep into my eyes. Then, with one move of her hips, she thrust the hard length of pleasure inside me. I felt every muscle in my velvet pussy walls tighten around it and try to clench it. It moved into the very depths of me, stretching and opening me.

- "Oh fuck," I moaned. "Oh fuck, that feels so good."

I wrapped my legs around Sister Monique's waist as she began to fuck me with a beautiful, intense rhythm. Her hands moved to my blouse and ripped it open, exposing my firm, swollen tits, held within the confines of a white lace bra, to her gaze. She began to caress them and pinch the engorged nipples tightly between her fingers, delivering an exquisite, searing pain. My mind no longer felt anything but wild abandonment to a depth of lust that I never knew existed. I bucked my hips and began to writhe on the rug, everything within me now lost to the goddess of sex.

As I moved towards my climax, I felt two fingers slide into my mouth, covered with the musk of sex. The taste and feel of fingers in my mouth only increased my need to surrender to the only thing my body wanted.

- "She's fucking you, Paola," teased Sister Martha. "She's fucking your needy, drenched, lust-soaked pussy and you are going to take it until you come hard, you little whore."
- "Fuck me, fuck me, fuck me," I moaned, over and over, through the fingers that were pushed into my mouth, probing it, and feeding it with the juices of Sister Martha's own desire. I felt Sister Monique's fingers move down onto my swollen little pearl and vibrate it. I began to scream like a wild animal, bucking and needing to be broken under the tidal wave of sensual pleasure crashing over me. Suddenly my entire body convulsed and went into spasm as between my legs the crescendo of my climax broke upon me. It felt as though it would never end.

Some moments later, when I finally regained some composure, I knelt up on the rug in front of Sister Martha.

- "Go with Sister Monique, Paola," Sister Martha said, smiling. "I now want you to give some serious thought as to whether you would like to join us here at the Convent School as a novice. You have much to learn, but I think you would be a perfect addition here." I smiled, silently rose to my feet, put my arm through Sister Monique's and walked with her in silence to the cloister garden. I viewed the prospect of joining the sisters now in a very new light, although I knew immediately that if I did take the oath, that I would inevitably be getting into habits I would probably never be able to get out of.

*"She's the flower I had never seen before and found a
home in me in places I'd never known before."*
Pierre Jeanty

BIKING IN THE MOUNTAINS

We are now at that time of year when here in Mexico you often get temperatures over thirty with glorious sun at midday and then storms and quite a chilly evening. Last week I went out on my bike as I have often done over recent weeks, trying to do some exercise in the now cooler evening air. Over the autumn I have had to go to the gym and exercise inside, where they at least had air conditioning, but now at last I can get out.

I was home early from work, instead of driving back to my flat in Barcelona I had taken my car to work with the express intention of driving out of the city to my village and my house there. I got there at around six in the afternoon, perfect timing. I parked the car in the road and let myself into the garden. My garden is small and perhaps a little overgrown, trees around the edges and well grown bushes, still I like it like that as no one can see in and it affords me privacy. I opened the front door, dropped my document case and computer, and happily ran up the stairs to my room.

There I stripped off my work clothes and pulled out my cycling stuff. I have a lovely outfit a friend gave to me of red cycling shorts with a matching sleeveless white and red top. They go with my cycling helmet and with my bike. I have even bought myself some red and white glasses! The whole things look surprisingly good, I know that it is for doing exercise, but it doesn't take much to coordinate these things, some male readers I know are scratching their head at this, but for me looking good is important.

I put on my shoes and climbed down to the garage, the pedal fastenings on the bottom making a racket on my wooden parquet floors. In the garage my bike hangs on a hook on the wall, I heaved it down and hit the remote for the garage door.

Brilliant sunshine spilled into the garage leaving me momentarily blind. Then I put my glasses on, and my eyes adjusted to it, I wheeled the bike out. Another clicks on the remote and the door silently closed behind me. My garage is at the back of the house, so I got on my bike, clicked my foot into the pedal and hit the button for the gate at the end of the drive. By the time I had ridden down there it was already open.

By gate I mean a large high aluminum door that shuts off the end of my drive. When the gate is open my garden is exposed, it is weird having the gate open sometimes as normally I always park outside. When I do the garden feels odd. As I rode out, I hit the button again causing the gate to slowly close behind me, the remote went into the pocket on the back of my shirt and I was off.

I had decided to head out of the village along a path past the cemetery and then to follow a track I know that heads up into the hills then loops around before returning by the same road past the cemetery. It was a long ride, but I was feeling strong and optimistic that it would not leave me too exhausted.

A lot of my female friends from Barcelona, and even some from the village, have told me that they would not feel safe cycling alone in the hills, but I have to say I have never had reason to worry about it and I love all the scenery. Most of the route is made up of tracks between olive groves, these are normally very stony wheel tracks with a high part in the middle and low stone walls on either side.

After about twenty minutes or so I got to the highest part of the ride where the road up into the mountains starts. I was hot and sweaty, and my legs were burning nicely. I had pulled down the zip on my cycling shirt, I could feel the Lycra sticking to my back and how the sides and straps of my cotton exercise bra were soaked. I paused briefly, drank some water, and then happily launched myself down the next track. This one is a long downhill run over stones along a dry riverbed which is really exhilarating. You must watch out for the larger rocks as if you hit them, you can come off with nasty consequences.

I bounced and shuddered down the track and as I neared my village, I could see dark storm clouds rolling in, you could not miss how much darker it was getting. I got to the turnoff towards the village and the first drops of rain started to splatter down wetly.

Where I live rain is not a terribly frequent thing, however when it does rain it often does so with great vehemence. This was one of those occasions as suddenly the heavens opened, and a real downpour started. The rain soaked me instantly, dripping off the end of my nose and running into my mouth when I opened it, it was hard to see but what there was to see was obscured by the downpour.

The track I was following would soon meet the cemetery road but in the meantime the quantity of rain falling was turning it into a small river rather than a negotiable track. I then saw just in front of me a big oak, Spanish oak that is, different from the US ones, but big, nonetheless. I headed for it; it was just off the track and took grateful refuge under its branches. I have to say I was not really annoyed about the rain; I was not cold or anything, in fact I left my bike there and stood out under it for a while enjoying the feeling of the big heavy drops impacting on my skin. I was dressed all in Lycra and I knew that when it stopped, I would be able to cycle home with no problems.

Then I saw another person appear, heading for the tree like I had, from the same direction I had come from.

She too was on a bike but unlike me hers was a typical old-fashioned type thing with a basket on the front. Also, unlike me, she was not dressed for the rain. She had on a sort of white hippy cotton top, sleeveless with bits of lace around the edges and the shoulders. This went with her long hippy skirt, right down to her ankles, which was made from a multicolored, tie died cotton material. She had on small, cute flip flops with seashells on the straps. I could see them easily as she had the skirt up round her knees as she tried to push her bicycle through the torrent towards the shelter of the tree.

In the basket on the front of the bicycle she had a large type of cotton sack woven out of a raffia type material. Like me she was totally sodden but unlike me her clothes stuck to her and made walking difficult for her. The Bicycle obviously weighed a ton and was getting stuck in the growing mud. Her blonde hair hung down around her face in rat tails plastered to her shoulders and back.

I had never seen her before. I could see that she was petite, her skirt was plastered to slim legs, and that she had an exceedingly small waist. Her soaked blouse showed me that firstly she wore no bra, and secondly, she had small breasts like a schoolgirl.

From what I could see of her face she had white skin with the typical flush of color over her cheeks, exaggerated in that moment from the effort of pushing the bike through the torrent. I could not see her eyes, but I bet to myself they would be grey or blue.

All of this I took in in a single glance because the next instant I was boldly splashing into the tumbling water to help her. She seemed startled when I grabbed hold of the handlebars, you push I will pull, I said to her, come on! She brightened a little and flashed me a smile as with a heave we got the bike moving again.

By now the water was over my ankles and it had quite a force on it. We struggled, heaved, and pushed and eventually the bike rode up the slight rise that was the roots of the oak. I helped her prop it against the trunk of the tree and she collapsed onto the ground next to me. She was muttering something and seemed to be swearing and cursing. I sat down next to her pulling my knees up and wrapping my arms around them. Finally, once she had vented her frustration, she turned to me, Muchas Gracias, she said in Spanish. I smiled back at her, I had lost my bet, her eyes were in fact green. A delicate light green that would probably seem to be an unusual color depending on the light. Her skin was indeed white, obviously a recent arrival as she had no tan at all, and this is the end of autumn. Hey that is ok, I answered, are you new around here? A lovely smile split her face; you speak English! She must have totally missed that I had already spoken in English to her. With a smile on her face, she was really lovely, delicate, and youthful with those lovely eyes that seemed to draw my gaze deep into them. Of course, I said, a lot of the locals do. Not many of the ones I have spoken to, she replied ruefully.

We chatted about the locals, about the weather, obviously, and how awful it was at that moment. She explained that she wanted to go to the next town over from my village, not too far by bicycle, and I said that the rain would probably peter out soon. The way it was pelting down made that seem unlikely, but I knew that these autumn storms never lasted too long. As I told her this the rain did indeed start to slack off. We stood up. I looked across at her, her blouse was now practically seeing through, and it was plastered to her chest outlining her small breasts and a pair of extremely hard nipples perfectly. Her dress was also clinging to her thighs and legs and dripped water pathetically. The bottom half of it was brown and plastered with mud.

She lifted one foot, I seem to have lost something, she said as she showed me one bare foot. Her sandals would by now be long gone in the flood and there was no way she could cycle along the main road looking as she did, she would be accosted at best or arrested at worst. I tell you what, I said brightly, why don't you come home with me for now, you can get dry, and I have some other sandals you can have. I only live about five minutes from here and, honestly, I do not think you are going to be able to carry on as you are. She smiled at me again and said happily, really? Oh, that's great, thanks a lot.

We waited a few minutes more chatting happily about innocent things. She told me her name was Sandra, I asked her if she was Spanish, and she told me that in fact she was Venezuelan. She had come over with her parents and was trying to learn English and then find a job. She had been at university in the US but had left as she had discovered she did not like it.

Her hippy-like appearance fitted with what she told me about wanting to be an artist or to work in the theatre. I reckoned she was about nineteen, maybe early twenties. She was impressed when I told her about me managing the family company but quickly made it clear that my type of highly stressed business life would be something she would not be able to stand. Finally, the rain fell to the point where we both felt we could try to make the village.

We got up and I suggested that she pull her skirt up through her legs and tuck it into the waistband. She liked this idea and said it made her feel she had been working in rice fields or something. She was bubbly and seemed incredibly happy despite the rude shock our weather had given her.

We pushed our bicycles down what was left of the track till we came to the cemetery road proper. That one was covered with cement, so we got on our bikes and headed down towards the village. We wheeled in past the first houses and soon arrived at my gate. I fished out the remote control and was delighted to see that it worked despite having been absolutely soaked. The gate slid open, and Sandra exclaimed, wow, when she saw the garden and the house. "This is really lovely, she said as she pushed her bike in through the gate. I hit the button again and the gate trundled closed again behind us.

As I said at the start, my garden is actually really cute, a riot of plants and trees that makes it look luxuriant and intimate. There are not many open spaces, but it is really attractive. We left the bikes in the drive and walked across the grass to my front door. The key I always keep inside a false stone in the flowerbed in front of the door, so I soon had the door open.

Sandra paused, looked in through the door at my polished parquet and said, I cannot go in there. She sounded quite despondent. Don't worry, I said, I'll go in and open up, you go round the back and I'll meet you at the back door." She set off round the house and I quickly went in and grabbed a couple of towels from the downstairs shower. At the back door I opened and ushered her into the kitchen, I have a shower here downstairs, you can clean off there, here, take a towel. Hang on, she replied and then to my amazement, and delight, she quickly unhitched her skirt and let it drop down her legs until it was a muddy pile on the floor, then she stripped off her white top pulling it up and off over her head. Her total lack of inhibitions gave me quite a buzz.

Her body, as I have said, was very slim, nymph-like if you know what I mean. Almost boyish apart from her small breasts and the minute bright red tanga she was wearing. She took the towel out of my hands; I had totally forgotten that I was going to hand it to her and stood there looking at me. It was only a couple of seconds, but it took me that long to click, oh yes, the shower is the second on the right, ok? Great, she said with a bright smile, and she picked her way down the corridor being careful not to touch anything with her muddy legs. Behind her she left a trail of small delicate wet footprints.

When I heard the water start, I snapped out of my idiot state and quickly grabbed her clothes, the skirt I put straight on to wash and the blouse I left soaking. Then I hastily headed upstairs to my bathroom and stripped off all my cycling gear. I jumped into my own shower and as the water cascaded down over me my mind was running at a thousand miles an hour. Was she? Could she really want...? Why had she stripped off like that?

I shampooed my hair and soaped myself all over, the water felt great, but I did not take my time as I wanted to get downstairs as soon as possible. Out of the shower and dry I left my hair damp hanging down my back and wondered what I should wear. Sandra would only have her towel, so I got hold of a cotton top and shorts of mine for her and then I put on a top and some shorts for me. I thought about underwear but then thought she probably would not want any of mine, as an afterthought I did not put any on either.

Then I went back down the stairs. The door to the shower was open and Sandra was not in the bathroom, I peeked round the door of the sitting room and there she was. She had wrapped the towel around her just under her arms and was walking around looking at my pictures and photos. Her hair, like mine, hung down her back still damp. The towel just covered her bottom but left her lovely slim legs bare. I walked in boldly and as she turned; I offered her the clothes. She made no move to take them but immediately asked me, is this you in this photo? The photo she was referring to is one of me taken on a beach by an old boyfriend of mine, it is almost sunset, and the light is illuminating my body in lovely tons of gold and yellow as I am lying on the beach just where the waves are breaking.

It is a great photo that I had had enlarged and has a definite erotic quality to it. Yes, yes, it is me. I replied, a little awkwardly as she was still staring at it. You are really beautiful, she said. I smiled in reply but said nothing.

Normally with other women I am the one who takes a more aggressive role, I often pick up my female partners and actively seduce them. Sandra was different, I knew she was no child, but she had this childlike air about her, of innocence and fragility that made me hesitate at the same time as it turned me on tremendously. Still smiling back at me she took the clothes from me but then dropped them onto the sofa behind her.

I have not thanked you for rescuing me, she said. In fact, as she said this, she dropped her eyes and tilted her face down, she looked almost ashamed but then she looked up at me coquettishly. There was no doubt, she was coming on to me. How can I possibly thank you? She asked me. She took a step closer and reached out to take the end of one of the strands of my hair, she was standing remarkably close to me now. The fabric of the towel over her breasts almost touched my top. Let me thank you properly, she breathed.

I was struck dumb and stood rooted to the spot, she leaned forward towards me and her lips reached up to mine, she brushed my mouth with her lips lightly and delicately. Then she did it again with slightly more pressure, I was about to respond when she ducked her

head, and I felt her lips on the skin of my neck on my left-hand side. She kept on giving me featherlight kisses, kisses that were more like a caress. I started to raise my hands but hers found mine and held me still.
- Please do not move, she told me.
She covered my neck with kisses, returning every few kisses to kiss my own lips. I had come out in goosebumps and was starting to feel aroused. I could feel my nipples hardening a little. She kissed down over my shoulders and then across the front of my chest above the line of my top. Her hands still lightly held my wrists, and her kisses landed delicately on the skin just at the top of the swell of my breasts.
She pulled away slightly and holding my wrists she swiveled me round to her right leaving me facing my fireplace. The mantelpiece was in front of me. She reached round me and placed one first one of my hands on the mantelpiece and then reaching round my other side she placed my other hand there too. I got the message that she did not want me to move.
Looking slightly back over my shoulder I saw the towel she had been wrapped in land on the sofa on top of the clothes I had brought down for her. She was now naked behind me. I played the game and made no move to look at her but inside I was dying to see her naked body. She started to rain kisses on my shoulders again, she delicately collected my hair and hung it over my right shoulder so she could continue kissing the back of my neck. The delicacy of her kisses and the thought of her naked behind me were now really exciting to me. I could feel the cotton of my top rubbing against my now hard nipples. I was starting to feel warm and very sexy. Then I felt her take hold of my top at the sides and start to pull it up. It caught on my breasts at the front, and she slipped her hands round me to help the front part of my top over my breasts so she could continue pulling

it up my body. Her hand lightly touched the skin of my breast, and I involuntarily shivered at the contact. I raised my hands, my movements synchronized to her wishes, and she slipped my top up over my head and off my arms.

It joined the other clothes and the towel on the sofa. I replaced my hands on the mantelpiece and stayed petrified, my mind spinning as I awaited her touch. She continued kissing me working from my neck down my spine. Her kisses now were not so light, they had more urgency and force, and I could feel the imprint they left on my skin.

A pause and then I felt something different, two hard points brushed my back. I realized they could only be her nipples rubbing against the skin of my back. She brushed my back with her nipples and then I felt her arms on either side of my chest, and she leaned into me. Suddenly after her ever so delicate kisses I overloaded on the intensity of feeling her naked chest and stomach pressed against me. I could feel her nipples, her breasts, and the warm skin of her stomach clearly, her hands on my ribs seemed hot to me.

She pressed against me and as she rubbed herself against me her mouth came back to my shoulders and neck. Once again, I made a move to turn, and she quickly reached round me and placed my hands firmly back on the mantelpiece. Then she ran her hands up from mine, up my arms to my shoulders and then onto my chest. Her hands were resting on my chest just above my breasts. She continued kissing my neck and shoulders and then slowly, so slowly she ran her hands down onto the swell of my breasts, down their slope and onto my erect nipples. She kept her palms flat and once she had my nipples centered on her palms; she teased them by rotating her palms across them. I have overly sensitive nipples, and her movements created waves of pleasure that ran all through me.

I moaned with pleasure and inclined my head back towards hers seeking more contact. She avoided me and continued the friction on my excited nipples. I pushed my pelvis back into her, pushing into her stomach and her own pelvic area. We fit together well, I could feel her thighs against mine, she pushed forward into me. Then she opened her fingers wide and cupped each of my breasts completely with her open hands. She gripped them firmly and pushed herself forward against me.

I felt so aroused, really excited, hot, ready for real contact, but I knew she wanted to keep on playing her game. She relaxed her grip on my breasts and used her fingers to pinch my nipples lightly, this made me wriggle against her and gasp a little. Then she pinched them really quite fiercely, this caught me by surprise, and I bucked against the pressure of her body on mine. She released one hand and gave me a sharp slap on the right cheek of my bottom. She then pinched my nipple again with her left hand and held on to it squeezing hard and then softly for a while. I guessed her right hand was ready to slap me again if I moved and then when I did not, she put it back on my breast and continued pinching both of my nipples. I have never been crazy about people tugging on my nipples, lots of guys think more pressure equals more pleasure and this is not my case but, in this situation, I found her rough treatment exciting.

Her nipples were hard against my back, and I knew that she was just as excited as me. Her fingers dwelt on my now afflicted nipples a while longer until each squeeze made me gasp then finally, she let go. She placed her hands on my hips, and I felt her body separate from mine. Then I felt her squat down beside me, looking down I could see her knees on either side of my feet, then she knelt on the carpet behind me. Her hands on my hips took hold of the waistband of my cotton shorts and started to inch them down over my bottom.

She took her time, and it was very provocative, all I could think of was what she was going to do next. When she had my shorts halfway down, she edged backwards and pulled me after her. I instinctively knew I should not take my hands off the mantelpiece and so as she pulled me backwards, I ended up bending over with my body leant over and my arse sticking out behind me. Once she was happy, she slowly continued pulling my shorts down. I could imagine the effect she was looking for, with by bum stuck out, my legs slightly apart and my shorts coming down she would get a lovely view of my rear with my sex exposed, peeking out from between the cheeks of my arse.

I was, as I normally am, totally waxed so nothing would stop her from seeing my sex, my excited sex. Its lips, by then a little swollen and probably shining lightly with my own wetness. Stood there with her behind me seeing just how excited she had made me was a really erotic sensual feeling.

I pushed myself backwards towards her, pushing my sex at her, blatantly asking for her to touch it. Sandra seemed to study me for a while, with that same smile on her face, then supposedly having liked what she saw she leaned forward, and I felt her tongue slide wetly over the tight puckered hole of my anus. She toyed with it, licking all round, and pushing lightly against it then she gave it a resounding kiss before taking her tongue downwards.

She reached the start of the lips of my sex and ran her wet tongue along their sticky wet outlines, down the left side and then up the right but without touching my clit at all. Then she wetly inserted her tongue between the lips of my sex and used it and her mouth to seek out each of my labia minor. The whole of my sex was responding to her touch and opening up with my excitement. She continues running her tongue around my different parts but avoided both the entrance to my pussy and my clit. I squirmed under her touch, but she held me firmly with her hands on my hips. I could feel her face pushed up hard against my arse as she pleasured my sex.

Finally, she used her tongue to penetrate me and excited as I was, I could feel, as she darted her tongue in and out of my sex, how she was coating her face with my wetness. I could feel how the cheeks of her face now slipped around against the cheeks of my arse. She tongue fucked me for a minute or so and then reached up with her hands to once again pinch my nipples, not expecting this again I once more bucked under her touch but this time it only drove my sex harder against her tongue and feeling her tongue slide inside me a little made me moan even more. I was getting really excited and started to desperately need her to work on my clit.

I need not have worried, she seemed to have my needs calmly calculated. She leaned back from me and pulled me away from the fireplace, she twirled me round, seeing as I was so worked up, I accepted her indications meekly. She pushed me towards one of my armchairs. She crawled after me and when I felt the armchair behind my calves she reached where I was and pushed me back so that I sat down heavily.

She was now kneeling on the carpet in front of me. My sofa and armchairs are old fashioned with high round arms and big cushions, very English in style. Predictably, and unconsciously fulfilling one of the fantasies I had had when I chose the sofa and chairs, she placed her hands on my knees, separated them and bent them back towards my chest. She then spread my legs even further apart until I had one leg draped over each arm of the armchair. Then she dug her hands in under my bottom and pulled me towards her. The final effect was that I was half lying in the chair with my bottom almost on the edge, my knees were up round my ears somewhere as my ankles rested on the arms. My sex lay open in front of her.

First, she reached up and played delicately with my nipples, she toyed with them caressing and flicking. She quickly brought me back to a state of high excitement and then she placed her hands on my thighs, effectively the underside of my thighs considering my position. She edged closer, her eyes locked on my sex. Her mouth lowered towards me, half open with the point of her tongue just showing.

I could see the wetness of my excitement still shining on her face. She was flushed, a red bloom showing in her face, down her neck and even across the top of her chest. I got a quick glimpse of her breasts, and I saw she had exceptionally long hard erect nipples. Her mouth settled onto my clit, I felt her breath on me, her lips brushed my sex. Then her tongue began to caress my hot needy clit. She flicked at it slowly, pushing with her tongue so that my clit was slightly flattened until by virtue of its own erect state it escaped the pressure of her wet tongue. Each flick was an explosion for me, a wave of pleasure that broke over my whole body and made me stiffen.

All the muscles in my thighs, legs, arse and stomach were tensed. I heaved mightily under each caress, but I could not possibly escape, just in case she moved her hands up and held onto my ankles imprisoning me. She started running her tongue in circles around my clit, running over it at the end of each circle. She pushed on it, caressed it, caught it with her lips, sucked on it. She played me like an instrument, and she was a master at this style of music. I was going crazy and inevitably I started to feel the beginnings of an orgasm.

Perhaps it was the way I was so tense, the way I could not keep my arse on the cushion, I do not know what, but she recognized that I was going to come. She kept up her attack on my clit but let go of my ankles. As my orgasm started to really build past the point where I could delay it, I felt a hard finger, or two, slip wetly inside me. She slipped them past my labia and deep inside me, my orgasm was now making me writhe and buck, she pumped her fingers inside me and then turned her hand upside down so that the ends of her fingers were facing upwards. As she fucked me with her hand, I could feel her fingers sliding over my g-spot every time they ran inside me.

This added buzz coupled with her tongue made me lift my arse and hips fully off the cushion. I felt my sex tighten on her fingers and just as I started to come hard with her free left hand she pinched me viciously on my left nipple, pulling at my nipple and twisting it too. The combination of sensations made me lose all control; I was almost convulsing as I came in a way I had never done before. Without realizing it I clamped my legs onto her head, trapping her face against me and her hand inside me. I took hold of her hand on my breast but did not break her grip on my nipple. I think I screamed, though I am not sure, I writhed and spasmed and jerked and ended up sliding off the sofa.

When I could once again think about who I was and where I was or anything at all I found myself on the floor lying partly on top of Sandra. I had my hips and legs on top of her, my shoulders, and head on the floor. Our faces were relatively close so when I opened my eyes, I was looking straight into hers. She had that same smile, though perhaps now even wider, on her face.

Her pupils seemed dilated, she smelled of me, she was wet with my sex and seemed so so sexy. I reached across and grabbed the back of her neck, I kissed her hard, passionately but also aggressively. My tongue invaded her mouth, and her tongue fought back against mine. I felt I wanted to almost hurt her with the kiss, to transmit to her the depth of pleasure she had given me in the way I kissed her. We kissed each other hungrily like this and then finally I let her go. We gazed at each other with idiot smiles on our faces.

Let us have a drink, she said. I have some cava, I answered. Wait a minute and I will be back, we can refresh ourselves and then..., then, I told her with a smile, then it is your turn.

Fine, she said as she rolled onto her back and stretched sexily, "I cannot wait".

THE AUTHOR

Juan Ramon Rodulfo Moya, **Defined by Nature**: Inhabitant of Planet Earth, Human, Son of Eladio Rodulfo and Briceida Moya, Brother of Gabriela, Gustavo and Katiuska, Father of Gabriel and Sofia; **Defined by society**: Venezuelan Citizen (Limited Human Rights by default), Friend of many, enemy of few, Neighbor, Student/Teacher/Student, Worker/Supervisor/Manager/Leader/Worker, Husband of K/Ex-Husband of K/Husband of Y; **Defined by the U.S. Immigration Office**: Legal Alien; **Classroom studies**: Master's Degree in Human Resource Management, English, Mandarin Chinese; **Real-World Studies**: Human Behavior; **Home Studios**: SEO Webmaster, Graphic Design, Application and Website Development, Internet and Social Media Marketing, Video Production, YouTube Branding, Part 107 Commercial Drone Pilot, Import-Export, Affiliate Marketing, Cooking, Laundry, Home Cleaning; **Work experience**: Public-Private-Entrepreneurial Sectors; **Other definitions:** Bitcoin Evangelist, Defender of Human Rights, Peace and Love.

Publications:

Books:

- Why Maslow: How to use his theory to stay in Power Forever (EN/SP)
- Asylum Seekers (EN/SP)

- Manual for Gorillas: 9 Rules to be the "Fer-pect" Dictator (EN/SP)
- Why you must Play the Lottery (EN/SP); Para Español Oprima #2: Speaking Spanish in Times of Xenophobia (EN/SP)
- Cause of Death: IGNORANCE | Human Behavior in Times of PANIC (EN/SP)
- Politics explained for Millennials, GENs XYZ and future generations (EN/SP)
- Las cenizas del Ejército Libertador (EN/SP)
- Remain Silent: The only right we have. The legal Aliens (EN/SP)
- Fortune Cookie Coaching 88 Motivational Tips Made Of Fortune Cookies, Vol I (EN)
- Vicky Erotic Tales, Vol I (EN)

Blogs:

Noticias de Nueva Esparta, Ubuntu Café, Coffee Secrets, Guaripete Pro, Rodulfox, Red Wasp Drone, Barista Pro, Gorila Travel, Fortune Cookie Coach, All Books, Vicky Toys.

Audiovisual Productions:

Podcasts:

Ubuntu Cafe | Vicky Erotic Tales | Fortune Cookie Coach | All Books, available at: juanrodulfo.com/podcasts

Music:

Albums: Margarita | Race to Extinction | Relaxed Panda | Amazonia | Cassiopeia | Caracas | Arcoiris

Musical | Close Your Eyes, disponibles en: juanrodulfo.com/music

Photography & Video:

On sale at Adobe Stock, iStock, Shutterstock, and Veectezy, available at: juanrodulfo.com/gallery

Social Media Profiles:

Twitter / FB / Instagram / TikTok/ VK / LinkedIn / Sina Weibo: @rodulfox
Google Author: https://g.co/kgs/grjtN5
Google Artist: https://g.co/kgs/H7Fiqg
Twitter: https://twitter.com/rodulfox
Facebook: https://facebook.com/rodulfox
LinkedIn: https://www.linkedin.com/in/rodulfox
Instagram: https://www.instagram.com/rodulfox/
VK: https://vk.com/rodulfox
TikTok: https://www.tiktok.com/@rodulfox
Trading
View: https://www.tradingview.com/u/rodulfox/

ENDNOTES

9 798330 522309